D0948712

Cambridge Studies in Speech Science and Communication

A perceptual study of intonation

In this series:

A perceptual study of intonation

An experimental-phonetic approach to speech melody

Johan 't Hart, René Collier and
Antonie Cohen

Institute for Perception Research, Eindhoven

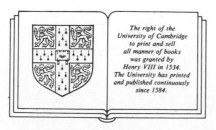

The right of the
University of Cambridge
to print and sell
all manner of books
was granted by
Henry VIII in 1534.
The University has printed
and published continuously
since 1584.

Cambridge University Press

Cambridge
New York   Port Chester
Melbourne   Sydney

Published by the Press Syndicate of the University of Cambridge
The Pitt Building, Trumpington Street, Cambridge CB2 1RP
40 West 20th Street, New York, NY 10011, USA
10 Stamford Road, Oakleigh, Melbourne 3166, Australia

First published 1990

Printed in Great Britain at the University Press, Cambridge

British Library cataloguing in publication data

Hart, Johan 't
  A perceptual study of intonation: an
  experimental-phonetic approach to speech
  melody. – (Cambridge studies in speech science
  and communication)
  1. Language. Intonation
  I. Title II. Collier, René III. Cohen, Antonie
  414

Library of Congress cataloguing in publication data

Hart, Johan 't
  A perceptual study of intonation : an experimental-phonetic
  approach to speech melody / Johan 't Hart, René Collier, Antonie Cohen.
  p. cm. – (Cambridge studies in speech science and communication)
  Bibliography.
  Includes index.
  ISBN 0 521 36643 7
  1. Intonation (Phonetics) I. Collier, René. II. Cohen, Antonie
  III. Title. IV. Series.
  P222.H37   1990
  414'.6—dc 20   89-33196   CIP

ISBN 0 521 36643 7

VN

Contents

Contents

Contents

Tables

Figures

Preface

Ever since the establishment, in 1957, of the Institute for Perception Research (IPO) in Eindhoven, The Netherlands, one of the main fields of interest in the research programme has been psychoacoustics. More particularly, the study of the perception of pitch in complex signals predominated right from the beginning. When, in 1959, a start was made with phonetic research, it was not immediately clear on which of the many potential subjects the efforts should be concentrated. After having attended the Fourth International Congress of Phonetic Sciences in Helsinki, in 1961, we concluded that, in those days, relatively little attention was paid to prosodic phenomena in general, and to pitch in speech in particular. Gradually, we began to appreciate that trying to explore the perception of pitch in speech not only could contribute to fill a gap in phonetic research, but also would link up our phonetic activities with the already existing psychoacoustic tradition at the Institute. And so, we decided to devote part of the work of the then small group of phoneticians at IPO to a perceptual study of intonation. In anticipation of the complication that speech pitch is highly dynamic, our first aim was to develop a method that would enable us to unravel systematically recurring characteristics of the various possible melodic lines in spoken language. This implied that, for the time being, an exploration of the linguistic substratum was considered premature.

We started with Dutch, in view of the abundant availability of native speakers and listeners. Once the method had sufficiently matured and been shown to be capable of laying bare the intonation system of the Dutch language, we expected that the same approach would be applicable to other languages as well: although intonation systems are known to be language specific, the auditory processing mechanism can be considered to be very similar in all people, irrespective of their native tongue. Near the end of the seventies, a start was made with the study of British English intonation, with a twofold aim:

1. Can it be demonstrated that the perceptual approach used in the analysis of Dutch intonation and the emerging theoretical framework are also applicable to British English as a representative of just an arbitrary language other than Dutch?

2. Is it possible to give a description of British English intonation which is explicit enough to be incorporated in a text-to-speech system? If so, the description may also turn out to be helpful in teaching English as a second language to Dutch students.

This project produced promising results, and as a consequence, two doctoral dissertations have been written on the intonation of yet two other languages, viz. Russian and German.

The reason why we decided to write this book is not only that the IPO approach has proved to be applicable more generally than for Dutch intonation only; a more important reason is that we felt it desirable, if not necessary, to overcome a shortcoming in the way we have published our results thus far, viz. piecemeal, and only in condensed papers in various journals, congress proceedings, and the like. A number of these publications are not easily accessible. This book should offer the reader a comprehensive view, in one volume, of the characteristics of our perceptual study of intonation.

This does not necessarily imply that it is merely a collection of previously published papers written ten to twenty years ago. For one thing, we have taken the opportunity to write in far more detail how we proceed in the analysis, and how we interpret the outcome of the experiments in a wider perspective than was possible in the earlier papers, which most often dealt with one experiment at a time. For another, we have been able to add new experimental findings, and, in a number of theoretical propositions, to reflect more on the link with linguistic structure than we have done in the past. Finally, we have attempted to comprise the entire undertaking, strongly perceptually oriented as it is, in one general framework, viz. 'modelling the listener'.

We take joint responsibility for every part of the text. Although the writing of a particular (part of a) chapter started with one author, depending on who had the greatest affinity to the subject, we have extensively discussed every contribution until agreement was reached.

We would like to thank our colleagues at IPO, who have supported our work with many technical facilities and fruitful exchange of ideas. In particular, we thank Herman Bouma, director of the Institute for Perception Research, for his firm belief in the success of our enterprise and his encouragement to pursue it. We are very grateful to Sieb Nooteboom, who has taken great pains to carefully and critically read and discuss with us an earlier version of the manuscript. We are also indebted to Diek Duifhuis for his critical comments on the psychoacoustical part of chapter two. Finally, we acknowledge the valuable comments and constructive criticism given by three anonymous reviewers, from which we have benefited considerably.

Acknowledgments

The following figures are taken from publications that have already appeared in the literature.

Fig. 2.2   R. Collier 1975. Physiological correlates of intonation patterns. *JASA* 58: 251.
Fig. 2.7   H. Bouma 1979. Perceptual functions. In J.A. Michon, E.G.J. Eijkman and L.F.W. de Klerk (eds.), *Handbook of psychonomics*, vol. I, 494. Amsterdam: North Holland.
Fig. 4.2   J. 't Hart and R. Collier 1975. Integrating different levels of intonation analysis. *Journal of Phonetics* 3: 252.
Fig. 4.3   As fig. 4.2, p. 253.
Fig. 4.4   As fig. 2.2.
Fig. 4.5   Is the same figure as fig. 2.2.
Fig. 4.6   R. Collier 1974. Laryngeal muscle activity, subglottal air pressure, and the control of pitch in speech. *Status report on speech research, Haskins Laboratories* 39/40: 160.
Fig. 4.7   As fig. 4.6, p. 163.
Fig. 4.8   As fig. 4.6, p. 169.
Fig. 4.12   R. Collier and J. 't Hart 1975. The role of intonation in speech perception. In A. Cohen and S.G. Nooteboom (eds.), *Structure and process in speech perception* 112. Berlin/Heidelberg/New York: Springer.
Fig. 4.14   J. 't Hart 1976. How distinctive is intonation? In Rudolf Kern (ed.), *Löwen und Sprachtiger* 373. Louvain: Edition Peeters.

1

Introduction

As humans' most sophisticated means of communication, the code of language exploits numerous formal devices in order to get the meaning of the message across. When words are strung together, the resulting meaning of the whole structure is a function of the semantic properties of the individual lexical items and of the syntactic relations that hold among them. It is also a function of the linguistic and situational context in which the utterance is produced. When speech is uttered, the vocal organs are set into motion in order to generate the sound pattern that corresponds to the underlying linguistic elements. In this generation process the speaker does not merely articulate the successive speech sounds that make up an utterance, but simultaneously controls other vocal features such as loudness, tempo, rhythm, pitch, voice quality, etc. The latter variations do not shape the phonetic identity of the segmental speech-sounds, but constitute a truly 'suprasegmental' or 'prosodic' layer in the sound pattern. The prosody of an utterance adds an expressive dimension to the communication process: by modifying the prosodic features the speaker can supplement his utterance with elements of meaning that are not explicitly contained in its lexical and syntactic make-up. This added meaning must be taken in the broad sense of 'communicatively relevant information', and may be given widely different paraphrases, such as: this is the topic of my discourse; this is a polite request; I don't believe you; I am bored; I don't mean what I say; I mean the opposite of what I say; I emphasize this word; this is the end of my message; etc. The communicative value of prosodic features is evidenced by the fact that novelists and playwrights are frustrated by the impossibility of coding them in conventional orthography (a defect already taken up by J. Steele, 1775, 1779), and by the fact that the same text can be said in many different ways. The few punctuation marks that are available, or the use of italics and capitals, are insufficient means to express the added shades of meaning conveyed by prosody. They have to be paraphrased in plain words.

Both linguists and phoneticians, in as far as they are interested in the communicative function of language and speech, have been convinced for a long time that prosody is a legitimate issue in their fields of interest, but they have also been aware that it is fairly elusive subject matter. By their very nature as utterance-long components, prosodic features are more difficult to observe, transcribe and analyse than are their segmental counterparts, and attested formal differences along any prosodic dimension cannot be given a functional interpretation as easily as is the case with a segmental contrast of the type /p^{h}i:k/ (*peak*) vs /bi:k/ (*beak*). Given the formal and functional complexities of prosodic features, one cannot investigate all of them at the same time.

We have chosen to concentrate on just one prosodic feature, viz. intonation, which we define as the ensemble of pitch variations in speech caused by the varying periodicity in the vibration of the vocal cords. Even with this limitation, the domain of our investigation remains vast and complex. Indeed, intonation can be approached from a variety of angles, all of which are equally indispensible if one wishes ultimately to understand how speech melody functions in human communication. Ideally, a theory of intonation should comprise a phonetic and a linguistic component. The phonetic part of the theory should account for the physiological, acoustic and perceptual aspects of intonation, and elucidate the relation between them. The linguistic component of the theory should aim at a phonological interpretation of the phonetic facts and at a pragmatic explanation of how intonation functions in the communicative interaction between speaker and listener. Finally, the theory should comprise a natural link between the linguistic and phonetic components: it should clarify how the melodic performance of the language user results from the interaction between his communicative intent and the peripheral means of his vocal and perceptual apparatus. Admittedly, to develop such a unified theory of intonation is a formidable task and our own research programme is a far less ambitious enterprise. In the remainder of this chapter we will first present a number of considerations that have led to our choice of goals and means. Secondly, we will give a survey of the contents of this monograph, thus offering a preview of the topics that we consider to be important in our work.

1.1 A dilemma

The most fascinating and intriguing thing about language is that it functions so eminently well in human communication. Therefore, the evident goal of linguistic analysis is to lay bare the properties of language that support its communicative role in the speech community. Undoubtedly, intonation is one of the vocal means that can be put to use in conveying a message from speaker to listener. However, in order to investigate how speech melody contributes to the overall meaning of an utterance, one needs a metalanguage in which one can talk about the phenomenon. The vocabulary of such a metalanguage should consist of suitable descriptive units with which one can refer to entities and structures at various levels of observation.

At the start of our efforts, some twenty years ago, it turned out that a reliable description of the formal properties of intonation was still lacking. There was no consensus regarding the way in which speech melody could best be described, much in contrast with the established agreement in the study of segmental speech phenomena. In the latter domain the units of description present themselves quite naturally. Indeed, it seems intuitively satisfying to assume that the individual speech sounds are the basic segments into which the stream of speech can be decomposed. Some notorious difficulties notwithstanding, many of these units can be recovered as discrete elements in both the waveform and the spectral representation of the signal. They can also be viewed as the consecutive targets in production and as the unitary percepts in the interpretation of the speech signal. The plausibility of the individual speech sounds as descriptive units is attested by the success of alphabetic writing, both in conventional and in phonetic notation. However, this fortunate state of affairs only holds for the segmental level of speech analysis. No such evident descriptive units can be thought of when intonation is the object of study. Speech melody is a continuously varying attribute that encompasses linguistic units as long as complete utterances, and it is far from evident whether, and if so how, it can be segmented into smaller units. The reason for the absence of self-evident melodic units may perhaps be found in the lack of a 'distinctivity criterion', comparable to the one that led to a breakthrough in segmental phonology. Indeed, the emergence of phonology in the late twenties led to a fundamental distinction between 'language' and 'speech', and the powerful concept of the phoneme provided a means to define the functional properties of speech sounds. At the heart of this functional definition was the criterion of *distinctivity*: a minimal phonetic difference between speech sounds is functional if it supports a semantic distinction in the language. In practice, this criterion appeared to be straightforward to apply in so-called 'minimal-pair' tests, in which the phonologist could rely on his phonetic knowledge, combined with either his own semantic intuition or that of a native informant. Phonology thus appeared to perform successfully a much desired reduction on the wealth of phonetic data: it abstracted the 'linguistic code' from the amalgam of physical distinctions, and it provided a principled criterion to decompose the flow of speech into phoneme-sized descriptive units.

Early attempts to apply the distinctivity criterion to speech melody have not been successful. The semantic distinction was commonly limited to the dichotomy of 'statement' vs 'question', which led to a typology of 'falling' vs 'rising' intonation patterns. Clearly, such an approach runs the risk of seriously underdifferentiating important melodic features. In retrospect, it seems as if the successes of segmental phonology have tempted the students of intonation to focus immediately on its distinctive function without going through the preliminary phase of systematic observation. Of course, scholars such as Jones (1909) and Armstrong and Ward (1926) have taken great pains over systematically observing pitch variations in speech, but their phonetic observations had a dubious empirical status: impressionistic auditory descriptions remain difficult to interpret and may not be representative of other listeners' perceptions.

Admittedly, in those days no techniques were available to measure speech melody in a simple way. The automatic extraction of fundamental frequency became possible only in the thirties, with, e.g., the 'pitch meter' of Grützmacher and Lottermoser (1937). In fact, the use of this device and of its more sophisticated successors created more problems than it solved: the minute physical variations that could be recorded were almost impossible to interpret in perceptual and communicative terms. Once more the researcher was confronted with the difficulty of finding suitable descriptive units.

In summary, the student of intonation faces a dilemma: either he chooses the linguistic approach at the risk of overlooking phonetically important features, or he opts for an instrumental-phonetic angle, thus increasing the chance of missing the communicatively relevant essentials.

1.2 A way out

In the preceding section we have argued that progress in the study of intonation cannot be achieved unless one has procured suitable descriptive units. The latter cannot be found by applying a gross linguistic criterion of distinctivity to unreliable auditory impressions, nor by carefully inspecting the acoustic details revealed by the use of a pitch meter. For one thing, whatever information is carried by speech melody may not be confined to linguistic distinctivity; for another, it is very unlikely that all the minute variations in a pitch curve have been intended by the speaker. Such considerations have led us to believe that a very promising solution to the multitude of linguistic and phonetic problems may reside in the development of a 'model of the listener'. Such a model should eventually answer the many questions subsumed under the more general one: *what does the listener make of pitch in speech?* To answer this question implies that one brings to light which melodic units the listener distinguishes, how he structures them to the overall percept of a pitch contour, how he relates perceived contours to more abstract melodic entities (intonation patterns), how he integrates melodic and textual information into one linguistic message, etc. To discover the kind of structure a listener imposes on the melodic variations in speech amounts to revealing major aspects of his intonational competence.

A language user's intonational competence not only comprises knowledge about melodic form, but also about melodic function. However, the assessment of the formal properties of intonation takes logical precedence over the study of its linguistic and expressive use. Eventually we want to come to grips with the communicative value of intonation, but our immediate concern is to develop a descriptive framework for the melodic properties of speech and for the intonational features of language. In other words, the task has to be approached from the bottom end, i.e. from the phonetic level of observation. But also at this level a further choice has to be made between a physiological, an acoustic, or a perceptual approach. Our predilection for the perceptual angle in the phonetic domain is based on the consideration that perception acts like a filter that performs a much needed reduction on data of acoustic or physiological origin, which are overspecified: they contain far more information than need be relevant for the purpose of communication. Thus, our ultimate aim of explaining the role of intonation in speech communication accounts for our immediate goal of unravelling the *perceptual* structure of intonation, captured in a model of the listener.

Our emphasis on the listener should not be confounded with a psychoacoustic approach to pitch perception. Of course, there certainly are acoustic variations that go unnoticed because they fail to reach the known thresholds of auditory perception. But it is to be expected that much larger tolerances exist in the domain of speech pitch and that they are of a phonetic-linguistic, rather than of a purely psychoacoustic nature. On the other hand, we do not anticipate that all the perceivable elements of speech melody fulfil a communicative function. Psychoacoustic thresholds and communicative relevance constitute the lower and upper boundaries that delimit the province of our perceptual quest.

To study intonation from the listener's point of view does not exclude a genuine interest in speech production and acoustics. We are convinced that the auditory impressions should be studied systematically in relation to the properties of the acoustic signal, in particular to those that result from voluntary physiological action on the speaker's part. Thus our central concern is not so much the question 'What melody do we perceive?', but rather 'Which properties of the acoustic signal are relevant for our perception of speech melody?' and, subsequently, 'Which physiological mechanisms control these perceptually relevant acoustic features?' Our concern with objective methodology does not force us to solely rely on electronic measurement techniques, but it does compel us not to study perception in isolation from the physiological and physical factors that control it. Objectivity might be sought in the domain of acoustic or physiological measurement, but such data seldom speak for themselves: they are hard to interpret in terms of what ultimately matters, viz. the contribution of intonation to the communication process. Indeed, physiological recordings do not tell us much about what pitch inflections the speaker actually intended to produce, nor do acoustic tracings foretell what information is relevant for the listener.

On the other hand, a perceptual approach is subjective *per se*. In order to formulate warranted generalizations about the perception of speech melody, one needs to ascertain whether a particular melodic impression can be reproduced in the same listener as well as in other listeners. This requires the use of reliable experimental techniques. Therefore, our approach can best be characterized as an experimental-phonetic study of how the listener's intonational knowledge is brought to bear on his perception and interpretation of spoken language.

1.3 Overview of the contents

This book offers a comprehensive treatment of the philosophy, the methodology and the major results of intonation research in the tradition of the Institute for Perception Research (IPO) in Eindhoven, The Netherlands. As such, this volume is not a textbook: it does not cover the subject matter of intonation study in a broad sense, offering a historical perspective in which successive or competing theories are juxtaposed. In fact, we will have little to say about the 'state of the art' in general, but will rather limit ourselves to an in-depth treatment of what has become known as 'The Dutch School' of intonation. Readers who are less familiar with the field may find general information on intonation studies in overviews by Cruttenden (1986), Ladd (1980), Bolinger (1986) and others.

In chapter 2, 'Phonetic aspects of intonation', we provide succinct information on the physiological mechanisms that determine the rate of vocal-fold vibration. We also discuss how intonation is embedded in the speech signal, and how the relevant information can be extracted from the signal in more or less automatic ways. Finally we devote attention to the perception of pitch. The latter treatment is more extensive, in accordance with our emphasis on the perceptual approach to the phonetic aspects of intonation. We start with an overview of psychoacoustic insights in the auditory impressions of pitch, of pitch distance and of pitch change, both in terms of absolute and differential thresholds. In particular, we examine whether these insights, based on experiments with rather short and simple signals, can help to explain the perception of pitch in longer and more complex speech stimuli. In many respects the answer is negative: in the dynamic and complex speech signal, the perception of pitch is, in general, less accurate than in the stimuli usually applied in psychoacoustic experiments.

Chapter 3, 'The IPO approach', sketches the general framework of our perceptually oriented analysis of intonation. It introduces our basic assumption and the descriptive units with which we operate at different levels of analysis. Most importantly, we give an exhaustive and explicit account of the experimental procedures that we use, so that they can be duplicated by interested researchers.

First we explain how the artificial manipulation of fundamental frequency (F_0) is at the core of a series of procedures that yield descriptive units of increasing complexity. Indeed, the *stylization* of an original F_0 curve and the evaluation of the perceptual consequences of such an operation are the basic tools of our approach. With this technique we are able to isolate perceptually relevant F_0 changes and to explore along which melodic dimensions they are distinct from one another. We can also examine within what limits the original and the stylized F_0 changes result in either identical or equivalent perceptions, so as to be able to propose *standard* acoustic specifications for each of the perceptually distinct *pitch movements*.

Next, we elucidate how the atomistic pitch movements can be used in the construction of a global *pitch contour*, through the intermediate unit of the pitch movement *configuration*. Again we explain how these sequential constraints of the pitch movements can be discovered, how they can be formalized in a *grammar* of intonation, and how the validity of the predictions made by this grammar can be assessed.

Finally, we discuss how perceptually distinct pitch contours may be related to more abstract categories, the *intonation patterns*. Here, too, we describe the experimental techniques with which one may explore the nature of this relationship.

Chapter 4 is entitled 'A theory of intonation'. The analytic and experimental techniques presented in chapter 3 have produced a fairly coherent body of results that we present as our theory of intonation. We formulate the acquired insights in the form of ten propositions. In support of these propositions we summarize the experimental findings that have accumulated in the course of our study of Dutch intonation, and we adduce additional evidence from more recent analyses of English, German and Russian intonation.

The first six propositions pertain to the *phonetic* part of our theory. They primarily deal with our melodic model of intonation and with the relation between the perceptual and the acoustic or physiological manifestations of intonation. The next three propositions concern our views on certain functional aspects of pitch in speech, viz. the role of intonation in sentence accentuation and syntactic-boundary marking, and its contribution to the overall meaning of an utterance. The last proposition regards a psycholinguistic issue, viz. the amount of preplanning that is required for a speaker to successfully integrate melodic and functional requirements in the control of his pitch.

Chapter 5 is devoted to declination. The theoretical issues raised in the propositions of chapter 4 all pertain to intonation in so far as it manifests itself in the form of conspicuous major pitch changes. Nothing has been said about declination, i.e. the actual or virtual tendency for a pitch contour to gradually drift downward in the course of an utterance. The chapter is subdivided in three phonetic sections (acoustics, production and perception), followed by a fourth in which some functional aspects of the phenomenon are at issue. The acoustics section discusses the difference between *topline* and *baseline* declination and illustrates how our stylization technique can be used to reliably measure the declination rate. Predictions about the variable rate of declination are stated in a formula. The first section ends with a discussion of *declination resetting*. The second section explores the possible physiological causes of declination and examines to what extent it may be actively controlled by the speaker. The perceptual side, dealt with in the third section, raises the issue of the psychological reality of declination. In the final section of this chapter we address the possible influence of declination on the overall interpretation of an utterance.

In chapter 6, 'Linguistic generalizations', we attempt to further reduce the phonetic structure of Dutch pitch contours to its essential properties. In the first part of this chapter we introduce and define a number of descriptive units and categories, and show how they apply to abstract intonational structures. Then we present a set of derivation rules that convert underlying intonation patterns into more elaborate, concrete melodic entities. Finally we show how melodic structures and textual elements can be mapped onto each other. In the second part of the chapter we compare our treatment to a more orthodox phonological analysis of Dutch intonation.

In chapter 7, 'Applications', we consider a number of actual and potential applications of our phonetic results. To date, actual applications are to be found in the areas of foreign-language teaching and aids for the handicapped. Our findings have been translated in non-technical terms in a 'Course of

Dutch intonation' and they have been incorporated in the design of an intonable electrolarynx. Our specification of the melodic possibilities of Dutch, English and German have also been implemented in algorithms that are components of full-fledged text-to-speech systems, still under development. Finally, our melodic models of Dutch and English intonation provide a formal phonetic description of sufficient detail to allow for further explorations of more functional, linguistic issues.

Finally, in chapter 8, 'Conclusion', we recapitulate the main points that we have tried to make in establishing the feasibility of our perceptual approach. We look back upon the considerations that have motivated our initial choices and we examine to what extent we believe our endeavours have contributed to a better understanding of the phenomenon of intonation.

Phonetic aspects of intonation

2.0 Introduction

Intonation, as we have defined it, is the ensemble of pitch variations in the course of an utterance. This perceptual impression of speech melody correlates, to a first approximation, with changes in the fundamental frequency (F_0) of the signal. These F_0 variations, in turn, reflect changes in the rate at which the vocal cords vibrate. Therefore, if intonation is approached from a phonetic angle, its form of appearance can be described in perceptual, acoustic and physiological terms.

This chapter is devoted to such a threefold characterization of intonation. In section 2.1 we present some basic insights into the physiological mechanisms that control the rate of vocal-cord vibration. Section 2.2 is devoted to the acoustic manifestation of this vibration and to some of the ways in which it can be extracted from the speech signal. Section 2.3 offers a rather detailed account of the psychoacoustic literature concerning the perception of pitch in pure and complex tones and in speech-like signals. The information in sections 2.1 and 2.2 is intended to provide the necessary background knowledge for the reading of subsequent chapters. The expert reader can skip these sections. In section 2.3 comparable background information is given, but it is shown in addition that the psychoacoustically defined thresholds do not account for the selective sensitivity of the listener when extracting pitch information from the speech signal.

We will round off the entire chapter (2.4) with considerations about which strategy can best be chosen in an attempt to integrate the three main aspects as they have been presented in this chapter, viz. those of production, of acoustic manifestation and of perception of speech pitch.

2.1 The physiology of intonation

2.1.0 Introduction

The physiological basis of intonation is vested in the mechanisms that set the vocal cords into motion and determine the variations in the rate at which they

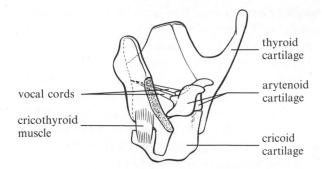

thyroid
cartilage

arytenoid
cartilage

vocal cords

cricothyroid
muscle

cricoid
cartilage

2.1 Perspective view of the larynx

vibrate. Since Van den Berg's pioneering studies (1968) it is generally agreed that vocal-cord vibration is a function of the myoelastic properties of the laryngeal musculature and of the aerodynamic forces in the upper airways.

2.1.1 The anatomy of the larynx

The vocal cords are situated behind the 'Adam's apple', in the cartilaginous structure called the larynx. As can be seen in figure 2.1, the larynx consists of several cartilages, the most important of which are the thyroid, the cricoid and the two arytenoid cartilages. The thyroid and the cricoid cartilages make contact in the cricothyroid joints, about which they rotate. The pair of arytenoid cartilages is situated on the posterior part of the cricoid. They can slide back and forth a little and they can rotate and rock on the cricoid. The cartilages of the larynx are covered with and connected by ligaments and membranes. They also support several (pairs of) laryngeal muscles, among which are the vocal cords themselves. The latter are called the thyroarytenoid muscles, since they run between the thyroid and the two arytenoid cartilages. Any muscular or mechanical force that changes the spatial configuration of the points of attachment of the cords is likely to also change their position, length and tension. For instance, the rocking and sliding movements of the arytenoid cartilages are responsible for the adduction and abduction of the cords. Thus they determine the amount of glottal aperture, i.e. the space between the cords. Glottal width is large during inspiration and narrow during phonation, and it also varies according to the articulation manner and the voicing feature of consonants.

2.1.2 Vocal-cord vibration

In order for the vocal cords to be set into vibration, two conditions must be met: they must be sufficiently approximated and there must be a large enough amount of air flow through the glottis. The air flow is caused by the difference in air pressure in the lungs and in the supraglottal cavities. During speech the subglottal air pressure (P_s) typically varies between 5 and 10 centimeters of water above atmospheric pressure, but in loud singing it can rise to some 50 cm H_2O. P_s is controlled by the respiratory muscles (the intercostals and the abdomen). The adduction of the vocal cords is accomplished by the contraction of the interarytenoid and lateral cricoarytenoid muscles, which pull the arytenoid cartilages together. One vibratory cycle of the cords can be decomposed in a number of phases, as summarized in Pickett (1980: 57ff.). The approximated cords form a resistance to the flow of air from the lungs and this results in an increase of the subglottal pressure. A sufficiently high P_s forces the cords apart, overcoming the muscular force that tends to keep them adducted. As the glottis opens more, the natural elastic tension of the cords increases and the kinetic energy, supplied by their outward movement, accumulates in their mass. Now the glottal aperture reaches its maximum and so does the flow of air. The stored elastic recoil energy then causes the vocal cords to move inward. As the glottal opening becomes narrower, the velocity of the air flow increases; the Bernoulli effect then causes a pressure drop in the space between the cords. This pressure drop produces a suction effect that snaps the vocal cords together and closes the glottis abruptly. The Bernoulli effect then ceases and the elasticity of the vocal cords restores them to their initial, loosely adducted position. A new vibratory cycle begins when the increasing P_s pushes the cords apart. Thus the cyclic repetition of the opening and closing of the glottis, called phonation, is primarily the result of aerodynamic forces that act upon the vocal cords after they have been sufficiently approximated by some of the laryngeal muscles.

2.1.3 Variation in fundamental frequency

The vocal cords can vibrate over a wide range of fundamental frequencies. In female speech F_0 may vary typically between 180 and 400 Hz and the fundamental frequency of a female singing voice may exceed 1 kHz. In the adult male the speaking voice ranges between some 80 and 200 Hz. How are F_0 changes brought about?

According to Van den Berg's (1968) myoelastic aerodynamic theory of phonation, the F_0 of vocal-cord vibration is determined by their elasticity, tension and mass and by the amount of air pressure below the glottis. Tension and air pressure are to a large extent under the speaker's control, in a way that is well explained in Borden and Harris (1983: 74ff.). We will summarize their account in the next subsection.

2.1.3.1 Muscular tension

Within the same speaker, the lengthening of the cords will stretch out and thin their effective vibrating portion. This will increase their tension and thereby produce a higher F_0. Since the vocal cords run between the cricoid cartilage and the arytenoid cartilages, their lengthening can be brought about by increasing the distance between these points of attachment. In order to do so, the speaker activates his cricothyroid muscles, which pull the cricoid and thyroid cartilages toward each other (see fig. 2.1). This rotation around the cricoarytenoid joint tilts the posterior part of the cricoid backward and the cords, which are attached to the arytenoids on the cricoid, become elongated. This stretching increases their extrinsic longitudinal tension.

Another way to increase the tension of the vocal cords is to contract the thyroarytenoid muscles themselves, in particular the portions that can vibrate and that are called the vocalis muscles. Such a contraction would, in principle, counteract the elongation caused by the activity of the cricothyroid and reduce the extrinsic tension of the vocal cords. However, if the distance between the points of attachment of the cords is kept constant, the isometric contraction of the vocalis muscle will effectively increase the intrinsic tension of the vocal cords.

Understandably, the rate of vibration of the vocal cords will be lowered whenever their intrinsic or extrinsic tension decreases. Following a rise in frequency, the tension is primarily reduced by the relaxation of the cricothyroid and vocalis muscles. However, in order to produce very low rates of vibration, the strap muscles of the neck, primarily the sternohyoid muscles, may be activated (Atkinson, 1978). The effect of these muscles on the physical state of the vocal folds is only indirect and not completely understood. Presumably, these muscles pull on the hyoid bone and lower the laryngeal structure, which is suspended from it. This lowering reduces the vertical tension on the membranes that form the lining of the larynx and are connected to the ligament of the cords (more particularly to the conus elasticus membrane). The resulting reduction of the vertical tension of the vocal cords would then slow down their rate of vibration (Maeda, 1976; Ohala, 1978).

2.1.3.2 Subglottal pressure

In addition to the muscular forces reviewed so far, variations in subglottal pressure also exert an influence on the rate of vocal-fold vibration. Frequently, a rise in P_s is seen to be accompanied by an increase in F_0. However, as remarked by Titze (1983), this correlation is not easy to explain, since the effect is only an indirect one. Indeed, higher P_s values primarily increase the amplitude of vocal-cord vibration, not its frequency. The effect on frequency may be explained by considering that the higher P_s forces the vocal cords wider apart and deforms them. This greater deformation leads to a greater mechanical stiffness, which in turn causes a higher F_0, since the stiffened cords bounce back faster. Furthermore, a higher P_s produces a larger amount of air flow through the glottis and intensifies the Bernoulli effect by which the cords are snapped together at the end of the closing phase of their vibratory cycle. All in all, the effect of P_s on F_0 is rather small: an increase in pressure of 1 cm H_2O will raise F_0 by not more than 3 to 7 Hz (Baer, 1979). Therefore, P_s changes can only account for a small proportion of an observed F_0 change. Only in exceptional cases, such as the production of emphatically stressed syllables, can P_s substantially contribute to the F_0 change (Van Katwijk, 1974: 61). On the other hand, there is some evidence that the slow and gradual decrease of P_s over the course of an utterance may be responsible for the equally gradual overall decrease of F_0, the so-called 'declination' phenomenon (Collier and Gelfer, 1984; Gelfer *et al.*, 1985; Gelfer, Harris and Baer, 1987; Collier, 1987). This issue is dealt with in greater detail in chapter 5.

Finally, it should be borne in mind that the respiratory system has fairly high inertia. It is ill suited to bring about such rapid P_s changes as would be required to shift F_0 by one octave in 100 ms or less (Sundberg, 1979).

In summary, a simple but reasonably realistic model of F_0 control in speech certainly has to ascribe the majority of the F_0 changes to the activity of the laryngeal muscles that determine the length and tension of the vocal cords. P_s remains at a fairly constant, gradually decreasing value and primarily provides the energy drive for phonation.

So far, we have concentrated on factors under the speaker's control. However, the fine structure of an F_0 curve results from more factors than those reviewed above. For instance, the anatomical coupling of the laryngeal sound source to the resonators of the supralaryngeal cavities causes the physical state of the vocal cords to be influenced by articulatory gestures such as jaw lowering, raising of the tongue body, elevation of the soft palate, etc. A well known effect is the so-called intrinsic pitch of the vowels: high vowels have a higher average F_0 than low vowels (Peterson and Barney, 1952; House and Fairbanks, 1953; Lehiste and Peterson, 1961; Hirst, Nishinuma and Di Cristo, 1979; Ladd and Silverman, 1984; Di Cristo and Hirst, 1986; Reinholt Petersen, 1986; S.A. Steele, 1986). One possible explanation is a mechanical link between tongue-body elevation and the vertical displacement of the larynx: a heightened larynx would result in greater tension of the conus elasticus membrane, which in turn affects the vertical tension of the vocal cords. On the other hand, there is also the influence of the varying degrees of constriction in the vocal tract on the air flow and on the size of the transglottal pressure drop. For instance, the closure of the tract during the production of a voiced stop decreases the transglottal air flow and slows down the vibration of the vocal cords. Therefore one usually observes major F_0 drops in the vicinity of obstruents. Such modulations of the F_0 curve may be termed 'microintonation' (House and Fairbanks, 1953; Lehiste and Peterson, 1961; Di Cristo and Chafcouloff, 1977; Di Cristo and Hirst, 1986; Silverman, 1986). Evidently, such perturbations, not intended by the speaker, cannot be considered as constituents of the pitch contour as a linguistic entity; but they make the interpretation of F_0 curves in terms of underlying intonation patterns all the more difficult.

The physiological aspects of intonation have been studied rather intensively since the late sixties. It is now possible to make rather accurate recordings of both respiratory and laryngeal muscle action.

Subglottal air pressure can be measured directly via a tracheal puncture into the space immediately below the vocal cords. The inserted thin catheter is coupled to an external manometer and the pressure variations are converted into an electrical signal by a pressure transducer. Another direct technique makes use of a miniature pressure transducer that is inserted through the nose and, via the pharynx, reaches down between the vocal cords, thus making a tracheal puncture unnecessary (Cranen and Boves, 1985).

To record the electrical potential that accompanies the contraction of the laryngeal muscles, use is made of very fine wire electrodes that are inserted into the muscles. Pairs of such electrodes are implanted transcutaneously at the neck, using a hypodermic needle to guide the wires (Basmajian and Stecko, 1962). The electromyographical (EMG) signals are recorded on magnetic tape (in analogue or digital format) and are later submitted to various forms of signal processing (Harris, 1981).

Figure 2.2 illustrates a simultaneous recording of P_S and laryngeal muscle activity, together with a recording of F_0. The F_0 contour of the utterance *Heleen wil die kleren meenemen* ('Helen wants to take those clothes along') contains two rise–fall combinations, which produce accents on the syllables *-leen* and *kle-*, and it terminates in an endglide. The corresponding physiological data that are plotted below it show the cricothyroid and sternohyoid muscle activity and the subglottal air-pressure variation for this particular utterance token (light line) and for an average over some twenty-five repetitions of the same contour type (bold line). Notice how the F_0 variations are closely mirrored by the pattern of CT contraction and relaxation. SH activity is suppressed whenever CT is active, but this muscle does not seem to be clearly involved in F_0 lowering. Indeed, the peaks of its activity lag behind the actual F_0 falls. P_S shows minor increases and decreases in synchrony with

15

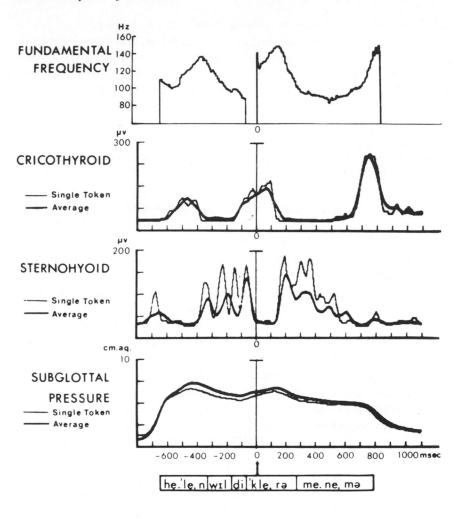

CONTOUR 9

2.2 Simultaneous recordings of fundamental frequency, laryngeal muscular activity and subglottal pressure during the utterance Heleen wil die kleren meenemen *('Helen wants to take those clothes along'). Bold lines: averages over ca twenty-five repetitions; light lines: the single token of which F_0 is plotted.*

the first two F_0 rise–falls. The excursion of the P_s fluctuations, however, is so small that it cannot account for the full extent of the observed F_0 change. Notice, finally, that the CT peak for the end-rise is extra high, probably to compensate for the utterance-final drop of P_s. A fuller explanation of these and similar measurements is given in Collier (1975a).

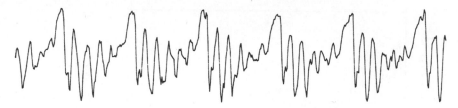

2.3 Oscillogram of 50 ms of the steady state of a vowel /a/

2.2 Acoustic manifestations of vocal-cord vibration and their measurement

2.2.0 Introduction

The various possible acoustic manifestations of vocal-cord vibration have given rise to many strategies in its quantitative analysis. For this reason this section will deal with both the acoustic manifestations (2.2.1) and the measurement of F_0 (2.2.2). As for the latter, we will make a subdivision into measurement by ear, measurement by eye and automatic measurement.

After a brief remark about the unit in which the measured values can best be expressed (2.2.3), we will raise the question to what extent the measurements are interpretable in terms of how the auditory system processes them (2.2.4).

2.2.1 Acoustic manifestations

The vocal-cord vibrations give rise to a sound to which pitch can be assigned. Quite obviously, this property is related to the fact that the physical result of the vibrating vocal cords is a complex, quasi-periodic signal. In the source-filter model for the production of speech, the periodicity of the source signal is, to a first approximation, not affected by the filter action of the vocal tract. Thus, the periodicity in the source vibrations can be made visible when the pressure variations of which the speech sound consists are transduced into electric variations by means of a microphone, and when the latter are displayed as a function of time. Figure 2.3 shows the waveform, or the oscillogram, of the steady state of a vowel. One of the most conspicuous features is the occurrence of peaks at more or less regular distances, and the nearly exact repetition of the fine structure between the peaks. The distance between any two successive peaks or, for that matter, between any two other clearly recognizable recurrent points in the wave form, corresponds to the period T_0. The inverse value of T_0 is the fundamental frequency, generally indicated by F_0.

17

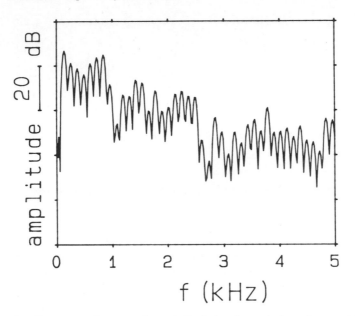

2.4 Spectrum of an exactly periodical signal, consisting of a repetition of one period extracted from the signal of figure 2.3

An alternative display is obtained by determining the spectrum of the signal. This results, for example, in a plot of amplitude as a function of frequency. If the signal is exactly periodical, this plot will show a large number of equidistant peaks (see fig. 2.4), corresponding to the fundamental frequency F_0 and the higher harmonics, at integer multiples of F_0. But the speech signal is not exactly periodical, and this has two consequences: (a) we will have to determine the spectrum for a period of time that is short enough to consider the signal to be stationary (which puts a limit to the resolving power); (b) we will have to determine a whole series of successive spectra, in order to make visible the variations of F_0 as a function of time. This poses the additional problem of how to present this now three-dimensional display in an elegant way. A reasonable solution to this problem is provided by a spectrograph (e.g. the Sonagraph), set to analyse the signal using a narrow filter band. Figure 2.5 shows the result of such an analysis. The fine lines represent the harmonics as separated by means of the filter. The lowest one is F_0, but it is not always visible separately, and its excursions are very small. In a spectrographic display usually a linear frequency-scale is applied, to the effect that the excursions of the nth harmonic are n times those of F_0; in this way, the speech melody can be seen reasonably well.

Both the oscillographic and the spectrographic representation of the speech

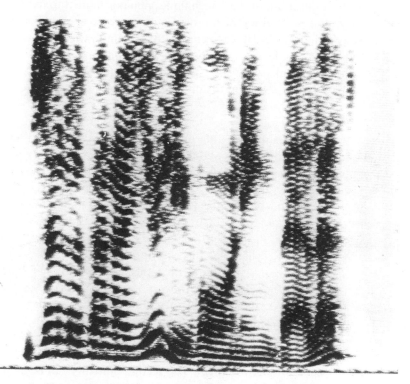

2.5 Narrow-band spectogram of the utterance Zullen we naar jullie woning bellen? *('Shall we phone your home?'), showing the courses of separate harmonics. The frequency ranges from 0 to 4 kHz.*

signal contain, of course, far more information than that with respect to F_0. This implies that attempts to determine F_0 in a quantitative way should start making an appropriate selection, such as only one peak per period, or only one harmonic, together with its rank number.

2.2.2 Measurement of F_0

In what follows we will confine ourselves to the measurement of F_0 in recordings of the microphone signal of speech. This is not because measurement from the microphone signal gives the most accurate results. In fact, refined techniques like electroglottography or glottal transillumination, or even the use of a throat microphone or an accelerometer, are generally capable of giving superior results. But, since methods in this category imply the attachment of electrodes or a probe to, or their insertion in, the body of the speaker, the application of these techniques remains limited to use within the laboratory, thus precluding the study of tape-recorded speech. The price we have to pay is that we shall have to cope with the complexity of the signal, with noise and with considerable variations in amplitude.

In the following subsections, we will mention a few measuring techniques from the past, and a selection of more recent, computer-based techniques.

2.2.2.1 Measurement by ear

Musically trained listeners are able to write down the course of a melody as produced by a musical instrument or by the human voice. The only restriction to this ability is that most people cannot hear in which key the melody is played or sung, unless from time to time an anchor point is given. This may have inspired Else and Willem Pée (1932, 1933) to try to determine pitch in speech using a harmonium as their reference, and gramophone records to enable them to make the speech fragments audible repeatedly. Pitch was transcribed taking the syllable as the descriptive unit. This procedure must have given difficulties, since, for one thing, F_0 need not be stationary during the entire voiced part of the syllable; for another, if it were nevertheless perceived as stationary in some cases, the corresponding pitch sensation need not coincide with any of the discrete tones of the harmonium. With respect to the first difficulty, one can imagine that the method can be improved if such short segments are taken that a stationary pitch is perceived (see 2.3.2.3, the absolute threshold of pitch change). The second difficulty can be avoided by taking a reference signal whose F_0 can be varied continuously.

At the start of our investigations on intonation, we made use of such a method. With the aid of an electronic gate, successive portions of 30 ms length were isolated from the speech utterance (as recorded on a tape loop) and matched auditorily for pitch with a three-formant vowel synthesizer, whose fundamental frequency was, subsequently, measured by means of a frequency counter. Provided that the artificial sound was given each time approximately the same timbre and loudness as the portions of speech to which it should be matched for pitch, the accuracy obtained by this method (as could be checked in a comparison with the measurement of successive periods) was of the order of 1 per cent. Only in rare cases (very low F_0, low amplitude) the interindividual disagreement was more than 3 per cent.

Of course, this method is very laborious and time consuming: one second of speech took about twenty minutes to analyse. But it has a number of advantages as well: it is a reliable and objective account of pitch perception; it overcomes the difficulty to relate F_0 values to segmental information, since the experimenter can always hear which segment is at stake, whereas segment-ation of an oscillographic or a spectrographic recording is much more difficult; finally, the method makes the investigators aware of the fact that speech pitch does not vary in an interesting way during fairly long stretches, whereas at some moments rather dramatic changes take place. This has inspired us to suppose that the listener applies selective attention in the perception of pitch in speech.

2.2.2.2 Measurement by eye

The measurement of the lengths of successive periods in the waveform became possible in the middle of the last century. 'According to Scripture (1902), . . . the first attempt at recording and vizualizing speech was done by Scott in 1856' (Hess, 1983: 95; Scott, 1861). Although instruments recording pressure variations were already in use in meteorology in the eighteenth century, and despite Scott's early attempt to apply the technique to the speech signal, it took another half century before Rousselot's (1908) kymograph became a leading measuring device in instrumental phonetics. Its limited bandwidth prevented the display of harmonics higher than the first one or two, but it was good enough to study the three prosodic parameters – duration, intensity and pitch (Léon and Martin, 1969: 86). The use of a smoked surface of a cylindrical drum, although advantageous because it could be used repeatedly, was gradually pushed to the background by the rise of electronics (for amplification of a microphone signal) and mirror-galvanometer techniques, so that the speech signal could be recorded on film. Probably the first publication on such an instrument is the one by Parmenter and Treviño (1932), and comparable apparatus has been used in The Netherlands as well (Ledeboer van Westerhoven, 1939).

Although F_0 measurement with the help of these devices is certainly objective and more reliable than the use of the unaided ear, it is very laborious. Much of this disadvantage could, however, be taken away by means of ingenious contraptions for a rapid conversion from length of period to frequency (e.g. Meyer, 1911; see Hess, 1983: 97). From these considerations, it may be understood why the technique of measurement of successive periods by eye remained popular for such a long time.

We applied a computer-aided waveform-measuring technique up to the end of the seventies, largely as a check on still rather unreliable automatic measurement (see 2.2.2.3).

As was mentioned before, the accuracy with which F_0 can be measured in a narrow-band spectrogram can be increased by selecting a higher harmonic. But there are two circumstances which make it risky to take it too high. First, for certain speech sounds, the energy in higher-frequency regions may be too low to create any visual effects. Second, if there is enough energy by virtue of the presence of a formant, there may be not enough energy in lower regions,

21

making it impossible to count the number of harmonics: taking the ninth instead of the aimed-at tenth causes an error of over 10 per cent. For this reason, it has been considered a safe compromise to take the fourth or the fifth harmonic.

2.2.2.3 Automatic measurement

Attempts to measure F_0 automatically date back at least to the thirties (e.g. Dudley, 1935; Hunt, 1935; Riesz, 1936; Grützmacher and Lottermoser, 1937; Obata and Kobayashi, 1937, 1938, 1940), and have still not found an entirely satisfactory solution. Before the application of general-purpose computers to speech research, large numbers of 'pitch meters' have been developed. Léon and Martin (1969) have published a list of no less than 145 titles on this issue. More recently, Hess (1983) produced a list of over 2,700 titles, many hundreds of which deal with pitch-measuring devices, including, of course, modern computer techniques. Since it cannot be our purpose to give even a condensed survey of the many products of human ingenuity in this field, we will confine ourselves to merely mentioning two very early computer techniques, and to giving a somewhat more detailed account of three methods used in our own investigations.

One of the two early techniques is Gold's (1962) multiple-criterion method, which attempts to find the most 'popular' period among the outputs of six pitch-period detectors, each of which works on different aspects of the waveform. The other one is Noll's (1964) cepstrum technique, which calculates the spectrum of the one-sided logarithmic spectrum with the aim of finding a peak in the so-called quefrency domain that corresponds to T_0.

The first computer-implemented automatic 'pitch detector' used in our laboratory was based on the autocorrelation technique (e.g. Gill, 1959; Fujisaki, 1960; Stone and White, 1963; Sondhi, 1968; Rabiner, 1977; 't Hart *et al.*, 1982). With this technique, a short (40 ms) fragment of the signal is correlated with the same fragment delayed by τ ms, τ varying from e.g. 2 to 20 ms in successive small steps. The resulting autocorrelation function will show a more or less pronounced peak at $\tau = T_0$. Of course, there will also be a peak at $\tau = 2T_0$; and if the signal contains a very strong second, third (etc.) harmonic, rather high peaks may occur at $\tau + \frac{1}{2}T_0, \frac{1}{3}T_0$ (etc.). Thus, unless special measures are taken, erroneous measurements, such as octave errors, remain possible. · Rabiner *et al.* (1976) have given a survey and an evaluation of the techniques of this kind. In order to speed up the measurement, auto-sign correlation is often applied, in which only the sign of the signal is taken into account.

More recently, an algorithm has become available to us, which in fact is a software implementation of a model of human pitch-perception, viz. the one proposed by Goldstein (1973; see 2.3.1), as modified by Duifhuis, Willems and

Sluyter (1978, 1982). Sreenivas and Rao (1979) have worked along comparable lines. The pitch meter consists of a spectral analyser together with a peak picker, and a harmonic-pattern recognizer. The latter classifies the peak frequencies provided by the former, and determines F_0 on the basis of the best fit of the classified peaks. The harmonic-pattern recognizer is, in fact, a harmonics sieve, with meshes around the harmonic frequencies. The procedure amounts to successively setting the sieve to all possible values (in discrete steps of 1/24th octave) of F_0 between 50 and 500 Hz. The best fit is the one in which the candidate set and the ideal harmonic pattern show the greatest resemblance. The performance of this pitch meter has proved superior to the autocorrelation algorithm used in our laboratory, which ranks among the best discussed by Rabiner *et al.* (1976). Nevertheless, the harmonics sieve is also prone to making octave errors, but these can fairly easily be detected by eye, or by ear after resynthesis (see ch. 3), and corrected.

The most recent development in our laboratory is an algorithm which, upon a suggestion by Schroeder (1968), shifts the spectrum downwards over successive harmonic intervals (octave, fifth, fourth, major third, minor third, etc.), and adds the shifted spectra to the original spectrum. The highest peak in this so-called harmonic-sum spectrum corresponds to F_0. One can show mathematically that this method is equivalent to the harmonics sieve. However, probably an important difference is that in the harmonic-sum spectrum the information about the amplitude of the spectral components is maintained. Indeed, this algorithm has turned out to perform better than the one by Duifhuis, Willems and Sluyter (see Hermes, 1988): in a sample of twenty-eight sentences, fourteen of which were spoken by male and fourteen by female speakers, the percentage of incorrectly measured frames was four times lower with the harmonic-sum spectrum algorithm than with the harmonics sieve.

This survey of various techniques of measuring T_0 or F_0 is, of course, by no means complete. Nor is it sufficiently detailed to help the reader find the relevant literature; for that purpose, we refer to Hess (1983). Our main aim has been to illustrate that, however simple the relation between pitch on the one hand, and F_0 or T_0 on the other may be, the measurement of either is very difficult, and its automatic extraction from the microphone signal has required half a century of intensive research to be brought to an acceptable, but still not perfect and general, solution.

2.2.3 Choice of units: Hz versus semitones

Although the internationally recommended unit of frequency is the Hertz, for a number of reasons we prefer to convert the data as obtained in the F_0

measurement algorithm into logarithmic units. The main reasons are that, with a view to the perception of pitch, we are more interested in frequency distances than in the absolute frequencies themselves, and that we want to express the magnitudes of these distances independently of the incidental frequency. This makes it possible to compare F_0 curves from different speakers, with different ranges of voice. If, for instance, F_0 in a male voice rises from 100 to 150 Hz, we experience it as a perfect imitation of a rise from 180 to 270 Hz in a female speaker. We are unable to express this effect if we talk about a frequency difference of 50 Hz in the former, and one of 90 Hz in the latter case. A conversion into logarithmic units does enable us to express the effect satisfactorily. The unit to be chosen is, of course, arbitrary, and among the numerous possibilities we have decided to choose the semitone. A distance D, in semitones, between any two frequencies f_1 and f_2 is calculated by means of the following formula:

$$D = 12.\log_2\frac{f_1}{f_2} = \frac{12}{\log_{10} 2}.\log_{10}\frac{f_1}{f_2}$$

If we apply this formula to the example given above, we obtain 7.02 semitones in both cases.

The choice of semitones is by no means dictated by a spurious wish to attribute a specific role to musical intervals in speech, nor by an ultimate desire to design a transcription system in terms of a musical notation with notes in a staff. This would be defendable if the outcome of the logarithmic conversion were to show (near) integer values in a disproportionally large number of cases, but as it appears, no such predominance exists in speech-pitch distances.

2.2.4 Concluding remarks

The satisfaction which phoneticians may feel with the enormous progress made during the last decades in the automatic determination of F_0 is overshadowed by the fact that the finer the performance of the techniques applied, the more it becomes apparent how irregularly the vocal folds vibrate. As has already been mentioned in 2.1.3.2, the local perturbations are caused by the varying acoustic coupling between the voice source and the vocal tract. As long as these mechanisms are not fully understood, the interpretation of F_0 curves remains a difficult task. But even if this problem had been brought to a solution, we would still be faced with the following two problems: (a) as long as it is unclear what are adequate descriptive units, an interpretation other than one in terms of values of F_0 as a function of time is not possible; (b) it is not possible, solely on the basis of a visual inspection of an F_0 curve, to decide how it is converted by the auditory system into a melodic continuum, let alone that it would be possible to know what is communicatively relevant and what is not. This implies that our understanding of the listener's interpretation can only be achieved in a study dedicated to the perception of speech pitch, which will be the topic of the next section.

2.3 Perception

2.3.0 Introduction

In this section, we will deal with the perception of pitch in general and of speech pitch in particular. We are especially interested in the limits of perceptibility of pitch phenomena in speech, in connection with the question of communicative relevance. No matter how systematically a phenomenon may be found to occur through a visual inspection of F_0 curves, if it cannot be heard, it cannot play a part in communication.

We will first (2.3.1) briefly discuss how and under which conditions pitch is perceived. Next (2.3.2), in order to answer the question of how accurately pitch can be perceived, we will select a number of experimental data to be found in the psychoacoustical literature. These data might make us apprehensive of very low thresholds in a number of respects also for pitch in speech; but since the objectives of psychoacoustics are essentially different from those we have in mind in this section, we must be aware of the possibility that a direct extrapolation cannot safely be made. Therefore, data will be added from experiments with more speech-like stimuli; and indeed, it appears that there are sometimes substantial discrepancies between these data and the results obtained in psychoacoustic experiments. In a later discussion (2.3.3) we will argue that 'psychophonetic' experiments too are not fully representative of the way in which pitch in real speech is perceived.

2.3.1 How and when is pitch perceived?

Modern theories on the perception of pitch (Goldstein, 1973; Terhardt, 1979) share the concept of a central processor which tries to detect the greatest common divisor of the frequencies of a number of harmonics. Most effective are the third up to the sixth harmonic, which have therefore been said to lie within the dominance region (Ritsma, 1967) for the perception of periodicity pitch (formerly termed the 'residue pitch', after J.F. Schouten, 1940). A contribution may also be made by harmonics outside this region. Thus, e.g., when presented with 300, 450, 600 and 750 Hz, the central processor will find 150 Hz. Note that the physical presence of the fundamental frequency is not necessary. Consequently, the term 'pitch' stands for the sensation brought about by either the fundamental frequency, or by the greatest common divisor of the harmonics, or by both. However, in signals in which higher partials are not integer multiples of the fundamental frequency there is an obvious discrepancy between the two. Furthermore, due to the irregularities of the vocal-fold vibrations, the phonated speech signal is not exactly periodical; but the corresponding inharmonicity is not very serious, and can therefore be neglected.

It has appeared that only two (adjacent) harmonics have to be supplied to the central processor to enable it to calculate the greatest common divisor reliably. Moreover, it constitutes no problem if one of these components is 20 to 25 dB weaker than the other (Cardozo, 1972; Houtsma, 1980), unless the distance between the two is so small that one is masked by the other.

A condition for the perception of pitch is that the fundamental frequency (physically present or virtual) is not lower than about 40 Hz. There is also a higher limit, in the sense that the accuracy with which pitch can be judged decreases sharply for frequencies beyond 4 kHz (Henning, 1966).

Pitch can be perceived in very short stimuli. Cardozo and Ritsma (1965) and Ritsma *et al.* (1966) have measured an accuracy of 1 per cent or better in stimuli of only 30 ms duration (unless F_0 is lower than 100 Hz). Our own experience with the pitch matching of gated portions of 30 ms length, as has been dealt with in the previous section, has amply confirmed the psychoacoustic findings of Cardozo and Ritsma. The fact that only 30 ms is needed to produce a reliable pitch sensation may not be significant: in the psychoacoustic experiment, as well as in our gating technique, the listener is given enough time after the presentation of the stimulus to process the information. In speech, however, the stream of information goes on continuously.

Preliminary conclusions with respect to F_0 in speech can be drawn on the basis of this subsection. The fundamental frequency of the human voice is well within the limits of 40 and 4,000 Hz. Harmonics in the dominance region are practically always present with sufficient energy. Although the speech signal is not exactly periodic, there is no need to consider the perception of pitch in a speech signal to be essentially different from the perception of pitch in a strictly periodic signal.

2.3.2 How accurately is pitch perceived?

The previous subsection, in which it was examined under which conditions pitch can be perceived, also touched upon the accuracy with which it is perceived. In the following subsections, we want to deal with accuracy more specifically. In particular, we want to examine to what extent results obtained in psychoacoustic experiments apply to the perception of pitch in speech. The aim of this examination is to try to estimate the accuracy needed in a description of F_0 variation in speech in view of the perceptual limitations of a listener. However, we must be aware of the fact that psychoacoustic research sets out to explore the extreme values of the system parameters; it is not necessarily true that everyday practice continuously requires the utmost performance. Thus, we should expect that the results supplied by psychoacoustics may be more detailed than needed for our purpose. Fortunately, apart from purely psychoacoustic experiments, a number of experiments have also been carried out that can be called 'psychophonetic'. A comparison between these and psychoacoustic experiments might give us an indication as to how serious the discrepancies may be between the limits of pitch perception and the perception of pitch in speech.

In the following subsections, we will deal with the differential threshold of pitch (2.3.2.1), the differential threshold of pitch distance (2.3.2.2), the absolute threshold of pitch change (2.3.2.3), and the differential threshold of pitch change (2.3.2.4).

2.3.2.1 The differential threshold of pitch

When asked to tell the pitch of only one tone, listeners are practically unable to perform this task. In an experiment by Bachem (1937) on the identifiability of individual musical tones, the average errors of the seven cases studied varied between five and nine semitones. Only subjects who possess so-called absolute pitch are able to yield an accuracy of a quarter of a semitone or better.

More relevant to the question about the accuracy with which pitch is perceived is the just noticeable difference (j.n.d.) in frequency between two successively presented (pure) tones, the differential threshold. Surprisingly, perhaps, the same people who cannot identify the frequency of a single tone with any accuracy, when confronted with two successive tones, may very well be able to discriminate between a tone of 1,000 Hz and one of 1,005 Hz (best performers come below 1Hz; see Ritsma, 1965; Nordmark, 1968; Rakowsky, 1971). If we take the j.n.d. relative to the reference frequency, we can see that at lower frequencies than 1,000 Hz, the sensitivity to frequency difference is lower. For instance, Nordmark found $\Delta f/f$ to be 0.00054 at 1 kHz, and 0.00136 at 125 Hz. And as we have mentioned already (Henning, 1966), also at high frequencies the sensitivity decreases: at 10 kHz, the relative j.n.d. is about ten times that at 1 kHz. Furthermore, for short stimulus durations, the precision of pitch sensation decreases as duration becomes shorter. For instance, Cardozo and Ritsma (1965) found, in an adjustment procedure, for 1 kHz a relative standard deviation of 0.6×10^{-3} at 60 ms or longer durations, but more than a doubling of this value each time the duration was halved. Complex signals contain more information, and therefore it should cause no surprise that the saturation point, as measured by the same authors, is situated at a duration of only 30 ms.

Flanagan and Saslow (1958) have measured the differential threshold in synthetic vowels, in a frequency region representative of male speech. Their outcome was 0.3 to 0.5 per cent. This is of the same order of magnitude as has been observed for sine waves (see Nordmark 1968 for 125 Hz), and it suggests that in speech, too, the auditory system is able to measure pitch very delicately. It should therefore cause no surprise that, on the basis of these results, Lehiste (1970) estimated that to take into account the perceptual abilities would require an accuracy in the specification of F_0 in speech of 1 Hz. But other authors come up with much higher values. Issachenko and Schädlich (1970) have found 5 per cent (of 150 Hz) with resynthesized speech material, and Rossi and Chafcouloff (1972) obtained 4 per cent (of 195 Hz) with a natural voice. This discrepancy implies that, in as far as the differential threshold is relevant in the perception of pitch in speech, we are still remote from a workable answer to the question how accurately pitch in speech is perceived.

2.3.2.2 The differential threshold of pitch distance
Musically trained listeners are generally capable of identifying the size of the interval between two successively or simultaneously presented tones. Stumpf (1890) already appears to have explored judgments of pitch distance; and Plomp, Wagenaar and Mimpen (1973) have found a standard deviation of about half a semitone in the identification of the musical intervals between simultaneously presented tones by musically trained subjects.

We have reasons to believe that the identification of musical intervals is not relevant to the question as to how accurately pitch in speech is perceived. Rather, we think that it may be important to know the conditions in which a listener is able to say that one interval is larger or smaller than a second one. This brings us to the differential threshold of pitch distance. Stumpf complains that participating in experiments set up to measure this threshold is a difficult task. Although in some conditions musically trained subjects could hear differences below a semitone, they were much less successful in most cases. Stevens and Volkman (1940) used a three-tone paradigm in which the subjects were asked to adjust a tone between two given tones in such a way that the distances to either of the given tones were equal; they found intra-observer variabilities of no less than 10–15 per cent. Burns (1974), using four tones, none of which were equal, asked his subjects (professional performers of classic Hindustani music, in which the octave is divided into twenty-two steps instead of twelve) to indicate whether they judged the interval between tones 1 and 2 larger than, equal to, or smaller than that between tones 3 and 4. Only one of his thirteen subjects was able to perform this task with any accuracy.

For speech, this threshold was measured ('t Hart, 1981) in experiments in which the subjects were deliberately not selected on grounds of their already known extraordinary acuity in pitch perception, nor had they been trained to do this particular psychophysical experiment. For the sake of comparison, additional data from psychoacoustically trained subjects were also collected. This study yielded a just noticeable difference of 1.5 to 2 semitones. The experiment was done using pair comparisons with so-called 'roving reference', i.e., in most of the stimuli, the starting frequencies and/or the final frequencies in a pair were unequal, as in the paradigm applied by Burns, and this condition made it very difficult for the listeners to do the comparisons. But exactly this condition is what one must expect to occur in speech pitch. The outcome suggests that only differences of more than three semitones can play a part in communicative situations. For instance, if an utterance contains two rises, the first of which starts at 125 and ends at 150 Hz (3.16 semitones), the second one, starting at e.g. 100 Hz, should finish at at least 143 Hz (6.19 semitones) in order to be heard as larger.

Apparently, the discrepancy found between the results of the psychoacoustic and the psychophonetic experiments on the differential threshold of pitch proper is much smaller in the case of the differential threshold of pitch distance.

2.3.2.3 The absolute threshold of pitch change

One of the striking properties of the fundamental frequency in speech is that it changes continuously. Therefore, it seems important to know in which conditions these changes are audible as such, and in which conditions they go unnoticed. This brings us to the absolute threshold of pitch change: how rapidly should, in a given interval of time, the fundamental frequency change in order to evoke a sensation of pitch change? The classic experiment was done by Sergeant and Harris (1962). Being interested in the possibility of incorporating in certain man–machine systems a frequency glissando to indicate change of position of a component, they paid more attention to the time needed for the detection of pitch change (in view of the time needed to give the appropriate reaction) than to the question as formulated above. At a duration of 75 ms, it is necessary to move about 30 Hz away from the initial frequency of 1,500 Hz, corresponding to a 390 Hz/s threshold found for untrained listeners. As the duration increases, the speed as well as the amount of frequency change decrease: plotting the results on double-logarithmic paper, Sergeant and Harris obtained a linear relationship over the whole range between 75 ms and 10 s, without any sign of an asymptote on the side of the shortest durations. Thus they feel entitled to suppose that the ear could still have reported pitch changes after durations of only a few milliseconds. Accordingly, they consider the sensitivity to (this type of) frequency modulation surprisingly good, although they admit that for slow frequency shifts, considerably longer times are required.

In the alternative viewpoint, taking duration as the independent and the rate of change of frequency as the dependent variable, one would conclude that if the stimulus is long (but not too long, since otherwise memory limitations pose a problem), the sensitivity is fairly good (about 1 Hz/s at 10 s duration), but as the stimulus duration decreases, the sensitivity deteriorates dramatically (150 Hz/s at 100 ms for best performers).

Regrettably, one cannot be sure whether, in experiments like these, the sensitivity to frequency change is measured, or merely to the difference between initial and final frequency of the sweep. In fact, Shower and Biddulph (1931) used frequency modulation with the aim of measuring the differential threshold of pitch. Pollack (1968), who repeated the Sergeant and Harris experiment with starting frequencies of 125, 250, 500 and 1,000 Hz, and with sweep durations of 0.5, 1, 2 and 4 s, reports that his data were adequately fitted by a slope of − 1. This means that the total frequency change (rate multiplied by duration) was independent of duration, which gives support to the hypothesis that the frequency difference is the important perceptual factor. Sergeant and Harris, however, found a slope of about − 1.3, indicating a higher sensitivity with the longer-sweep tones. This can also be illustrated by comparing the total frequency change of 10 Hz at 10 s duration for best performers with the one of 15 Hz at 0.1 duration. Incidentally, by this comparison, the 'dramatic deterioration' as mentioned above is literally explained away.

Pollack's data show that, each time the initial frequency is taken an octave higher, the thresholds, if expressed in Hz/s, go up by a factor of about 1.75; however, this implies that in relative terms, performance is better at the higher initial frequencies. For instance, the amount of frequency change relative to the initial frequency is 2.5 to 3 per cent for 125 Hz, and only 1.7 per cent for 1,000 Hz.

Recently, H.E.M. Schouten (1985) has measured this threshold for the very short durations between 20 and 50 ms, with starting frequencies of 400, 1,300 and 2,700 Hz. Now, if Sergeant and Harris were right in their supposition that the linear course in their data does not show a tendency towards an asymptote at shorter durations, we would expect, by linear extrapolation, a threshold of about 1,500 Hz/s (or an amount of frequency change of 30 Hz) for a sweep of 20 ms starting at 1,500 Hz; and using the transposition rule as derived from

Pollack, these values would be 500 Hz/s (10 Hz) with a starting frequency of 375 Hz (two octaves lower than 1,500 Hz). Schouten's findings are very much higher: with 1,300 Hz, he needed a speed of 18,000 Hz/s (or an amount of about 350 Hz); and with 400 Hz, the speed was about 13,500 Hz/s (amount 275 Hz). If we were to base our extrapolation on Pollack's observation that the total frequency change is independent of duration, we would obtain a threshold of only about 45 Hz/s for 20 ms duration and a starting frequency of 500 Hz. These figures illustrate that a linear extrapolation is not feasible for shorter durations; rather, it seems that the slope of -1 in Pollack's data, and of -1.3 in those of Sergeant and Harris, becomes steeper with decreasing duration, particularly for lower frequencies, as can be observed in a comparison of Schouten's data for the three different starting frequencies. The latter effect is to be expected, since in very short sweeps at low frequencies, the number of 'periods' becomes too low to enable the auditory system to detect a pitch difference between beginning and end.

The absolute threshold of pitch change in speech-like signals has been measured by Rossi (1971) for upward, and later (1978) for downward glides. In one of his experiments, stimuli were made from glides produced by a male voice, starting at approximately 135 Hz and ending at various frequencies from 0 up to about 60 Hz higher than the onset frequency. Durations were 200, 100 and 50 ms. The reported threshold values are 19 Hz (14 per cent), 25 Hz (18.5 per cent) and 44.5 Hz (33 per cent) respectively. Klatt (1973), however, reported that a glide in a synthetic vowel /ɛ/ from 119.25 to 120.75 Hz in 250 ms could just be distinguished from one going from 120.75 to 119.25 Hz. This can be interpreted in terms of an absolute threshold, a glide from 120 to 123 Hz being just distinguishable from a stationary tone. Now, in terms of speed of pitch change, Rossi's data boil down to 95 (200 ms), 250 (100 ms) and 890 (50 ms) Hz/s, whereas Klatt's result corresponds with only 12 Hz/s (in 250 ms). A (small) extrapolation of Rossi's data to 250 ms would give about 60 Hz/s, five times as much as the value found by Klatt. Ironically, Klatt did his experiment with the aim of demonstrating that when the dynamic-situation characteristic of speech was taken into account, the various thresholds would be considerably higher than those obtained in psychoacoustic research. We cannot conclude that Klatt's experiment remained too close to psychoacoustics; we may equally well suppose that Rossi's thresholds are exceptionally high.

In an attempt to decide between these two possibilities, we can convert the values for the threshold slopes, including those obtained in the psychoacoustic experiments by Pollack and by Sergeant and Harris, into semitones per second (ST/s) instead of Hz/s (Schouten's data were already given in octaves per second), in order to make them independent of the frequency region in which

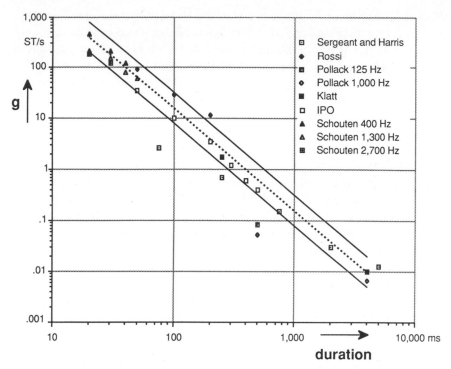

2.6 The absolute threshold of pitch change. In order to be audibly distinguished from a stationary tone, a short glide of 50 ms duration should have a rate of change of F_0 (g) of sixty-four semitones per second (ST/s). Each doubling of the duration decreases the threshold value by a factor of four. The dashed line connects the points that meet this condition. The solid lines are drawn at distances of a factor of two from the dashed line.

the experiments had been done. If these values are plotted on double-logarithmic paper, a pattern emerges as is shown in figure 2.6. Added to this figure are the results of a small-scale experiment done at IPO with a synthetic vowel /œ/ starting at 135 Hz, with durations 50, 100, 200, 300, 400 and 500 ms.

The dashed line in figure 2.6 represents a glissando threshold satisfying the equation:

$$g_{thr} = .16/T^2,$$

in which g_{thr} is the speed of frequency change at threshold in ST/s, and T is the duration of the sweep in s. This seems to be a reasonable compromise: twenty-five of the thirty-three data points lie within a distance of a factor of two from that line, over the entire range from 20 ms to 5 s. It appears that, particularly for the longer durations, Rossi's thresholds are indeed rather high, but more

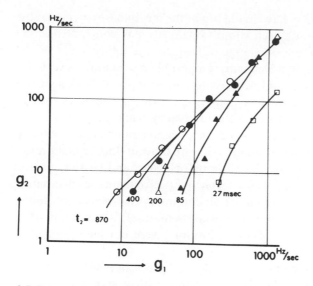

2.7 *Just noticeable differences in frequency glides with rates of change g_1 and g_2, as replotted by Bouma (1979: 494) on the basis of Pollack's (1968) data*

serious deviations from the general trend are Sergeant and Harris at 75 ms, and Pollack's data for 0.5 and 1 s.

This partial reconciliation seems to suggest that for the absolute threshold of pitch change there is no essential discrepancy between 'psychoacoustic' and 'psychophonetic' stimuli.

2.3.2.4 The differential threshold of pitch change

The differential threshold of rate of change of frequency has been measured by Pollack (1968) for sine waves. The question was, how much the rates of change in two glides, presented one after the other, should differ in order to be just audibly distinguishable. Pollack worked around a central frequency of 707 Hz with frequency differences between onsets and offsets of the glides of 4, 8, 16, ... up to 512 Hz, which took place in time intervals varying between 0.1 and 870 ms. The difference in rate of change in a stimulus pair was brought about by the difference in these time intervals.

The results can be interpreted as follows: for the longer durations, the value of g_1/g_2 (quotient of the two rates of change in Hz/s) is about 2, although close to 3 for the slowest changes. For shorter durations, this value is considerably larger (up to about 10 for slow changes), although it tends to be about 2 again for the most rapid changes. For durations shorter than about 50 ms it remains high (between 10 and 30), irrespective of the speed (see fig. 2.7). Considering that the (single) subject may have made use of the inevitable extra cue of the difference in duration within each stimulus pair, we may conclude that the differential sensitivity to rate of change of frequency is rather low.

Nabelek and Hirsh (1969) have made comparable measurements with five subjects instead of only one and, whereas the majority of Pollack's stimuli covered frequency intervals of less than two semitones and were located around 707 Hz, these authors varied the interval systematically (two, seven and twelve semitones), and they studied the phenomenon at 250, 1,000 and 4,000 Hz. Their results agree reasonably well with those of Pollack in the range of intervals covered by both studies, although Nabelek and Hirsh's subjects performed somewhat better (g_1/g_2 for seven and twelve semitones fluctuating around 1.6, for two semitones around 2.3); optimum performance was found for 1,000 and 4,000 Hz, with seven and twelve semitones, at a duration of 30 ms, g_1/g_2 being as low as 1.3. These conditions were not incorporated in Pollack's stimulus material.

The differential threshold of rate of change of F_0 in a speech-like signal has been measured by Klatt (1973). In comparison with a standard stimulus (synthetic /ɛ/) in which F_0 descended from 135 to 105 Hz in 250 ms (-120 Hz/s), a variable stimulus, having the same average value of F_0, but different initial and final values of F_0, could just be distinguished from the standard if it changed from 139 to 101 Hz in the same duration (-152 Hz/s). The value of g_1/g_2 is 1.27, even slightly better than the optimum result reported by Nabelek and Hirsh (1969) for high frequencies and larger intervals at 30 ms duration, as we have discussed above. Their stimulus best comparable to the one used by Klatt is the downward glide from 250 to 167 Hz in 300 ms, which yields a value of $g_1/g_2 = 1.71$.

Once more, it seems as if there is no serious discrepancy between the psychoacoustic and the more speech-like conditions. But yet, we cannot be sure that these results are generally valid in actual speech. For one thing, Klatt's stimulus has in common with those in the psychoacoustic studies that the phenomenon is listened to in isolation. Moreover, whereas the paradigm used by both Pollack and Nabelek and Hirsh offered the potential extra cue of the difference in duration of the glide, Klatt has tried to circumvent this problem by making stimulus pairs of equal duration, but, as a consequence, the initial and final frequencies were bound to be different. And it is easily verifiable that in this paradigm the difference between the initial frequencies is already detected by the ear in the first 30 to 50 ms, irrespective of what happens later in the stimulus. In an attempt to avoid this direct cue, we used essentially the same paradigm, but now on a $V_1CV_2CV_3$ stimulus, with voiceless consonants (see fig. 2.8). The variable rising (or falling) sweeps were on V_2, whereas in each of the members of a pair, the courses of F_0 in both V_1 and V_3

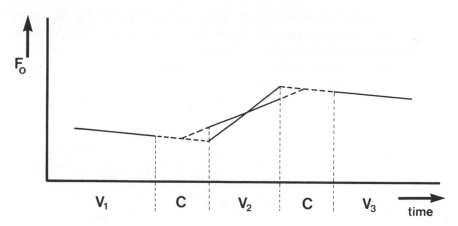

2.8 Measurement of the differential threshold of the rate of change of F_0 in a speech fragment

were identical, viz. slowly falling, as is the case in normal speech. In this way, the frequency differences at either side of the sweep are of course still present, but they may be obscured by the common attributes of the remaining parts of the stimulus. In particular, the varying on- and offsets of the sweeps are made inaudible by the voiceless consonants. We found that differences in slope characterized by a factor of less than two were inaudible. In conclusion, we feel safe to say that in actual speech two just distinguishable rates of change of F_0 will differ by a factor of at least two.

2.3.3 How accurately is pitch perceived in real speech?

In section 2.3.2 we have seen that, except with respect to the differential threshold of pitch, no substantial discrepancies exist between the results from psychoacoustic and 'psychophonetic' experiments. This may cause some surprise, since, as we have argued before, we cannot expect that the results of psychoacoustic experiments are representative of the way in which pitch in speech is perceived. The main reason for this is that such experiments are designed to explore the ultimate limits of the performance of the auditory system, on which to base a model of this system.

To what extent can we expect the results of psychophonetic experiments to be representative of the perception of pitch in real speech? For several reasons, it should be suspected that even such experiments may not be adequate for finding a conclusive answer to this question. One reason is that such experiments still suffer from enabling the listeners to concentrate too easily on mere pitch. And we should take into account that in a communicative situation the listener does not perceive pitch in its proper sense: the variations of F_0 are translated into prosodic properties of the linguistic code, such as accentuation and the like. Although physical properties are, of course, at the basis of linguistic interpretation, the perceptual activity of the listener takes place at a higher level of abstraction.

A second reason for our suspicion is that the dynamic situation of speech is characterized not only by continuous variation of F_0, but also of formant frequencies and, above all, of amplitude. In our experience, a drop in amplitude of 10 to 20 dB in several tens of milliseconds, as can often be found in transitions from vowels to consonants, can entirely obscure the presence of changes in F_0 of up to half an octave.

From these considerations it follows that the stimulus material to be used in experiments aiming at finding out how accurately the variations of F_0 in speech should be specified in view of the limitations in speech perception should consist of entire speech utterances. Admittedly, if in the experiment comparisons have to be made between pairs of utterances in which only the course of F_0 differs, listeners can still concentrate on pitch, since the content of the message need not distract them, but anyway, memory is loaded considerably more realistically than with isolated vowels. And entire utterances contain all the variations of amplitude and formant frequencies. In chapters 3, 4 and 5, a number of such experiments will be dealt with, most of which have been done with the general purpose of obtaining data reduction, a central issue in our analysis of intonation.

2.4 Integration

Ideally, a phonetic description that would be as complete as possible, would combine in itself the three aspects given in this chapter. In analogy to the study of segmental phenomena, one could begin with production, subsequently give an acoustic description of the signal, and next try to establish the relationship between these two. Afterwards, one could concentrate on perception, and examine which acoustic properties contribute to what extent and in what way. If both the relationship between production and the acoustic characteristics and that between the latter and perception are sufficiently understood, then, in addition the bridge from production to perception can be built.

However, the study of the production of intonation, by means of electromyography and measurements of subglottal pressure and lung volume, has appeared to be very complicated. Apart from technical problems inherent in all these measurements, there is a more fundamental problem, viz. that the physiological mechanisms involved have far less transparent relationships with what is produced than, e.g., the tongue tip, the jaws and the velum have with the various speech sounds. Part of this intransparency is caused by the lack of adequate units for a phonetic description. To address the specific question of the relationships mentioned above, one needs a selection criterion in order to decide what to look for in the abundance of possible physiological recordings. Such a criterion can only be based on hypotheses about the correspondence between the muscular activities on the one hand, and as many discrete events in the acoustic signal on the other. Thus, the first problem is to find a way to describe the F_0 curve in terms of discrete events.

For these reasons, we opted to start with the measurement of F_0, and next to consider the question as to which aspects of F_0 variation give substantial contributions to the perception of speech melody. It was only in a later stage, when we had gained enough insight into the relative importance of the F_0 variation for perception, that we found it meaningful to take up physiological measurements, and to try to look for muscular and respiratory activities that might correspond to the observed F_0 variations as far as these are pertinent for perception.

3

The IPO approach

3.0 Introduction

As was mentioned in 2.4, and also suggested at other places, one cannot hope to establish the full relationship between the production, the acoustic manifestation and the perception of intonation at a blow. Therefore, it has been our deliberate choice to first concentrate on the study of the acoustic phenomena, and to try to develop a method of data reduction on the basis of perceptual tolerances. Data reduction in itself would already make the data more manageable, but if it is done on the basis of perceptual tolerances, it might provide us with perceptual units in a melodic description. This, in turn, might enable us to interpret these data so as to reflect how the human listener processes them. Ultimately, this may help to offer a solution to the problem of finding suitable descriptive units.

In this chapter, we will give an account of how we have tried to find such units at three different levels of the analysis of intonation. Since it seems impossible, in a phonetic approach, to establish a direct link between recordings of F_0 on the one hand and the abstract mental categories of the basic intonation patterns possibly underlying them on the other, it is, in our view, necessary to make a detour. In each of the steps of this perception-guided detour, subjective similarity is at stake, from auditory identity in the first, to a more abstract kind of resemblance in the last step.

3.1 Pitch movements

Upon inspection of F_0 recordings as they can now be obtained using modern, sophisticated pitch-extraction algorithms, one observes far more detailed fluctuation than became visible in the measurements by means of the old 30 ms-fragments pitch-matching method. In view of the perceptual restrictions that have been dealt with in 2.3, especially those found in dynamic situations, we cannot believe that even the lesser detail obtained in the old measuring method is relevant to the perception of speech melody, let alone the much finer detail to be seen nowadays. Neither do we believe that all those fluctuations are actually voluntarily programmed in production. On the contrary, it has been generally accepted meanwhile that, as a result of changes in the resistance as encountered by the air flow, which occur due to variations in the articulatory configuration of the vocal tract, the pressure drop over the glottis is influenced in such a way as to bring about certain involuntary fluctuations in F_0. These fluctuations, or microintonation phenomena, are thus dependent on the incidental segmental content of the speech utterance, and it is therefore reasonable to presume that they contribute less to the perception of speech melody than do the systematically programmed changes of F_0. This implies that it is important, in the analysis of speech-pitch fluctuations, to try to separate these two categories of F_0 changes, according to their origin, voluntary or involuntary.

Again, the most obvious way to achieve this purpose seems to be to perform physiological measurements on the laryngeal musculature, supplemented with measurements of the subglottal and intra-oral pressure. Such a method has a number of unattractive aspects. If one sets out to map out the main characteristics of the intonation of a language, it is not sensible to restrict the number of speakers beforehand to the few who want to volunteer for such experiments; besides, the possibilities of producing spontaneous speech under such circumstances are rather limited; consequently, the inclusion in the observations of less frequently occurring intonation phenomena may not be guaranteed. Moreover, there is every reason to fear that collecting physiological measurements without foreknowledge will lead to even greater interpretative difficulties than are encountered in acoustic measurements. Therefore, it seems better to postpone physiological measurements until it is known what to look for in the recordings.

3.1.1 Basic assumption

Our choice of concentrating on the acoustic and perceptual aspects before turning to production, together with our hope that data reduction on the basis of perceptual limitations and tolerances may help to interpret F_0 curves in a meaningful way, leads to the first task of trying to introduce the distinction between programmed, voluntary F_0 changes and physiologically determined, involuntary fluctuations. For this purpose, we formulated the following basic assumption (Cohen and 't Hart, 1967: 177–8):

We believe that ... pitch movements that are interpreted as relevant by the listener are related to corresponding activities on the part of the speaker. These are assumed to be characterized by discrete commands to the vocal cords and should be recoverable as so many discrete events in the resulting pitch contour, which may present themselves at first sight as continuous variations in time.

This assumption does not necessarily include any presupposition about the way in which the listener operates in order to retrieve the relevant aspects from the signal. For instance, we do not claim that the listener must have direct knowledge about the laryngeal activities on the part of the speaker. Moreover, our enunciation is not meant to be a postulate; its status of an assumption implies that at the time we expected that, in later research, the relevant pitch movements would appear to be related to the speaker's voluntary activities.

A consequence of the basic assumption is that the involuntary fluctuations do not make an essential contribution to the perception of the speech melody: their omission (we will describe later how this can be realized technically) should not bring about any substantial change in the perceived speech melody. On the other hand, the F_0 changes that do contribute essentially to the perception of the speech melody are just those changes that are programmed and voluntarily executed by the speaker. Omission of any of these leads to a substantial change or distortion of the identity of the speech melody. From a perceptual point of view, we will henceforth use the terms 'perceptually relevant pitch movements' versus 'irrelevant detail'.

It should be added immediately at this point that, generally, it is not the case that the distinction discussed manifests itself in the F_0 curves in a simple way, e.g. by the size or the steepness of the F_0 changes. In an actual recording of F_0 the desired separation between perceptually relevant pitch movements and irrelevant detail cannot be indicated with certainty.

Nowadays, there is general agreement on making a distinction between macro- and microintonation (Kaiser, 1940: 111). Our position thus boils down to a consideration of macrointonation as built up of the perceptually relevant pitch movements, whereas microintonation would constitute the irrelevant detail. However, to what extent this can be shown to be the case remains to be seen. This will come up for discussion later in this chapter (see pp. 43f., 47f.).

3.1.2 Manipulation of the course of F_0

The most important characteristic of our approach in the analysis of speech pitch is the continuous confrontation of the measurement of F_0 with the way in which the speech melody is perceived. Therefore, one needs a way to manipulate or modify the course of F_0, in order to examine the effect on the perceived speech melody. In view of the basic assumption, the kind of changes in the course of F_0 that we are after should be such that they lead to a simplification or stylization in the first place (by omission of irrelevant detail), and to a possibility of describing the F_0 curve in terms of a number of discrete events in the second place.

Straight-line segments are taken as building elements, since these can be specified in the most simple way, and they constitute the most straightforward discrete events; the procedure thus boils down to a piecewise linear approximation of the F_0 curve, but not just that, as we shall explain further on (pp. 42–4; 46–53).

Meanwhile, wanting to study the effect on the perceived speech melody, we needed a way to make the thus processed F_0 curves audible, together with the underlying lexical material, in order to be able to compare the resulting speech with the original utterances.

In 1965, the Intonator was built for that purpose (we named this instrument after the one developed at Haskins; see, e.g., Borst and Cooper, 1957; F.S. Cooper, 1962). The Intonator, a special kind of channel vocoder, offered the facility of constructing, in the output signal from the resynthesis part, an entirely artificial F_0 contour (see Cohen and 't Hart, 1967). The input signal was a natural speech utterance, recorded on a loop of tape with a revolution time of 4–5 seconds. Parameters available to specify the straight-line segments were direction, rate of change, duration and starting point with respect to the segmental structure of the speech utterance. Changes of F_0 were superimposed on a slowly downdrifting baseline (the lower declination line, see ch. 5) which was controlled automatically. Since duration multiplied by rate of change gives the magnitude of excursion, the latter can be adjusted by means of variation of either the duration or the rate of change. In practice, we preferred to do it by means of duration, leaving the rate of change at some feasible standard value for all abrupt F_0 changes. For typically gradual changes it was, of course, necessary to adapt the rate of change, but as we have demonstrated in the previous chapter (2.3.2.4), the differential sensitivity to rate of change is rather low.

Whereas the number of specification parameters per line segment was reduced to four deliberately, by our own choice, there was also a limitation of the number of controllable segments to twelve. This accidental limitation of the Intonator turned out to be a blessing in disguise, since it helped us in our intention to achieve a data reduction as strong as possible. This parsimony is, of course, needed in order to remove all the irrelevant detail.

The later introduction of an analysis–resynthesis system, as implemented on a computer and based on Linear Predictive Coding (LPC) provided us with an instrument with far better segmental quality of the resynthesized speech, but also with much greater versatility. Moreover, algorithms became available which, for the first time, enabled us to measure F_0 in a reliable way. Thus, it would have been possible to make much closer approximations to the original F_0 curve; but we preferred to maintain our tendency to parsimony in spite of the abundant facilities.

41

3.1.3 The search for descriptive units

We will now explain in detail how we proceed nowadays in order to separate the perceptually relevant pitch movements from the irrelevant detail after F_0 has been measured. As it was said in the Introduction, the aimed at separation takes place in a number of steps. The first step, to be described here, is the measurement of F_0, together with analysis and resynthesis by means of LPC (see Atal and Hanauer, 1971). A speech utterance is fed into the computer and stored on disk. It is analysed by means of LPC, and the analysis data are also stored. Next, a program is run to measure F_0, and the resulting data are – time-aligned – connected to the other parameter values. The measured F_0 curve is displayed on a screen for visual inspection and detection of errors; octave errors, for instance, are recognizable visually in many cases. In general, errors are traced and corrected by means of a program which enables the experimenter to listen to any resynthesized fragment, selected with a cursor on the screen, of the analysed utterance, and to compare it with the same fragment of the stored input speech. In this way, a smooth F_0 curve can be obtained which is entirely correct in the sense that the – usually small number of – errors in the measurement are replaced by values that are, within the perceptual limits, equal to the genuine values. Finally, the thus corrected whole file is resynthesized and stored. This version is called the resynthesized original.

3.1.3.1 Perceptual equality

(a) Making close-copy stylizations
After the resynthesized original has been made, the procedure is repeated, but now with the aim of making a stylized version, which should eventually be auditorily indistinguishable from the resynthesized original. But it should meet the additional requirement that it must contain the smallest possible number of straight-line segments with which the desired perceptual equality can be achieved. A stylized pitch contour that meets these two conditions is called a close-copy stylization, or in short, a close copy.

Understandably, there is not just one close copy for a given F_0 curve. The limits of dynamic pitch perception, together with restrictions of human memory capacity, make it possible that a second close copy would show small deviations if visually compared with the first one. Due to perceptual tolerances, however, they sound equal to each other, and to the resynthesized original. We may therefore conclude that, if we make a combined recording of an F_0 curve and its close-copy stylization, we are confronted with an acoustic

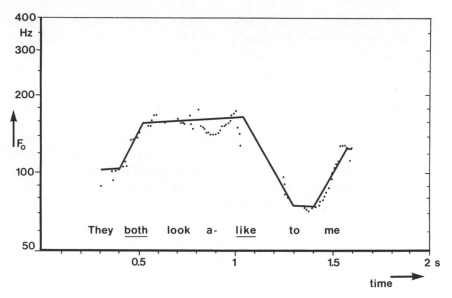

3.1 F₀ curve and close-copy stylization; perceptual equality

representation of the course of F_0, together with a picture of the way in which the speech melody is perceived, mapped onto it. (See figure 3.1.)

Since a close-copy stylization is, by definition, auditorily indistinguishable from the resynthesized original, it contains all the perceptually relevant pitch movements; and since it is made with the smallest possible number of straight-line segments, it contains only the perceptually relevant pitch movements, whereas irrelevant detail has been removed.

At this point, we feel we should become more explicit about the relationships between irrelevant detail, involuntary fluctuations of F_0 and microintonation. As for the latter, there is a good deal of agreement in the literature on making a distinction between two types of microintonation (see, e.g., Reinholt Petersen, 1986). The common property being that the fluctuations are determined by the segmental content, the difference is that, in one type, the influence exerted on F_0 in a given segment (more particularly, a vowel) originates from the segment itself, whereas, in the other type, it originates from an adjacent segment (usually a consonant). The former type is generally called (vowel) intrinsic pitch, the latter is named by different terms, but could be called coarticulatory F_0 fluctuation (Reinholt Petersen, 1986).

Both types of microintonation are reported to be acoustically and physiologically determined, and therefore belong to the involuntary changes of F_0. But it does not necessarily follow from this that these effects are always inaudible. As we have put it earlier (in 3.1), we may presume that they contribute less to the perception of speech melody than do the voluntary, programmed changes of F_0. As for vowel-intrinsic pitch, the differences in F_0 between closed and open vowels may amount to three semitones. Thus, it is plausible that such a difference can be perceived, even in the dynamic situation of speech melody, and even though it has been reported (e.g., Hombert, 1976) that listeners tend to at least partially compensate for the effect. If pitch differences between closed and open vowels due to intrinsic pitch can be perceived, it follows that a close-copy stylization still contains this inform-ation, since, otherwise, there would be no perceptual equality. As a consequence, this effect cannot be separated from the voluntary, planned movements.

The effect of vowel-intrinsic pitch is negligible in unaccented syllables (Ladd and Silverman, 1984: 31). And indeed, the practice of making close-copy stylizations has shown us that it is generally possible to make straight lines over successions of unaccented syllables, irrespective of the presence of an alternation of closed and open vowels. At the same time, this very possibility implies that, at least in close-copy stylizations of the course of F_0 in natural speech, the absence of the coarticulatory fluctuations is not audible. We will come back to this implication in 3.1.3.2.

(b) Experimental verification

Whether or not a close copy is really indistinguishable from the resynthesized original can only be verified by eliciting judgments about their perceptual equality from a number of independent listeners. During our study of Dutch intonation, such a verification could only take place in an informal way, due to the instrumental limitations of that time. Later, we undertook a study of British English intonation, which started with an attempt to verify that English intonation, too, could be satisfactorily approximated by means of straight-line segments. On this occasion, we felt that the auditory acuity of the – native Dutch – experimenter should be tested in such a way that the result would be beyond doubt. Now, obviously, it would be asking too much to follow such a laborious procedure for each speech utterance to be analysed. For our purpose, however, it is sufficient to do such a verification once, provided that it is done thoroughly. De Pijper (1983) ran a formal test to make sure that his close copies were indistinguishable from resynthesized originals, using sixty-four native speakers of British English. We will discuss this experiment in some detail here, mainly to demonstrate that the very first step in the IPO approach is sound, but also to make it clear why the instrumental

Table 3.1 *Total number of responses, and number of cases in which members of a pair were judged equal or different. Objectively, the members in a pair were different in categories A and C, and equal in category B*

Category	Number of responses	Number 'equal'	%	Number 'different'	%
A	1,280	1,111	86.8	169	13.2
B	1,280	1,222	95.5	58	4.5
C	1,280	75	5.9	1,205 ·	94.1

limitations prevented us from doing the experiment earlier, in the study of Dutch intonation.

The main characteristics of the experiment were as follows. Sentences, varying in duration between one and three seconds, were each made in three versions: viz. a resynthesized original; a close copy; and a so-called 'alternative' contour. Alternative contours typically had a number of pitch accents different from those in the original, or pitch accents on other words, or an audibly different timing of one or more of the pitch movements with respect to the syllables in which they occurred. Sixty pairs were formed, in three categories: (A) a resynthesized original and a close-copy stylization; (B) two identical versions; (C) a resynthesized original or a close copy, and an alternative contour. In the instruction, the subjects were made familiar with the notion of close-copy stylizations, also by means of demonstrations on tape. After that, they were asked to judge each pair as 'equal' or 'different'. Table 3.1 summarizes the results of the test.

Category A shows a very high number of responses 'equal'. In fact, in almost 87 per cent of the pairs subjects thought that the stylized versions of that category were exactly equal to the resynthesized originals. One reason for this behaviour could be that, since the pairs of category C differed much more clearly, the subjects' criteria might have been biased in favour of judging the pairs of category A to be equal. But in that case there would be no reason why the numbers of judgments 'different' in categories A and B would differ from each other. The null hypothesis that the scores for both 'equal' and 'different' are the same for A and B (viz. 1,166.5 and 113.5 respectively) can be tested by means of e.g. chi square. This shows that the actual outcome differs highly significantly ($p < 0.0005$) from the null hypothesis. The fact, moreover, that the number of judgments 'different' is higher in category A than in category B, and not lower, illustrates that the subjects must have been very attentive, and that they certainly would have scored a higher number 'different' for category

A if the objective differences had been only slightly bigger than they actually were. It can be considered a small weakness of this experiment that it did not contain stimulus pairs with such slightly bigger differences. The alternative contours had differences clear enough to be heard in 94 per cent of the cases. Moreover, as has been explained above, the differences were of various kinds. Therefore, we intend to do the experiment once more, with less conspicuous, uniform deviations for category C, e.g. an overall shift in time of 50 ms. Nevertheless, we feel entitled to conclude, on the basis of the outcome of De Pijper's experiment, that it is possible to stylize British English intonation by means of a restricted number of straight-line segments, and still maintain perceptual equality.

It is essential in this experiment that the pairs of category A contain a resynthesized original rather than the genuine original; otherwise, the difference in speech quality will prevent the listeners from judging the two members as exactly equal, even if the two courses of F_0 are identical. This is the reason why we could not do this experiment in earlier days: the lack of facilities for measuring F_0 sufficiently reliably made it practically impossible to make resynthesized originals.

3.1.3.2 Perceptual equivalence

(a) Operational definition
Apart from perceptual equality, other kinds of perceptual similarity, at a number of different levels, can be observed to exist between two objects. For instance, two hand-made prints of one photographic negative may be physically different, but perceptually equal. However, two different pictures of one and the same person, taken with a time interval of five years (as with passport photos) will show more or less clearly visible differences, but can nevertheless be said to possess a large amount of similarity.

In our view, the perceptual equality between close copies and resynthesized originals comes about by virtue of perceptual tolerance: the auditory system is unable to detect the objective differences between the two. As a consequence, the experiment just described could have been done equally well with non-native listeners.

Let us now suppose that we ask somebody to imitate the intonation in an utterance spoken by someone else. Generally, this results in a number of more or less clearly audible differences. But nevertheless, we can ask a panel of listeners to judge whether or not the imitation is successful. If we were to take non-native listeners as judges, they would have to rely on the same strategy as the one applied in the close-copy experiment. The differences between the two versions must remain within the limits set by perceptual tolerance, since these listeners do not know how much an imitation may deviate from the example before being called unsuccessful. Native listeners, however, can base their strategy on linguistic tolerance. For instance, some of the excursions may be audibly larger or smaller in the imitation than in the example, without an entire loss of similarity.

On the basis of these considerations, we propose the following operational definition of perceptual equivalence: if for a speech utterance two different courses of F_0 are similar to such an extent that one is judged as a successful imitation of the other, we say that there is perceptual equivalence between the two. In the following subsection, we will deal with perceptual equivalence in more detail, with the aid of some examples.

(b) Standardization

The various movements in close-copy stylizations all have their individual sizes, slopes, durations and positions with respect to the syllables in which they occur. The values of these parameters lie on continuous scales. By virtue of linguistic tolerance, however, it should be possible to quantize these values. If, for example, three rising movements in a close copy have slopes of 30, 40 and 90 ST/s respectively, we can already be sure that, on the basis of – smaller – perceptual tolerance, those of 30 and 40 ST/s will not be distinguished from each other. Taking linguistic tolerance into account might even provide the possibility that the three different slopes can be replaced by one of 55 or 60 ST/s for all three movements without the loss of perceptual equivalence.

Thus, close copies are used as the starting point for further stylization, with the aim of replacing the movements by movements with standard specifications for their various characteristic parameters. The ultimate aim of standardization is to enable the investigators to make generalizations: to take together, in a restricted number of categories, the various different movements as they are found in the close-copy stylizations. A second aim of standardization, for later application, is to gather a manageable set of precepts for synthesis by rule.

At this point, we should come back to microintonational phenomena. As will be clear, standardization removes all the microintonational differences originating from vowel-intrinsic pitch, together, of course, with the intended, macrointonational variations in peak height and valley depth. This may have audible effects, but not necessarily: the various influences may cancel each other out, to the effect that in a sequence of a low syllable with /i/ followed by a high one with /a/, the covered interval will be closer to the standard value for the size of a rise than might have been the intention of the speaker (Greiffenberg and Reinholt Petersen, 1982).

Coarticulatory F_0 fluctuations, too, are absent as a result of standardization;

they had already been removed in close copies. As has been said in 3.1.3.1, the absence of these fluctuations in a close-copy stylization is not audible in a comparison with the resynthesized original. This does not imply, however, that their absence in standardized stylizations is similarly unobservable. It may be that the greater liveliness of a resynthesized original and its close-copy stylization obscures the differences with respect to coarticulatory fluctuations, whereas such a masking effect could be cancelled by the use of standard movements. Recently, experiments have been run with standardized, straight-line contours on the one hand, and, on the other hand, standardized contours in which microintonational phenomena of either type had been reintroduced artificially. The results of these experiments indicate that such contours can be auditorily distinguished from each other, but only if they contain relatively long stretches without macrointonational F_0 changes, only in direct pair-comparison and only by trained listeners. With respect to the first aim of standardization, it follows that microintonation does not play a part of any importance: its presence or absence will not influence the perceptual equivalence. With respect to the second aim, synthesis by rule, we might expect that in the long run, when most people have been frequently exposed to synthetic speech, the presence of microintonation will be desirable in some conditions.

In attempts to obtain standard stylizations, two principles have to be followed. First, the generalization should not go so far that it would do away with possible categorical differences between types of pitch movements. To this end, we demand that the standard stylizations are perceptually equivalent to the close-copy stylizations. A second, independent principle is that the standard stylizations should sound acceptable, in the sense that they can be considered fair representations of the intonation of the language at issue. For instance, the stylizations applied by Issachenko and Schädlich (1970), with two levels and abrupt tone switches, although good enough to be used as stimuli in their experiments, are not sufficiently acceptable to be used in a system for synthesis by rule. As we shall see later, under (c), the requirement of acceptability plays a predominant role in a later phase of the investigations.

We might illustrate these two points with some examples. Figure 3.2 shows the F_0 curve as measured in the utterance *Alan's in Cambridge, studying botany* with accents on the underlined syllables, together with its close-copy stylization. Although all the straight-line segments used in the stylized contour have different slopes and sizes, a certain overall structure seems to emerge: viz. a succession of two shapes, both consisting of mid-range pitch before the accent, a rise and a deep fall in the vicinity of the accented syllable, and low pitch in the syllables following it. Half-way through the utterance, there is a switch from low pitch to mid pitch to the effect that, in the second part too, the

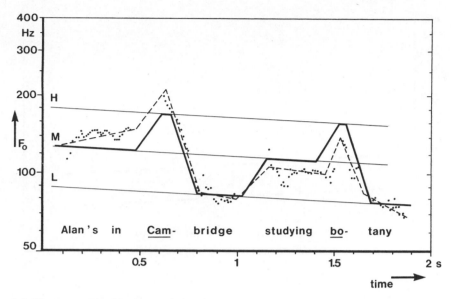

3.2 Close copy (broken line) and standardized stylization; perceptual equivalence

syllables before the accent have mid-range pitch. Standardization is obtained by taking the following measures. Full-size rises and falls are taken to cover an octave and are executed in 160 ms (this means that the rate of change of F_0 is plus or minus seventy-five semitones per second). Half-size rises and falls have the same slope, but their duration is only 80 ms, and hence their size is only half an octave. As a consequence, a grid can be set up to provide three equidistant lines (half an octave apart from each other). This grid is tilted downwards from beginning to end, to account for the phenomenon of declination (see ch. 5). The effect is that, in principle, in all stretches where no abrupt changes of F_0 take place, F_0 is supposed to drift down slowly.

Figure 3.3 depicts the situation in an utterance which contains only one accent: *You knew I didn't want you to do it.* The standard stylization has mid-range pitch before the accent, a rise and a deep fall around *knew*, and low pitch after it, just as in each of the two halves of the utterance of figure 3.2. In both utterances, the fully standardized stylizations do not sound exactly equal to the corresponding close copies (or originals), but they are perceptually equivalent to them.

Although the standardized versions of figures 3.2 and 3.3 have much in common, they are not mutually perceptually equivalent. Yet, the fact that we may use the same ingredients to build the standard stylizations (and that is what standardization is all about) reflects that they can be interpreted as

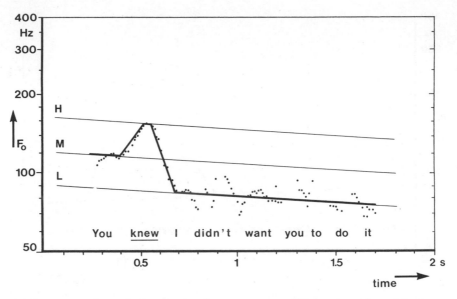

3.3 F_0 curve and standard stylization for an utterance different from that of figure 3.2 (only one pitch accent), but using the same ingredients

sharing a common origin on a higher level of abstraction (see also ch. 4, proposition 5). That this is not an automatic result of the procedure of standardization, and hence is a property already present in the originals, can be illustrated by means of the next example. If, once more, we try to apply the same combination of rise and fall to make a standard stylization for the F_0 curve of figure 3.4, the result may very well sound acceptable as such, but it appears not to be perceptually equivalent to the original. It turns out that the delay in the position of the rise–fall combination with respect to the accented first syllable is the essential property of these movements which ensures perceptual equivalence between the standard stylization and the original. A second, probably less important property is that, this time, the rise should start at the low, rather than the mid level.

The fact that we cannot always use the same standard movements in our attempt to obtain standard stylizations shows that not just any pair of courses of F_0 can be interpreted to have a common, more abstract origin. We take it as an indication that that of figure 3.4 belongs to a different 'melodic family', so to say, from those of figures 3.2 and 3.3. This is in line with the British tradition, which has always shown a tendency to classify intonation into a number of categorically different groups (e.g. Halliday's (1970) tones). There is a conceptual difference, though. Figures 3.3 and 3.4 can be considered to

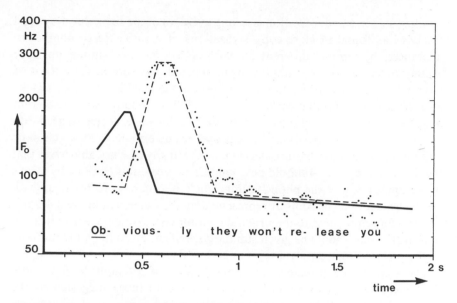

3.4 Using the same ingredients as in figure 3.3 leads to a dissimilar melodic impression. The late position of the rise–fall is responsible for this effect, rather than the larger excursion

constitute a kind of melodic minimal pair. This could invite the investigator to see an analogy with (segmental) phonemes. But if such an analogy is taken in a strong form, differences between intonation groups should reflect distinctivity. In chapter 4, we will explain why we are not convinced about an association between the 'melodic family', or the basic intonation pattern as we will call it later, and distinctive function. In quite a number of intonation studies, distinctivity appears to have been the starting point; in our approach, the introduction of the basic intonation patterns is a necessary last step in the analysis, rather than a preconceived notion. In chapter 4, we will present evidence in favour of a way of separating these classes without the need to use the notion of distinctivity. We will come back to intonation patterns in section 3.3.

It may seem strange that, while we are dealing with standard specifications of perceptually relevant pitch movements, we apparently need to take into consideration far more abstract and global aspects of intonation, viz. basic intonation patterns. We will therefore explain why, in trying to establish suitable values for the sizes, the durations and the positions in the syllables of the standardized pitch movements, the interrelationship between movements and patterns has to be accounted for.

51

A first step in standardization is taking averages of the sizes, durations and positions as found in close-copy stylizations of a rather large number of utterances, by various different speakers. However, one should not take averages over items that do not belong to the same population. Thus, it would be unwise, e.g. when the position with respect to the syllable is at stake, to take an average over items that contain both rise–fall combinations as are present in figures 3.2 and 3.3, and the one in figure 3.4. But since, at this stage, we do not yet have knowledge about what properties determine from which basic pattern a given pitch contour is derived, we are in any case not able to see that the rise–fall of figure 3.4 should be excluded. This can only be done by means of the application of the phonetic-linguistic criterion of perceptual equivalence. The fact that the contour represented by the full line in figure 3.4 is not perceptually equivalent to the original contour constitutes a clear indication that the rise–fall should be given standard specifications different from those of the previous figures.

The second step in standardization consists of attempts to find more convenient values for the various parameters than those suggested by the averages mentioned above. In line with the second requirement of standard stylizations, their acceptability, it is of paramount importance that it is checked continuously whether arbitrary pitch contours built on the basis of the more convenient values remain acceptable. This is verified during the process by the experimenters themselves, and can be tested later in a more formal way (see subsection (c) below).

The round figures mentioned earlier (one or half an octave, 160 or 80 ms, seventy-five semitones per second), do not in any respect reflect a wish to express the idea that equal-tempered musical intervals play a part of some special kind in speech pitch; rather, the fact that the exact size of pitch movements in speech is of minor importance for acceptability makes it possible not only to work with averages, but also to round them off.

Taking only one standard value for the slope, and varying the size only by means of duration is a deliberate simplification supported by acceptability tests. It neglects the general tendency observable in natural speech, that larger movements are – less than proportionally – longer, but also steeper than smaller movements.

The choice of standard sizes is not meant to suggest that speakers produce the same excursions always, or, more specifically, throughout an utterance. For one thing, a speaker would, for example, typically use larger excursions when he is excited or delighted, than when he is sad or dull. For another, it is true in general that the excursions become smaller later in an utterance than they are in the initial part. Both effects can easily be accounted for, of course, but we want the fully standardized stylizations to be as simple as possible, provided that they sound acceptable.

Since standardization is governed by language-specific, linguistic tolerance, it should cause no surprise that the parameter values are language-bound. The figures given above are those found for British English. In Dutch intonation, excursions most frequently vary around six semitones, durations around 100 or 120 ms. The corresponding slopes are 50 and 60 ST/s, somewhat less than that of British English. In German intonation, the excursion (for full-size movements) can be taken as ten semitones, only slightly less than in British English intonation, but in speech at normal speed, the movements tend to be even less steep than in Dutch, resulting in a long duration of over 200 ms (the standard is taken as 240 ms for full-size movements). It seems to be the case that in French intonation too, pitch changes less rapidly than in Dutch and British English.

(c) Experimental verification

As was mentioned earlier (p. 48), standard stylizations should be perceptually equivalent to the close-copy stylizations or to their originals, and they 'should sound acceptable, in the sense that they can be considered fair representatives of the intonation of the language at issue'. However, the combination of these two requirements is only at issue in the search for the standard movements. In a later stage, it is examined if the standard movements found thus far are more generally applicable. This can, for example, be done using utterances of which the original versions may have courses of F_0 different from those aimed at in the artificial contours. In such cases, only the second requirement is relevant.

It seems very difficult to devise an experiment in which perceptual equivalence can be measured properly. Whereas in the verification of a close copy the criterion is simply equal or not equal (as set by the limits of perceptual tolerance), perceptual equivalence applies a somewhat broader criterion (based on language-specific linguistic tolerance), and although even perceptual acuity may differ interindividually, we can almost be sure that the 'somewhat broader criterion' opens the way for considerably more variation between subjects.

In view of the verification of the validity of the analysis, viz. synthesis-by-rule of standard stylizations, it is of decisive importance that their acceptability is tested. From various experiments it has turned out that eliciting acceptability judgments in a direct fashion is possible in principle, for instance on grammaticality, but also on a typically low-level phenomenon such as vowel durations (e.g. Nooteboom, 1972: 78ff.). It presupposes that subjects are able to make use of an internal representation, an implicit knowledge, of how a grammatically well-formed sentence is constructed, or how long a certain vowel should be in a given context. If applied to intonation, such experiments presuppose that the listeners use their internal representations about how the speech melody of their mother tongue should sound. And as it has appeared, the acceptability of intonation can rather easily be experimentally verified in a reliable way.

In our study of British English intonation, we have run formal experiments on acceptability. De Pijper (1983) and Willems (1982), working on two different aspects of British English intonation, were the first to design, in close co-operation, fully-fledged experiments to measure acceptability of artificially generated sequences of pitch movements in such a way that a statistical analysis of the outcome was made possible. De Pijper's experiment being the one most related to the problem at issue here, we will take it as an example to illustrate the procedure. A limited number of test utterances are selected on the basis of a number of criteria, one of which is that their intonations are well assorted (another one is that their durations should not be too long). Of these utterances, a number of versions are made by means of the LPC analysis–resynthesis system. One of the versions is the resynthesized original, other versions are stylizations, in, for instance, various degrees of standardization; still other versions are also stylizations, but these are built on the basis of rules different from those developed so far for the language at issue. For instance, De Pijper used rules for Dutch intonation in his experiment. The test items are recorded on tape in random order, and presented to a fairly large number of listeners (e.g. fifty or more). These are asked to rate the acceptability of each of the test items on, for example, a five-point scale, from 1 for very bad to 5 for very good.

Special measures can be taken to make it possible to perform a parametric statistical analysis on the data. Such an analysis aims at finding out whether, in any significant way, the conditions (versions) have had an influence on the acceptability judgments. More particularly, one hopes to verify that the acceptability of the standard stylizations does not significantly differ from that of the resynthesized originals, and that the rule-violating contours are significantly less acceptable than any of the former.

De Pijper (1983) developed standard precepts for the approximation of the examples of the seven primary tones as given by Halliday (1970), and as recorded on the tape accompanying that course of intonation. De Pijper's outcome was that the fully standardized contours were not significantly less acceptable than the resynthesized originals: in fact, half of them were more acceptable (not significantly). But as soon as the rules were violated, as in the versions made according to the rules for Dutch intonation, the overall acceptability dropped significantly.

The technique has been applied on a number of occasions. Willems (1982) used it to evaluate deviations from 'correct' English intonation as produced by Dutch speakers of English. Of a list of nine presumably systematic melodic differences as measured in the productions of English material by British and

Dutch speakers, he was able to show that six of these deviations led to unacceptability to a greater or lesser extent. After the introduction, by means of the LPC analysis–resynthesis system, of a number of standardized pronunciation corrections, a second acceptability test showed much higher acceptability scores.

Later, Willems (Willems, Collier and 't Hart, 1988) developed standardized approximations to specimens of the intonation in spontaneously spoken English, and applied the test once more, for the necessary perceptual evaluation. This time, he used close-copy stylizations as the reference instead of resynthesized originals, in order to exclude a possible effect from the presence of microintonation in resynthesized originals and its absence in standard stylizations. Third versions were approximations based on the rules for Dutch intonation. These were carefully selected to come as close to their English counterparts as possible (in spite of the general difference between the two intonation systems, there is a certain partial overlap); furthermore, the excursions were blown up, in order to match those usually present in British English. Despite these measures, taken in order not to flatter the outcome by the presence in the stimulus material of too obviously deviating items, the result was again that there was no difference in acceptability between the close copies and the standard stylizations, whereas the 'Dutch' versions differed highly significantly from both close copies and standardized versions.

Once the feasibility of the various standardized movements has been tested in an acceptability experiment, their characteristic properties can be given an official status. As was mentioned before, these are: direction, position in the syllable, rate of change and duration, the latter two determining the size. Yet another characteristic of a perceptually relevant pitch movement is whether or not it is involved in accentuation. On the basis of these properties, the standardized movements are distinguished from one another, and accordingly, a transcription code can be developed by means of which each of these movements can be specified uniquely.

One remark has to be added here. The number of mutually different standardized pitch movements to be included in the standard inventory is, of course, deliberately limited by the very measure of standardization. But it is also dependent on the amount and, more particularly, the diversity of the speech material examined by the investigator. And, as it happened, the frequencies of occurrence of the various different pitch movements diverge strongly. Thus, in order to encounter rarely occurring phenomena, one has to examine large amounts of material. To cope with this problem, we applied a strategy in which the experimenter(s), while listening to recorded speech material, would typically leave aside all the utterances in which the pitch movements were auditorily recognized as already 'known'. Thus, a selection is made of specimens of which it is presumed that they contain something peculiar. This presumption can subsequently be verified or falsified using the techniques of the stylization method as explained above.

3.2 Pitch contours

In the experiments described in the preceding subsection, although meant to verify claims about properties of individual pitch movements, use was made of stimuli consisting of entire utterances. This is fully in line with our views, as have been given in 2.3. In these entire utterances, although they were rather short, generally more than one pitch movement occurred. We have felt the need for introducing a separate term for strings of standardized pitch movements. These will be called 'pitch contours' henceforth. A pitch contour can thus be distinguished from the 'course of F_0' in an original or a resynthesized original, and from the close-copy stylization.

In 3.2.1, we will put forward a number of questions about the possible structural properties of pitch contours and deal with a particular strategy for finding out what these properties may turn out to be. In 3.2.2, we will present the experimental verification with the aid of a large corpus, and discuss the validity of the outcome.

3.2.1 Possible structural properties of pitch contours

The procedure for finding the various different standard pitch movements has confronted the experimenter with a vast amount of pitch contours. With this extensive experience, he might well be able to try to give answers to the following questions:

1. Are there any restrictions to the ways in which these pitch movements may combine to form pitch contours, or can they simply be concatenated in any desired order?
2. If there are such restrictions, can these be formulated in some set of rules?
3. If so, what is the domain of these rules? In other words, are there units of language material within which the rules are operative, whereas the restrictions are no longer valid beyond the boundaries of these units?

The answers to these questions will be dealt with in the next chapter. In what follows now, we will discuss the ways in which we have attempted to find the answers.

One seemingly obvious way of finding possible restrictions in the combinability of the pitch movements is to make up a list of digrams, trigrams etc. of the combination observed in the material analysed thus far, and to try to work that out in a more or less formal way towards a kind of augmented transitional network. We decided, however, to take a shortcut. We adopted a strategy in which we postulated which combinations would be permitted and which not, and subsequently predicted that the former would, but the latter would not, be found in a new, independent corpus of considerable length. The postulates were based on experiences with previous material, but extended with expectations about the possibility of certain new combinations being permitted or not. This strategy led to what might be called a 'tentative grammar', an algorithm intended to generate all permitted strings of movements, and none but these ('t Hart and Collier, 1975).

This twofold aim was checked by means of a transcription of fresh material. The confrontation took place in two rounds, the first of which was meant to check the tentative grammar for omissions. In view of the first aim, the speech material had to be contiguous: we were no longer allowed to make any selection, or to discard any item of which we had the impression that it was a 'known' type. When the tentative grammar was not able to cope with a particular sequence of pitch movements encountered in this material, it was extended accordingly. At some point, we decided to close the first round, and to declare the grammar finished. In the second round, it was examined to what extent the grammar covered the phenomena observed in the remainder of the corpus.

3.2.2 Experimental verification

For our study of Dutch intonation we resorted to a selection of fragments of modern theatre plays in which it was apparently intended to represent spontaneous conversation. Six such fragments were chosen, from four different plays, of about ten minutes' length on average. As a seventh fragment, we took ten minutes of a recording of spontaneous speech (of a total duration of one hour) by four different (male) speakers, each with his own microphone visibly in front of him, on four different tracks.

This collection contained 1,359 utterances in all, varying from one to forty-eight words in content. The intonation was transcribed by ear, in terms of the standardized perceptually relevant pitch movements, by two of the authors. A number of safety measures were observed: for instance, part of the material was coded by each of the transcribers independently, and later compared; doubtful cases were submitted to the stylization procedure. The tentative grammar was fed into the computer, programmed to either recognize each input string as capable of being generated by the grammar, or signal that it could not be generated. Executing the confrontation on the computer was done on purpose, viz. to avoid even the scantiest undue tolerance. After having made the necessary adjustments, we undertook the second-round confrontation, this time for the entire material, of which 76 per cent was new. The outcome was that the grammar accounted for 94 per cent of the total number of contours.

A few comments have to be made about this in itself undeniably high percentage. First of all, in our approximation to Dutch intonation by means of the standard stylizations, the size of the pitch movements is also standardized. In making the transcription of the corpus, we regularly needed to indicate that certain movements or groups of successive movements had a typically larger or smaller excursion than 'normal'. Such local deviations from the standard values were not accounted for by the grammar, but were nevertheless noted down systematically. This made it possible to examine whether the combination possibilities for larger movements would differ typically from those found for smaller movements. This turned out not to be the case, indicating that combination rules are independent of the size of the movements.

Secondly, it is rather easy to obtain a high score with a grammar which is too unspecific, and therefore too powerful. Such a grammar will generate an almost infinite number of strings, of which it is impossible to show that they all may occur in a corpus of limited length, and of which it is also otherwise hard to prove that they are all well-formed. A probabilistic study, based on the frequency of occurrence of certain combinations ('t Hart and Collier, 1975) revealed that, to have a fair chance that all predicted contours, and particularly those containing rare combinations, will occur at least once, we would need a sample about a hundred times larger than the corpus investigated.

Yet we can easily illustrate that the grammar is not too powerful, by means of some calculations. As we shall see in chapter 4, ten pitch movements are distinguished for Dutch intonation, four of which are involved in accentuation. If we think of an utterance with two pitch accents, there are sixteen possible combinations of two movements in the most simple contour. Of these, four will be recognized by the grammar as well-formed. If we allow a third movement to occur (without giving an extra accent), the number of possible combinations increases to 288, but the number of permitted combinations is only three. More complicated contours, still with only two pitch accents, may contain a so-called Prefix, or a Suffix, or both (see ch. 4, proposition 4.2), in addition to the Root. Under still rather strict limitations with respect to the number of pitch movements in such contours, one can calculate that there are almost 300,000 potential combinations, of which only 125 are generated by the grammar.

Nevertheless, that the grammar is powerful enough originates from the fact that it contains a principle of recursiveness of certain combinations of movements, and that a maximum number of repetitions of such combinations has not been specified. Relatively low numbers of repetitions have all been observed in the corpus. This holds for Dutch intonation. Recently, Willems (in Willems, Collier and 't Hart, 1988) developed a grammar for British English intonation, based on a corpus of spontaneous speech (interviews). He did specify a maximum number of repetitions, basing it on what he had actually seen to occur in his corpus. As a consequence, his claim that the grammar generates only the permitted strings is stronger than ours for Dutch, but the complementary claim that it generates all the permitted strings is weaker.

3.3 Intonation patterns

In the preceding sections, we have made mention of a development in our analysis starting with single pitch movements, and ending up with entire contours. That development was made possible by introducing a number of generalizations, and by gradually raising the level of abstraction. In this operation, an important part is played by similarity, in three degrees, two of which were main issues in the preceding sections, viz. perceptual equality and perceptual equivalence. In addition to this, we have mentioned that it seemed possible to distinguish a third degree, since contours that lack mutual perceptual equivalence may still give rise to the impression of a kind of similarity at a higher level of abstraction. In the following subsections, we will discuss this kind of similarity in some detail, and since the phenomenon gave rise to the hypothesis that the various melodic shapes in a language can be subdivided into a limited number of 'melodic families', we will mention some experimental techniques with which this hypothesis can be verified. The experiments themselves, and their outcome, will be dealt with in chapter 4, proposition 5. In anticipation of that outcome, we will henceforth use the term 'intonation pattern' instead of 'melodic family'.

3.3.1 The introduction of a more abstract similarity

As it has appeared, between the courses of F_0 in two speech utterances with the same word content, a kind of similarity, or resemblance, can be observed despite differences which preclude perceptual equivalence. These differences may be of varying nature, as will be illustrated in the following examples.

(1) number of pitch accents.

De vergadering heeft drie uur geduurd
(The meeting has three hours lasted)

De vergadering heeft drie uur geduurd

(2) position of pitch accents

De vergadering heeft drie uur geduurd

De vergadering heeft drie uur geduurd

(3) additional pitch movements, not associated with accents

De vergadering heeft drie uur geduurd

De vergadering heeft drie uur geduurd

(4) size of pitch movements

(5) position of one type of pitch movement not involved in accentuation

De vergadering heeft drie uur geduurd

De vergadering heeft drie uur geduurd

(6) gradual vs steep falls

De vergadering heeft drie uur geduurd

De vergadering heeft drie uur geduurd

(7) different course of F_0 before syntactic boundary

... heeft drie uur geduurd, maar toen was het afgelopen
(... has three hours lasted, but then was it finished)

... heeft drie uur geduurd, maar toen was het afgelopen

(8) different course of F_0 between penultimate and last pitch accent

Iedereen was blij dat het afgelopen was
(Everybody was happy that it finished was)

Iedereen was blij dat het afgelopen was

The same kind of similarity can also be observed between utterances with different word content, e.g. (9) and (10):

(9)

Heb jij hem vandaag nog gezien?
(Have you him today at all seen?)

(10)

Maar dat heb ik echt niet beweerd!
(But that have I really not alleged!)

This is, in fact, an extreme example, since these two sentences have equal numbers of syllables, and in both cases the single-pitch accent is on the second syllable.

But it has turned out that this kind of similarity can also be heard between utterances with much greater differences. The following examples are derived from recordings of spontaneous speech:

(11)

Ze zitten daar met z'n allen in één huis
(They stay there together in one house)

Daar moeten ze dan maar even op wachten, op die boeken
(There must they then for a while for wait, for those books)

Ben jij nou geabonneerd op een opinieblad?
(Are you now a subscriber to an opinion weekly?)

(12)

Ja, daar heb ik ook al eens over gedacht
(Yes, there have I also one day about thought)

Sommige mensen vinden het geweldig wat-ie doet
(Some people find it marvellous what he does)

(13)

Dat heb ik altijd al willen vertellen
(That have I always wanted to tell)

En dan kan er ook niks meer fout gaan natuurlijk
(And then can there nothing any more wrong go naturally)

Items within each of the categories (11), (12) and (13) are judged to have similar intonation, but the intonations in (11) and (12), (11) and (13), and (12) and (13) are judged entirely dissimilar. This has appeared to be the case in the experiments described in 3.3.2, and which are treated in detail in chapter 4, proposition 5.

Earlier in this chapter, when dealing with attempts to stylize the F_0 curves of figures 3.2, 3.3 and 3.4, we suggested that the lack of perceptual equivalence between a stylization of 3.4 using the same precepts as applied in 3.2 and 3.3, on the one hand, and its original, on the other, could be attributed to a hypothetical membership of 3.4 to another melodic family. Upon confrontation with the similarities and dissimilarities as exemplified above, this supposition becomes increasingly stronger. But, of course, it is not enough for investigators to have only a supposition, even if it is strong.

3.3.2 Experimental verification

In order to verify our supposition about the existence of abstract categories of intonation, or basic intonation patterns, we devised and carried out a number of experiments of two kinds, to be called 'sorting' and 'matching'. These have in common that the subjects have random access to any of the stimuli in the set at issue. This can be achieved by recording each stimulus on a separate Language Master card, to the effect that each individual stimulus and every possible pair of stimuli can be played back on the (Bell and Howell) Language Master. This can, of course, also be simulated on a computer, but in case transportability is desired, the rather poor quality of the Language Master system does not constitute an essential handicap.

In a sorting experiment, the number of stimuli in the set is typically several tens, e.g. twenty. Subjects (about fifteen is sufficient) are instructed, by means of some examples, to pay exclusive attention to melodic similarity and dissimilarity; they are told that they are supposed to refrain from taking into account (semantic aspects of) the word content, and the number of accents. Their task is to sort the cards with the stimuli into as many piles as they wish, as long as that number is not too close to one or, worse, to twenty. The data of such an experiment can be submitted to a hierarchical cluster-analysis (Johnson, 1967), which may yield clusterings at relatively high levels of items with great similarity, and at only low levels of groups showing dissimilarity between the items. An alternative way of processing the data is applying a multidimensional factor analysis (MINISSA).

The experiment can best be done with short, original speech utterances, or their close copies. The use of standardized stylizations would introduce some of the differences in the precepts applied by the experimenter for making approximations to specimens of different basic patterns as distinguished by him. And that would make the dissimilarities between representatives of different patterns greater than they may be in natural speech, as is often the case in caricatures. On the other hand, the stimuli under examination should preferably contain specimens of at least three or four different hypothetical patterns. If only representatives of one pattern are present, the subjective dissimilarities between various items are judged greater than when more patterns are included. If a large number of patterns are used in one test, some minor differences easily go unnoticed. In a good compromise, it is just the experimenter's own notions about basic patterns that are put to the test.

The task is not easy for the subjects to do, and although some of them finish it in less than ten minutes, for others it takes more than half an hour to come to their final decision. The outcome provides us with a more or less clear separation of the stimuli into a limited number of classes, but it does not tell us what exactly is the analytic detail that may be held responsible for this classification.

To find an answer to that question, we have proposed another experiment, which may be called a matching experiment. Stimuli were again recorded on Language Master cards, but this time they consisted of naturally spoken utterances and standard stylizations, mixed together. Moreover, the task was different, in the sense that groups of four were formed, of which one was marked 'X', the other 'A', 'B' and 'C', respectively, and subjects, instructed in the same way as with the sorting experiment, were asked to find, among A, B and C, the item or items that had melodic similarity to X (finding none was also allowed). Note that this situation is different from that in a triadic comparison, in which subjects are asked to find the two most similar and the two least similar.

This experiment is easier to do for the subjects, and, as a consequence, it is quite possible to use ten to fifteen quartets, and hence, to incorporate more melodic variations in one test. Also, it has turned out to be possible to have the stimulus material contain naturally spoken utterances mixed with stylized resynthesized items. This makes it easier to find the connection between overall pattern identity and the responsible analytic detail.

As already mentioned, the results of these experiments can be found in the next chapter, under proposition 5. Meanwhile, we may add here that a matching experiment can, of course, also be done by means of a recording of all possible pairs of a number of stimuli, selected on the basis of their belonging to the various hypothetical basic patterns. In fact, we did one such experiment. In view of the obvious advantage of the random-access facility in the Language Master system, and since the results of the alternative experiment did not differ from those obtained in the other experiments, we will make no further mention of this pair-comparison experiment.

3.4 A schematic survey

For a kind of summarizing survey of the various steps and experiments described in this chapter, we can make use of the scheme of figure 3.5.

Starting with a number of speech utterances, and going anti-clockwise, we can measure F_0 in order to obtain their F_0 curves. These are hardly interpretable in terms other than the values of the fundamental frequency, since they still contain all the involuntary variations. With the criterion of perceptual equality, close copies are made, which contain all and only the perceptually relevant pitch movements. With the criterion of perceptual equivalence, the close copies are transformed into standardized stylizations. Once their acceptability has been established, the standardized perceptually relevant pitch movements can now be considered as the minimal descriptive units. These units can subsequently be used to characterize the perceptual structure of observed pitch contours. In order to give an account of the combinatory possibilities of pitch movements, a grammar is designed and tested, which should eventually generate all the kinds of pitch contours that may be found in the language at issue.

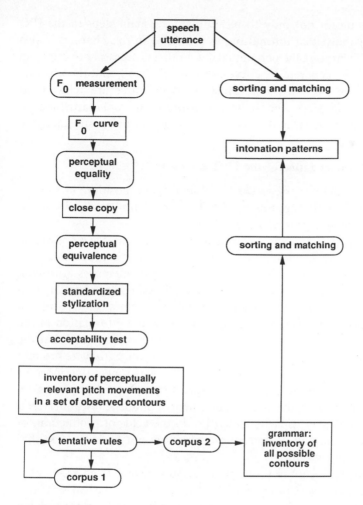

3.5 Summarizing survey of the method. Rectangular boxes represent products, rounded boxes represent processes or experiments

Meanwhile (again starting with the speech utterances, but now going clockwise), the investigator's preoccupation with the intonation of large samples of speech may have led to a supposition that there is more than one basic pattern. Whether these are mutually exclusive patterns can be corroborated in sorting and matching experiments, in the first instance with natural speech. But that does not answer the question as to what analytic detail is representative for the identity of a pattern. For that purpose, these experiments are also carried out using stimuli with artificial intonation, viz. standardized stylizations.

This survey is meant not only to recapitulate the main steps in the IPO approach to the analysis of intonation, as presented in this chapter; it also aims at literally illustrating the perceptual detour that is necessary to establish the link between the concrete F_0 curves, on the one hand, and the abstract intonation patterns, on the other. Since only the latter are relevant to communication, and since the former constitute the only attribute of intonation that can be measured, such a link is indispensable in the analysis.

3.5 A general characterization of the IPO approach

To conclude this chapter, we want to pinpoint our position in a brief characterization of the IPO approach, with the aid of a number of well-known terms whose meaning is generally agreed upon.

It is an experimental-phonetic, bottom-up approach, but it is more than a mere instrumental, acoustic analysis followed by statistic processing that examines the potential significance of certain postulated differences. Although our starting point certainly consists of measuring F_0, the centre of gravity is in perception. The motivation of this choice is not only to achieve data reduction in an effective way, but, moreover, to examine how the information in the speech melody is processed by the listener. Since we have assumed that the perceptually relevant information resides in those F_0 changes that are brought about voluntarily by the speaker, we must try to find experimental support for this assumption by studying production aspects by means of physiological measurements. In this way, the usual requirement of phonetic research is met: viz. that it should deploy tripartite activities, in the fields of production, of acoustic manifestation and of perception, although not necessarily in that order, nor with equal weights.

If we borrow the dichotomy of broad versus narrow from segmental-phonetic transcription, we can say that the IPO approach is narrow-oriented; but not too narrow, because it strives at data reduction by means of the application of perceptual criteria. It is not as broad as the 'Tune' approach. In fact, it does aim at trying to establish a link between concrete and atomistic features and more abstract and global structures, for example by examining what analytic detail is responsible for the identity of an intonation pattern.

The approach is, furthermore, characterized by a firm belief in a hierarchical organization of intonation. As will be explained in chapter 4, proposition 7, we do not adhere to the view that it is generally possible to generate an entire pitch contour solely on the basis of considerations of a local nature. It will be made clear that it is the intonation pattern which dictates the local choice among the various pitch movements, and the order in which they may appear.

The intonation pattern thus may seem to be a theoretical construct, introduced merely to implement the highest level of the hierarchical organiz-ation, but such a strategy would be contrary to the IPO approach. Neither is it our intention to lay bare the subdivision of speech melody into a limited number of intonation groups on the basis of any kind of linguistic categorization, such as statement vs question, or of paralinguistic, for instance attitudinal, features. Rather, our experimentation is directed towards getting insight into the listener's internal representation of the intonational system of his native language. If in the experimental outcome the listeners give evidence of sufficient agreement on the categorization of melodic shapes, we shall have to incorporate it in our theoretical account. But in the absence of such evidence, we do not feel entitled to introduce a categorization on *a priori* grounds.

We think that this concise characterization of the IPO approach also shows how it relates to the ideas and starting points of our fellow researchers of intonation, without creating the necessity of reviewing them one by one, which we consider to fall beyond the scope of this book.

4

A theory of intonation

Introduction

In chapter 2, we elaborated on how intonation manifests itself phonetically at the three usual levels of description: production, acoustics and perception. We emphasized that, ideally, these three phonetic aspects should be studied in a complementary fashion, with the aim of integrating these various forms of appearance into one coherent phonetic description that also allows a natural link with a more abstract, phonological characterization of intonation.

In chapter 3, we presented the major features of the IPO approach to the study of intonation. One salient characteristic of this approach is its emphasis on perception. From a historical point of view, our perceptual vantage point was, at first, a practical option. Indeed, in the absence of physiological research facilities, the production aspect could not be the natural starting point of the investigation. Secondly, in the early sixties the acoustic analysis of F_0 still caused great difficulty and, whenever it produced a qualitatively satisfactory result, it confronted the investigators with a wealth of physical detail that could not be interpreted in any straightforward way. Indeed, the measured F_0 curves did not suggest by themselves a suitable descriptive unit whose application would result in some form of data reduction. Such a unit offered itself quite naturally in the perceptual domain where – impressionistically at least – the course of pitch could be decomposed into a sequence of discrete pitch movements. This impression led us to believe that a thorough understanding of the perceptual structure of pitch contours would ultimately give us the indispensable clue to the interpretation of their physiological and acoustic counterparts. Thus, the perceptual approach became a methodological tenet.

In this chapter we present the major results that we have obtained in the analysis of intonation, following the principles and research strategies described in chapter 3. These results mainly pertain to the intonation of Dutch; however, their validity has been strengthened in recent years, when the application of our approach to British English, German and Russian intonation has resulted in a similar outcome.

We will formulate our insights in the form of propositions. For each proposition we will explain its meaning and implications, and we will adduce whatever direct or circumstantial evidence we have gathered in support of it. Taken together, these propositions can be viewed as a 'theory of intonation', i.e. a reasonably coherent body of explanatory statements concerning the production and perception of pitch in speech.

The first five propositions (1–5) regard the perceptual organization of pitch contours in relation to the physical attributes of the speech signal and to the linguistic categories of the intonation patterns. The sixth proposition deals with the physiological implementation of the pitch contours. Taken together, these first six propositions constitute the melodic-phonetic core of our theory. The next three propositions (7–9) address issues of a more linguistic nature: the relation of intonation to accentuation, syntax and meaning. Finally, proposition 10 regards a psycholinguistic question, viz. the integration of linguistic and phonetic knowledge in the speaker's programming of a pitch contour.

This chapter deals with *intonation* proper, i.e. with the salient pitch changes in the course of an utterance. Issues that relate to the much-debated phenomenon of *declination* are addressed in chapter 5.

Proposition 1: In the phonetic perception of pitch in speech the listener is sensitive to a highly restricted class of F_0 changes only: viz. those that have been intentionally produced by the speaker

In the present state of our knowledge, the extensive stylization to which the natural course of F_0 can be submitted without any perceptual consequences cannot be explained on purely auditory grounds. Admittedly, some of the minute F_0 variations that occur in speech cannot be resolved by the ear because they are below the absolute or differential thresholds that have been established in psychoacoustic experiments (see ch. 2, section 3). However, the listener also appears to be insensitive to certain F_0 changes that are well above the established thresholds. One possible explanation for this may be that the spectral complexity of the speech signal makes its auditory analysis more difficult than that of the sinusoidal stimuli used in most psychophysical investigations. In particular, the amplitude and the spectral features of the speech signal (including F_0) are constantly changing over time, so that the auditory analysis has to evaluate relative differences between non-stationary signals. Supposedly, this is a more taxing task than, for instance, to detect a glissando in a sine wave, or in a spectrally homogeneous signal with constant amplitude, such as a sustained vowel.

In chapter 2, we summarized the results of experiments found in the literature, from which one gathers an impression of how surprisingly large a difference in size or slope has to be for two F_0 changes to be perceived as unequal. Yet, the conclusion cannot be that the thresholds for speech-pitch perception are merely higher than those in the auditory analysis of simpler signals. Indeed, some F_0 changes that are well above these higher thresholds may still be perceptually irrelevant. Therefore, speech-pitch perception appears to be qualitatively, not merely quantitatively, different. Admittedly, much more psychoacoustic research on pitch perception in speech-like signals is needed. But we are inclined to believe that, in order to explain why speech-pitch perception is so *selectively* sensitive, we will still need an additional principle that is not auditory but phonetic in nature. That principle is stated as our basic assumption: viz. that only those F_0 changes are relevant for perception that have been intentionally produced by the speaker as physical properties that are cues to the intonation pattern that he wants to produce. Then, for an F_0 change to be detected as such a cue, it should not only be above some psychophysical threshold, but at the same time be recognized as the result of some purposeful action on the speaker's side. This distinct, 'phonetic', mode of *pitch* perception in speech echoes a similar claim for *segmental* perception, embodied in the revised 'motor theory', as formulated by A. Liberman and Mattingly (1985: 2): 'The first claim of the motor theory, as revised, is that the objects of speech perception are intended phonetic gestures of the speaker.'

Applying this claim to the perception of intonation, we do not mean that the listener perceives the intended laryngeal manoeuvres of the speaker, but rather that his perception is constrained by his knowledge of two sorts of production facts: (a) what is physiologically possible; and (b) what is allowed by the language-specific rules for intonation.

Knowledge of the first type plays a similar role in segmental perception, which – according to Dorman, Raphael and Liberman (1979: 1518) – 'is constrained as if by some abstract conception of what vocal tracts can do when they make linguistically significant gestures'.

Later on in this chapter (in proposition 6) we will elaborate on the evidence we have in support of our basic assumption. At this juncture we want to introduce two other propositions that are subsumed under the first.

Proposition 1.1: Those F_0 variations that are relevant for the perception of speech pitch can be approximated as strictly linear changes in the (log) F_0 versus time domain

As a consequence of proposition 1, it is to be expected that certain F_0 changes can be smoothed out without any perceptible difference between the original F_0 curve and the simplified one. And indeed, whenever no perceptually salient

F_0 rise or fall occurs, the natural course of this variable can be stylized as a straight, slightly tilted line, the so-called 'declination line' (see ch. 5). However, the stylization process has revealed that a comparable simplification can be applied to the perceptually relevant F_0 changes, too. The latter need not be left intact in their minute detail, but can likewise be grossly approximated by straight lines that depart from or return to the tilted baseline. This concatenation of straight lines thus effectively reduces the continuously changing F_0 to a sequence of discrete movements. De Pijper's experiments, discussed in chapter 3, have clearly shown that these linear approximations, when made audible in resynthesis, are perceptually indistinguishable from their natural counterparts. Straight lines may not be the only possible elements for the stylization of an F_0 curve (see, e.g., Fujisaki and Sudo, 1971). However, they do offer the advantage that they reveal neatly segmented, discrete units (see also proposition 2).

Proposition 1.2: The linear changes that approximate the natural course of F_0 have to be 'glides' rather than 'jumps'

The stylization procedure has revealed that the time course of a simplified F_0 curve must not show any abrupt discontinuities between adjacent values. This is to say that all perceptually relevant F_0 changes require a certain amount of time, so as to give the impression of a pitch *movement*, not of a jump in pitch. The introduction of an F_0 jump immediately leads to a loss of perceptual equality with the original curve. Moreover, it can be easily demonstrated that stylizations with abrupt transitions sound very unnatural (Issachenko and Schädlich, 1970). Apparently, the ear does not integrate a sudden discontinuity in F_0 as a pitch glide.

The indispensable gradualness of the stylized F_0 changes is not a coincidence: in accordance with our basic assumption, it reflects the fact that, in production too, F_0 changes require a certain amount of time – even if the subject is instructed to produce a sudden jump in pitch. Moreover, it turns out that F_0 changes in natural speech are effected more slowly than the maximum speed allowed by the laryngeal control (Ohala and Ewan, 1973; Sundberg, 1979). This is an indication that the speaker really intends to produce an audible glide, not a jump in pitch.

In conclusion, the propositions 1, 1.1 and 1.2 summarize the findings that have emerged from the application of our stylization method. These findings appear to be in accordance with the basic assumption from which our research programme originally started. The next propositions (2, 2.1 and 2.2) emanate from the application of the second step in our procedure, viz. the standardization.

Proposition 2: At the first level of description, the smallest unit of perceptual analysis is the pitch movement

Since intonation is a speech attribute that encompasses utterances of considerable length, even paragraphs, it may seem unavoidable to analyse it in fairly 'global' terms, viz. with descriptive units that are co-extensive with a clause or sentence. In fact, early analyses such as the well-known Tune approaches by Armstrong and Ward (1926) or Jones (1957) described pitch contours as overall structures that spread over entire sentences. However, as early as 1933, Palmer advocated an alternative approach in which the Tune is decomposed into its constituent elements, the pitch movements. The analytic detail that is introduced by the choice of a small-size descriptive unit may entail the risk that one can no longer see the wood for the trees. 't Hart and Collier (1975), however, have made proposals as to how the 'atomistic' and the 'global' levels of analysis can be integrated and reconciled.

In any case, the pitch movement shares with the segmental descriptive units (speech sounds, phonemes) the attractive feature of its discreteness: it is bounded in all its relevant dimensions. Moreover, its choice as the smallest descriptive unit naturally follows from the results of our stylization and standardization procedures. Indeed, the straight lines that we use are the simplest case of approximation that produces easily definable beginnings and endpoints, both in frequency and in time. As such, they elegantly delimit discrete perceptual events. At the same time they capture the essence of the physical phenomenon that gives rise to these perceptual impressions. Therefore, the pitch movement is at the same time a perceptual and an acoustic unit: it is the output of perceptual analysis and the input of (stylized) acoustic synthesis of intonation.

Proposition 2.1: Pitch movements can be decomposed into perceptual features along the following dimensions: their direction; their timing with regard to syllable boundaries; their rate of change; and their size

The stylization procedure brings to light along which possible dimensions pitch movements actually differ from one another. As shown in chapter 3, the standardization procedure, on the other hand, reveals into how many categories each dimension has to be divided and what the standard specifications for each category are. Presumably, the dimensions themselves are universal, whereas the categorization is language-specific (but see also proposition 2.2).

As an illustration, we present the inventory of the relevant pitch movements of Dutch, decomposed into features (table 4.1). A similar inventory has been

Table 4.1 *The pitch movements of Dutch*

	transcription symbol									
	1	2	3	4	5	A	B	C	D	E
Direction										
rise	x	x	x	x	x					
fall						x	x	x	x	x
Timing										
early	x					x		x		x
late			x				x			
very late		x							x	
Rate of change										
fast	x	x	x			x	x	x	x	x
slow				x						x	
Size										
full	x	x	x	x			x	x	x	x	
half					x						x

established for British English, for German and for Russian intonation (De Pijper, 1983; Adriaens, 1984; Odé, 1986, 1987, 1988, 1989; Willems, Collier and 't Hart, 1988).

The categories used in table 4.1, such as 'early' or 'fast', are more than suggestive impressionistic labels. They have a precise phonetic content, derived from the standardization procedure. Thus, for instance, a 'fast, early rise' (symbol '1') stands for an increment of 50 ST/s, with a duration of 120 ms (thus amounting to a rise of 6 ST), and timed in such a way that the peak of the excursion is reached 50 ms after the onset of the vocalic nucleus of the syllable. A 'half rise' (symbol '5') is characterized by a duration of 60 ms only, so that its excursion amounts to 3 ST. A 'very late rise' (symbol '2') has exactly the same duration and rate of change as an 'early' one, but it is timed in such a way that its peak coincides with the end of voicing of the syllable. In a similar fashion all the other pitch movements in the inventory receive an explicit acoustic definition. In the actual practice of perceptually analysing a pitch contour, each syllable of the utterance is assigned at least one of the symbols of the inventory (or the symbols 'O' or '∅' for the lower and upper declination lines, respectively). In case two or three movements occur on one syllable, their symbols are linked by means of an ampersand, '&', e.g. 'A&2', '5&A', 'B&1'. Because all the notational symbols have a known phonetic content, it can be claimed that for any contour transcribed with these symbols the pitch impression will be equivalent to that of the sequence of stylized F_0 changes that have the physical properties defined by the symbols. Consequently, the correctness of a transcription can be verified by making it audible through resynthesis, using the standard specifications inherent in the transcription symbols. If the analysis is correct, the original utterance under analysis and the resynthesized version should sound perceptually equivalent (for an explanation of the notion of perceptual equivalence, see ch. 3). Of course, the standard acoustic definition of the pitch movements is also a prerequisite for intonational synthesis-by-rule (see ch. 7, 'Applications').

Proposition 2.2: The maximum number of categories along each melodic dimension is limited by universal constraints

Languages may differ in the ways in which they exploit the possible distinctions along the various melodic dimensions. However, in doing so they are constrained by non-linguistic factors, such as the limited resolving power of the auditory system. For instance, pitch movements may differ in their timing with respect to syllable boundaries. Or they may be different in their rates of change. However, there must be an upper limit to the number of categories any language can distinguish along these dimensions. Collier (1983) presents an overview of some of the perceptual and physiological constraints that define the class of possible tone and intonation systems.

As far as the variable speed of pitch movements is concerned, it appears from data by, for example, Sundberg (1979) that rises that cover an interval of four to twelve semitones require a minimum duration of 85 to 100 ms, which amounts to a physiologically constrained maximum rate of change of 120 semitones per second. However, rises and falls in speech pitch are not usually effected so fast: for instance, the most abrupt pitch changes in Dutch have a rate of change of some fifty semitones per second only. Of course, they could be effected even more slowly. Then the question arises whether, within a single language, tonal contrast could be based on a difference in rate of change among otherwise identical pitch movements. In other words, can one discriminate – within the bounds of a single syllable – rises or falls that differ in slope?

't Hart (1976a) has examined the discriminability of different rates of change as a function of duration. The conclusion appears to be that if two rises are shorter than 250 ms (as they usually are) and cover an interval of more than 3.5 semitones (which they usually do), then any difference in their rate of change will remain below the threshold. Only gradual rises that extend over several syllables may perceptibly differ in rate of change (see also ch. 2).

A comparable question can be asked concerning the discriminability of pitch movements that differ in size. 't Hart (1981) has shown that in the perception of running speech a pitch range of one octave can be quantized into no more than three or four distinguishable intervals (see also ch. 2). This perceptual constraint suggests that, in tone languages, the number of contrastive pitch levels per octave cannot exceed four. And, indeed, very few tone languages exploit this maximum number of contrasts among so-called 'register tones'. Many more have tonal systems in which a contrast between two or three 'register' tones is supplemented with a contrast between dynamic 'contour' tones. Thai, for example, has a contrast between a low, a mid and a high tone, in combination with a rising and a falling tone (Abramson, 1978).

Finally, it appears from an experiment by Hill and Reid (1977) that there is also a perceptual limit to the number of pitch movements that can be discriminated on the basis of their position in the syllable. In an average syllable of 200 ms duration, no more than three distinct positions can be kept apart perceptually.

Proposition 3: There are no pitch 'levels'

According to proposition 2, rises and falls are the smallest units of melodic description. They are also the basic units, in the sense that we assume them to be the true targets of intonation production. As we have explained under proposition 1.2, a given pitch distance is covered as a function of time, not only because it is physiologically impossible to produce a jump in pitch (which is true, except in yodelling), but also because the speaker *intends* to produce audibly gradual pitch-transitions. One indication of this intention is that rises and falls are effected more slowly than what is physiologically possible.

By positing pitch movements as the basic melodic targets we reject the alternative view that the speaker primarily intends to hit a particular pitch level and that the resulting movements are only the physiologically unavoidable transitions between any two basic levels. The latter view has been cherished in most American structuralist approaches to intonation (e.g. Pike, 1945; Trager and Smith, 1951), and, despite Bolinger's (1958) criticism, it has recently been revived by Ladd (1983b), Pierrehumbert (1980) and others. We think that our rejection of pitch levels is not a matter of taste.

Admittedly, pitch movements may start or end at audibly different heights, which can be ordered on a scale and transcribed with digits. However, our standardization technique has revealed that, in Dutch, the 'full-size' pitch movements can all be given the same fixed size without changing their identity (e.g. six semitones). In other words, the excursion of a pitch movement does not enter into the definition of its basic melodic characteristics, except if it is conspicuously smaller than standard (e.g. the 'half fall' 'E' in Dutch). Moreover, the observable variation in the size of pitch movements within a single utterance in natural speech is not an intonational feature in the strict sense: with prominence-lending pitch movements the excursion size is determined by quite a different prosodic variable, viz. degree of accentuation (Rietveld and Gussenhoven, 1985). Similarly, differences in the average range of the pitch movements from one utterance to the next correlate with changing paralinguistic factors, such as the emotional state of the speaker.

It could, nevertheless, be argued that the standardization procedure, as applied to Dutch, does not deny the notion that this language operates with basic pitch levels: the procedure may only show that the number of pitch levels is just two. Indeed, the standardized rises and falls of Dutch move between two reference lines (a baseline and a topline), which are then the only two basic pitch levels. Furthermore, in the stylization of English and German intonation a 'midline' has to be distinguished, which suggests that these languages operate with three pitch levels. However, we think that the primacy of pitch levels can be refuted on the following grounds. If the levels themselves were the primary targets of intonation production, one would expect the transitions between them (i.e. the pitch movements) to have invariant melodic properties, such as a fixed rate of change (e.g. close to the physiological maximum), and a fixed timing with respect to the syllable structure (e.g. with a peak at the CV-boundary). We have seen that this is not the case: pitch movements differ among each other in many ways and these differences contribute to their melodic identity, so that their standard specifications for synthesis have to differ accordingly. In other words, the pitch movements have properties that are not merely accidental and predictable consequences of their putative function of bridging two pitch levels.

So, if one wants to predict correctly the relevant melodic properties of the pitch movements, while defending the primacy of the pitch levels, then these target levels will have to be specified in greater detail. Indeed, a specification such as 'low', 'mid' or 'high' will not suffice to differentiate, for instance, 'early', 'late' and 'very late' rises or falls. These three types differ in their timing with respect to the syllable boundaries, but there is nothing in the concept of a high, mid or low pitch level that will automatically entail these relevant differences. To account for these differences, then, the concept of levels will have to be enriched with a temporal dimension. In fact, this is exactly what Issachenko and Schädlich (1970) felt obliged to do in their attempt to synthesize German pitch contours with sudden jumps between two fixed levels. They had to differentiate between 'ictic', 'pre-ictic' and 'post-ictic' tone switches (ibid.: 20–3). But to enrich the 'levels' concept with a temporal dimension deprives it of its simplicity, which was its major *raison d'être* in intonation analysis.

Clearly, if the 'mid level' that appears indispensable in the characterization of British English and German contours is considered as a basic descriptive unit, it is subject to the same limitations as the low and high levels of Dutch.

The introduction of such a third level is a necessary ingredient in the definition of half-size pitch movements. Apart from a specification for direction (rise or fall), they also require a specification for range: half-size rises and falls can be either 'high' or 'low', depending on whether they cover the range above or below the midline. This means that the mid level enters into the definition of an additional dimension of pitch range, as required by certain pitch movements. The concept of pitch level may play a role in the typology of pitch movements, but it cannot be substituted for them as a descriptive unit.

From what precedes, it appears that the 'levels' approach cannot cope with relevant timing-distinctions in speech pitch. Ladd (1983a) has attempted to provide a solution while arguing that the time dimension can be incorporated in the 'levels' approach, not as a basic feature, but as a 'modification'. Late rises are 'scooped' variants of the canonical ones, and they receive the additional feature [+delayed peak]. The problem with Ladd's analysis, when he applies it to Dutch, is the following: 'scooped' pitch movements are not just 'variants'; they have distributional properties that cannot be expressed in terms of free or combinatory variation. For instance, as will be explained in greater detail under proposition 4, the 'late' rise '3' in Dutch is not a scooped variant of the 'early' rise '1', to the extent that only '3' can be followed by the 'very late' fall 'C', whereas either can be followed by the 'early' fall 'B'. Conversely, if the sequence '3C' is preceded by a combination of a rise '1' and a fall 'B' then the latter have to occur on the same syllable, whereas if the same combination precedes the sequence '1A', no such constraint exists.

A further problem with Ladd's analysis is, that [± delayed peak] only allows for a two-category distinction, whereas Dutch differentiates three positional categories.

To summarize our position, we believe that the use of 'levels' in a phonetic analysis of intonation is an oversimplification. And, even though it may be a commendable attempt at *phonological* data reduction, its application on the phonetic level runs counter to the phonetic facts of pitch-change production and perception.

Proposition 4: The combinatory possibilities of the pitch movements are highly constrained and can be expressed formally in a 'grammar' of intonation

In order to describe the melodic possibilities of a language it is not sufficient to establish the inventory of its perceptually relevant pitch movements. The distribution analysis of the pitch movements reveals that some of them combine with some others into higher-order structures and that, in turn, these structures can only be concatenated in compliance with specific rules of sequence.

In order to explicitly specify the combinatory possibilities of the pitch movements, a 'grammar' can be designed that generates all and only the permissible sequences of pitch movements in a given domain, e.g. that of the clause. In the following propositions (4.1, 4.2 and 4.3) we further explain the notion of intonational structure, and subsequently we present a 'grammar of Dutch intonation'.

Proposition 4.1: At the second level of description, pitch movements combine into 'configurations'

Pitch movements only occur in very specific melodic environments. A particular type of rise or fall can only be found just before or after one of a limited set of other rises and falls. In Dutch, for instance, rise '1' can be followed by fall 'A' or 'B', but never by fall 'C'. Fall 'C' has to be preceded by rise '3', but the inverse is not true: rise '3' can also be followed by fall 'B'. Rise '1' can be followed by rise '2', but it cannot be followed by either rise '1' or rise '3', unless fall 'B' intervenes. Unitary sequences such as '1A', '1B' or '3C' are called *configurations*. In the limiting case, a single pitch movement can occur as the only one in an utterance or stand alone amidst other configurations. In that case it is considered as a (one-unit) configuration all the same.

It is logically conceivable that a particular sequence of pitch movements can be structured in more than one way. For instance, the sequence '1B45A2' can be grouped as '1–B4–5A–2', '1B–45–A2', '1B–45A–2', etc. The grouping of movements into configurations is then guided by the consideration that, in order to function as a coherent structure, a particular sequence should

(a)   be possible as the only one in an utterance; or
(b)   be recursive in a clause.

In our example, condition (a) is met by the sequences '5A', 'A2', '45A' and by the single pitch movements '1' and '2', but not by 'B4', or '45'. Condition (b) is met by the sequence '1B', not by any other. Therefore, the third grouping is to be preferred over the other two. Another consideration that is relevant for the grouping into configurations is that the combinatory possibilities within a configuration are far more restricted than those at its boundaries. For instance, fall 'B' can only be preceded by rise '1' (very seldom also by '3' or '4'), whereas the resulting configuration '1B' can be followed by the rises '1', '3' and '4'.

Proposition 4.2: Pitch-movement configurations belong to one of the following paradigmatic classes: 'Prefix', 'Root' or 'Suffix'

The distributional analysis of the configurations reveals that there are several restrictions with regard to their concatenation into contours. If we take the contour to be the largest overall structure that is co-extensive with a clause, we notice that certain configurations only occur in contour-final position. Some configurations are optional and recursive, others are not. Therefore we have introduced the following typology of configurations:

(a)   ROOT configurations: they are obligatory and non-recursive; a contour must contain one such configuration, and not more than one.

(b)   PREFIX configurations: they are optional and some of them are recursive; they always precede another Prefix or a Root.

(c)   SUFFIX configurations: they are optional and non-recursive; they always follow a Root.

This terminology clearly reminds one of the possible structure of morphemes, but this should not suggest that we consider configurations as 'pitch morphemes'. Rather, we only want to make clear that any contour can be described with the following rule:

(1) Contour→(Prefix)^n Root (Suffix)

where ^{n} indicates recursiveness.

In a former publication ('t Hart and Collier, 1975), we have described the internal structure of contours in somewhat different terms, using categories labelled 'Prefix block', 'Continuation block' and 'End block'. Blocks were combined into contours according to the following rule:

(2) Contour → ((P) C) (P) E

in which P and C are recursive.

We now believe that this analysis unduly mixes melodic and functional aspects, in the sense that Continuation blocks may indeed signal clause boundaries, while they may have the same melodic appearance as End blocks. Therefore, we prefer to drop the category Continuation block altogether. As a consequence of this, the domain of application of the contour is no longer the complete utterance, but the clause.

By a further elimination of partial melodic overlappings between the former so-called blocks, we now retain the following configurations in Dutch:

Prefix	Root	Suffix
1B	(1) (E)^n(5)A	2
3B	4(5)A	
4B	(1)(E)^n(5)E	
B	3C	
	1	
	2	

Proposition 4.3: At the third level of description, pitch-movement configurations combine into contours in accordance with syntagmatic constraints

The rule for contour structure, presented as (1) above, merely states which general types of configuration should precede or follow each other. However, many sequences of Prefix, Root and Suffix are unlawful, exactly as in word-formation processes (where combinations such as *re+jump+ness* are excluded, even if they comply with a general rule for word structure, e.g. prefix + stem + suffix). Therefore, if one wants to specify all and only the well-formed contours of the language, a more elaborate set of rules is necessary.

We have designed a 'grammar' of Dutch intonation that incorporates the rules of sequence for configurations of pitch movements at the level of the contour, i.e. for melodic structures that are co-extensive with one clause. As explained above, the movements are first grouped into permissible configurations; then the configurations are combined into lawful contours. Figure 4.1 presents the grammar in the form of a transition network. The bold vertical bars are meant to indicate that every horizontal line arriving from the left may be continued by any of the horizontal lines departing at the right side. In this way, following the arrows, one generates all and only the acceptable contours of Dutch. Figure 4.2 shows some examples of such contours.

In previous publications (Collier and 't Hart, 1971; 't Hart and Collier, 1975) we have already presented a similar grammar. The present version is an improvement in the following respects. First, in the older version some of the grammatical rules were not stated in formal terms, but were paraphrased in plain words. Now this has been partly remedied. Second, as already explained, we have eliminated most of the melodic overlappings between configurations (by a more extensive use of parentheses and braces), and we have avoided the interference of functional considerations (by eliminating the former Continuation blocks). Third and foremost, we have regrouped the Roots and reduced their number in accordance with the intuitive clustering of contours into intonation patterns. Indeed, as will be explained under proposition 5, such a grouping is supported by experimental findings. By bringing the structure of the grammar into line with the observed intuitions of language users, we have increased its 'observational adequacy' (Chomsky, 1957).

We have verified the predictions of the grammar against a corpus of some 1,500 spontaneous and semi-spontaneous utterances. We found that our rules accounted for 94 per cent of the contours in the corpus ('t Hart and Collier, 1975).

Also on the basis of a corpus, a similar but more elaborate grammar of intonation has been designed for British English (Willems, Collier and 't Hart,

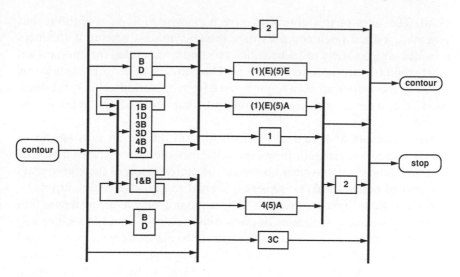

4.1 Grammar of Dutch intonation

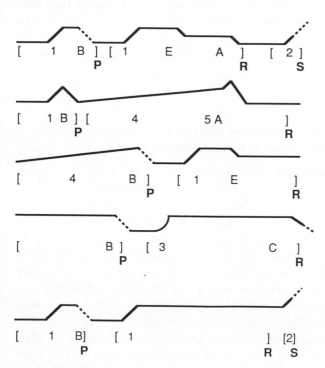

4.2 Illustration of a number of possible contours, generated by the grammar in figure 4.1

81

1988). The rules of this grammar have been written as an algorithm that generates stylized pitch contours in a speech-synthesis scheme. Utterances provided with a variety of such artificial contours were rated for intonational acceptability by thirty native listeners. The subjects valued the contours as highly as those that had been resynthesized from natural speech. On the other hand, they consistently rejected contours that violated the rules of the grammar.

The grammars of Dutch and British English intonation thus appear to capture significant generalizations about the melodic rules of these languages. Of course, the good agreement between the performance of these grammars and that of native speaker–listeners is limited to the observable outputs.

We also want to make clear that the grammar is only a formal device that generates structured sequences of pitch movements. It does not include any instructions as to how such sequences have to be mapped onto the words and phrases that make up an utterance. This mapping will be elucidated in propositions 7, 8 and 10, and will also be discussed in chapter 6. Let it suffice, at this point, to mention that the pitch movements that make up a contour need not always occur on adjacent syllables: on some occasions they may combine on a single syllable, in other cases they may be separated by a large number of syllables. But the 'elasticity' (see fig. 4.10) with which they are distributed over an utterance is of no consequence for the melodic identity of the contour they build.

Proposition 5: The unlimited number of different pitch contours are manifestations of a finite number of basic intonation patterns

The number of different pitch contours that can occur in any language is unlimited. Moreover, any individual utterance of some length can be intoned in more than a dozen different ways. This diversity stems from two sources: on the one hand, the actual sequence of pitch movements may be different from one contour to the other; on the other hand, the same sequence may be distributed differently over the utterance. The latter variation is caused mainly by differences in the location of the sentence accents. Indeed, as we will explain under proposition 7, those pitch movements that have a prominence-lending capacity can be flexibly moved around in the contour, so as to co-occur with the accentuated syllables which, by the same token, receive a pitch accent. For instance, as we have already illustrated in chapter 3, in the sentences (4) and (5) below three sentence accents are realized by the same sequence of pitch movements which occur in different positions in the contour.

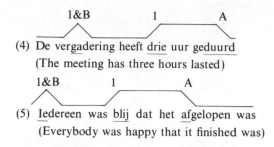

(4) De vergadering heeft drie uur geduurd
(The meeting has three hours lasted)

(5) Iedereen was blij dat het afgelopen was
(Everybody was happy that it finished was)

It is not surprising that listeners will intuitively feel a strong resemblance between the contours of (4) and (5). But (4) and (5) can be intoned in many more ways, e.g.

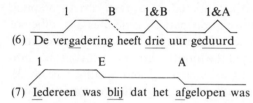

(6) De vergadering heeft drie uur geduurd

(7) Iedereen was blij dat het afgelopen was

Despite the increasing diversity, listeners will still consider the contours in (6) and (7) as very similar. Moreover, they will feel that (6) and (7) resemble (4) and (5). In other words, according to listeners' intuitions, the contours in (4) to (7) form a 'family'. However, if the same utterances are intoned as in (8) and (9), the intuitive similarity is lost.

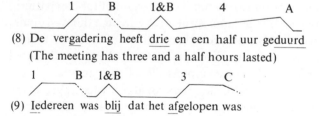

(8) De vergadering heeft drie en een half uur geduurd
(The meeting has three and a half hours lasted)

(9) Iedereen was blij dat het afgelopen was

In this case, no resemblance is felt between (8) and (9), and neither of them is intuitively related to the contours in (4) to (7). In other words, (8) and (9) belong to different 'families' of contours.

In order to account for these different groupings, one cannot refer to the degree of purely melodic similarity. Rather, the intuitive resemblance must have its origin in a more abstract organizational principle, viz. the existence of underlying melodic categories which we call 'intonation patterns'. Each

Table 4.2 *Results of a matching experiment*

Patterns	No. responses	Resembling	%	Not resembling	%
cap/cap	96	89	93	7	7
valley/valley	96	92	96	4	4
hat/hat	96	76	79	20	21
cap/valley	96	20	21	76	79
cap/hat	96	8	8	88	92
valley/hat	96	24	25	72	75

pattern is characterized by a unique combination of invariant abstract melodic properties, but these are instantiated in a great variety of pitch contours. In other words, each intonation pattern generates a number of 'variants' and all of these form a set of similar contours by virtue of their common origin. We have investigated the intuitive grouping of contours into patterns in two experimental paradigms: 'matching' and 'sorting' (see ch. 3).

In one of the matching experiments, objectively different contours were presented in pairs and subjects had to evaluate them as 'resembling' or 'not resembling'. In this experiment (Collier and 't Hart, 1972), we used contours that were hypothetically related to three different basic intonation patterns: the hat pattern (i.e. Root configuration '1A'), the valley pattern (i.e. Root configuration '4A') and the cap pattern (Root configuration '3C'). Examples of the hat pattern are the contours of (4) to (7) above; contour (8) is a variant of the valley pattern, and contour (9) exemplifies a variant of the cap pattern.

All the contours were read by the same speaker. We created thirty-six pairs of stimuli in which a contour was matched either with one of the same 'family' or with one of the other two, different 'families'. Sixteen subjects participated and gave a two-category, forced-choice response. Table 4.2 summarizes the results. It appears from table 4.2 that the listeners could consistently group the variants of the same pattern and discriminate the variants of different patterns.

In a similar experiment (Collier and 't Hart, 1972), we made use of utterances with both natural and stylized F_0 curves. Again, the contours were hypothesized to belong to one of three basic intonation patterns: hat, valley and cap. The material consisted of three sets of four sentences, each set being provided with a contour that was derived from a different intonation pattern. All the stimuli were recorded on Language Master cards (Bell and Howell). The cards were then grouped into fifteen quartets (X – A,B,C) such that each quartet contained two intonationally resembling stimuli, viz. X and one in the

Table 4.3 *Results of a matching experiment. Scores are percentages of the total score per pattern (n = 40)*

	Judged as resembling		No reaction
	predicted as *same*	predicted as *different*	
X = Cap	93	5	2
Valley	83	12	5
Hat	74	14	12

A–B–C group. Ten subjects were asked to match the X stimulus with A, B and C, and to indicate which of the three resembled X. They were allowed to indicate more than one item as 'resembling X' or no item at all. Subjects were free to play back the cards as often as necessary, in any order.

Table 4.3 summarizes the results, expressed as percentages of the total score per pattern (i.e. 40). The results in table 4.3 corroborate those in table 4.2: listeners can fairly consistently evaluate the melodic resemblance among sets of different contours. Their pairing of resembling contours is in accordance with our predicted grouping of pitch contours that derive from the same intonation pattern. Conversely, the fact that there is little confusion supports the notion that contours that belong to different patterns are consistently distinguished.

In a series of 'sorting' experiments, we studied the relation between contours and patterns in a more direct way: viz. by having subjects literally build piles of Language Master cards on the basis of perceived similarity. For one of these experiments ('t Hart and Collier, 1975) we took the Dutch sentence *Dat heb ik al gedaan* ('I've already done that') and provided it with twelve different stylized F_0 contours that essentially consisted of a prominence-lending rise 'l' on the syllable *heb* and a falling pitch movement on the syllable *-daan*. The size of this fall was varied stepwise, as shown in figure 4.3, so as to include instances of the 'full-size' fall 'A' on one end of the quasi-continuum, and representatives of the 'half-size' fall 'E' on the other end. The hypothesis to be tested was that the subjects would divide the ensemble of the stimuli into two groups: one set would include variants of the hat pattern ('1A'), the other would contain variants of a different pattern ('1E'). To the twelve stimuli we added four more that were exact copies of some of the original twelve (viz. 7 = 8, 10 = 11, 12 = 13 and 15 = 16). All sixteen stimuli were recorded on Language Master cards and ten listeners were instructed to group the stimuli in 'less than sixteen' piles, on the basis of subjective melodic resemblance. In other words, they were not told into how

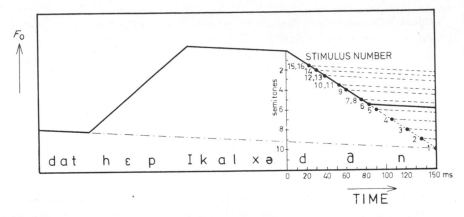

4.3 Contours with quasi-continuous variation of the excursion of the falling pitch-movement as applied in the sorting experiment

many categories they were expected to divide the stimuli. Of course, they were allowed to listen to the utterances as often as they wanted.

The results were submitted to a hierarchical clustering-analysis (Johnson, 1967), the outcome of which is presented in figure 4.4. The minimum method of analysis suggests the existence of two groups, whereas the maximum method reveals three clusters. So, both methods agree in distinguishing at least two groups (viz. the predicted contrast between '1A'- and '1E'-like contours). The stimuli numbers 6 to 11 may correspond to a region of ambiguity which clearly stands apart in the maximum method, but is eventually assimilated, in the minimum method, to those stimuli that definitely have a 'less than full-size' final fall.

Similar experiments with up to twenty different contours have produced comparable results (Collier and 't Hart, 1972; Collier, 1975b). Together with the matching experiments they all appear to support the hypothesis that listeners do not treat all melodically different contours as if they were merely variants of one and the same underlying intonational category. On the contrary, listeners feel the need to assign them to a number of different intonation patterns.

In the sorting experiments with Dutch contours, the pool of stimuli contained representatives of no more than two or three (out of six) hypothetically different intonation patterns. In a similar experiment with British English contours the number of potential categories was increased to seven. Yet again listeners showed the ability to group a large variety of contours into a limited set of melodic categories (Collier, 1977a, 1977b). Using the same experimental procedure, Odé (1986) found up to ten distinguishable basic patterns for Russian.

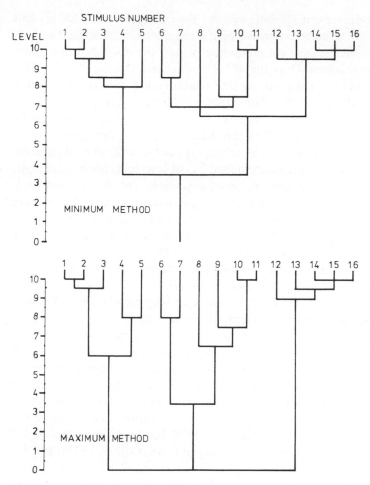

4.4 Outcome of the hierarchical clustering-analysis as applied to the results of the sorting experiment

Our studies of Dutch intonation have revealed that there are six basic intonation patterns in this language. Apparently, both in Dutch and in English, the categorization of contours into patterns is based (mainly) on the melodic properties of their Root configuration. The latest version of our grammar, as presented under proposition 4.3, reflects this categorization: the six different types of Root configurations are the phonetic manifestation of an equal number of basic intonation patterns.

In order to make a distinction between 'pattern' and 'contour' we now introduce the following notational convention: the patterns are transcribed with the pitch-movement symbols that are their obligatory ingredients and these symbols are given between slashes; the contours are transcribed with all the pitch movements they are composed of and these symbols are given between square brackets. Thus, the six basic patterns of Dutch are: /1A/, /1E/, /4A/, /3C/, /1/ and /2/. The set of possible contours that are associated with a given pattern is defined in the grammar by all the paths that go through the Root that corresponds to that pattern. For instance, pattern /1A/ can be realized as contours [1A], [1B1EA], [1B1&B15A], etc. The fact that contours derive their 'pattern identity' from the properties of their Root configuration means that this identity is not determined by the last single pitch movement, but by some (near) final melodic structure as a whole. This observation lends independent support to the configuration as a descriptive unit. The sorting experiments have also confirmed the status of Suffix [2] as a non-essential option. Indeed, contours with the same Root were grouped together irrespective of the presence or absence of the Suffix.

Our claim about the existence of intonation patterns as the abstract melodic stratum of observable pitch contours is by no means a new one. In the tradition of intonation analysis of a variety of languages, such as English, German, French and Russian, 'pattern'-like notions have been used to refer to melodically distinct families of contours (Tune, Tone, Intonations de base, Melodiegestalt). Intonation courses for foreign-language teaching in fact all purport to elucidate how a given basic 'Tune' can be realized in a number of variant ways. However, our experiments have produced empirical support for the long-standing claim that basic Tunes or patterns constitute a psychological reality. They have also given rise to the suspicion that some of the proposed classifications (e.g. by Halliday (1970) for English) are not in full agreement with the intuitions of the language users (Collier, 1977a, 1977b).

Proposition 6: All the relevant features of pitch movements are controlled by the activity of the laryngeal muscles

Taken together, the propositions that we have formulated so far constitute the essence of the perceptual component of our phonetic theory of intonation. We consider this component to be the central one, because the perceptual analysis of intonation appears to be a necessary condition for the interpretation of its acoustic and physiological manifestation. Indeed, the inspection of EMG tracings of the laryngeal musculature or of subglottal pressure curves does not allow one to predict in any detail which F_0 curve has resulted from the recorded production activity. And even when that F_0 curve is made available, it is not always possible to map it directly onto the production data. This interpretative difficulty does not arise solely from the already complex physical relation between, for instance, EMG activity of the laryngeal muscles and the frequency of vocal-fold vibration; the difficulty is compounded by the fact that one cannot always differentiate in the EMG recording of a single muscle those laryngeal gestures that were intended to produce the successive ingredients of the pitch contour and those that are not related to intonation production. The interpretation has to be mediated by insight into the perceptual relevance of the F_0 changes that have been produced.

In chapter 2 we explained that the fundamental frequency of vocal-fold vibration is, in principle, dependent upon two factors: the tension of the vocal folds themselves and the amount of subglottal pressure. There is an increasing body of production data to show that the control of F_0 is sited in the larynx and that P_s has a negligible effect on the production of F_0 rises and falls.

Our own physiological observations on the production of pitch contours in Dutch have amply confirmed the hypothesis that all pitch movements have their origin in the activity of the laryngeal muscles, predominantly in that of the cricothyroid (CT) muscles. There is not only a gross correspondence between CT activity and F_0 change; the time course of CT contraction and relaxation also shows a direct relation to the detailed properties of F_0 variation, such as excursion size, rate of change and timing.

Figures 4.5 to 4.9 illustrate this point. They are taken from the data presented in Collier (1974, 1975a), and show five different F_0 curves with the corresponding physiological data: the EMG tracings of the cricothyroid and sternohyoid (SH) muscles and the variation in P_s. In each figure the thick lines represent averages of about twenty-five repetitions of the same pitch contour. The thin lines correspond to the one single token whose F_0 curve is shown in the upper part. The physiological signals were sampled and processed as described in Harris (1981). The data pertain to one subject (RC).

In the first part of the contours 9, 10 and 19 we see a rise–fall sequence, and this F_0 variation clearly correlates with the pattern of increasing and decreasing CT activity. In contours 5 and 13 we notice a rise in F_0, followed by sustained high pitch. Here, too, we see a close correspondence with the CT curve: the activity of this muscle suddenly increases, and its contraction continues as long as F_0 is to be kept high. Contour 5 terminates in a sudden fall that correlates with the relaxation of CT. Contour 13 ends in an upward wriggle, which is caused by an additional burst of CT activity. The same utterance-final rise is observed in contours 9, 10 and 19, and there, too, we notice a momentary increase of CT activity. Finally, in the second half of contour 10 we see a more gradual increase of F_0, which finds its most evident correlate in the equally gradual increase of CT contraction.

In all the figures the activity of the SH muscle is somewhat antagonistic to that of CT, but only in the sense that this muscle tends to be less active

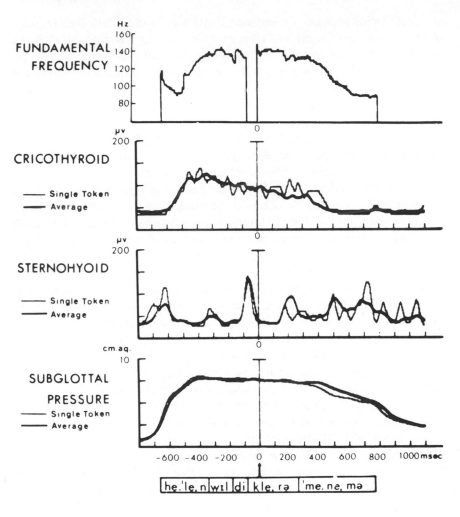

CONTOUR 5

4.5 Contour 5: simultaneous recordings of fundamental frequency, of EMG measurement of cricothyroid and sternohyoid muscles and of subglottal pressure. Heavy lines: averages over ca twenty-five repetitions; light lines: the single token of which F₀ is plotted

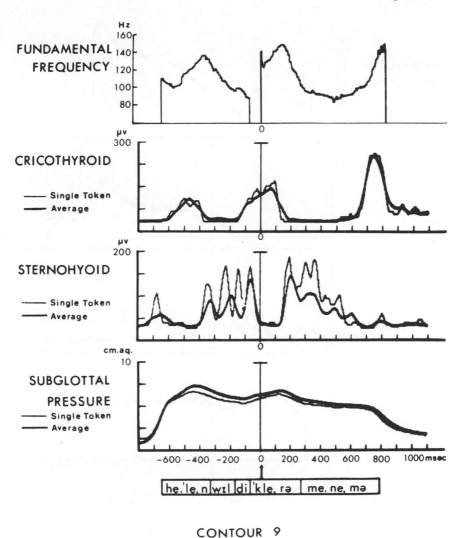

CONTOUR 9

4.6 Contour 9: see caption to figure 4.5

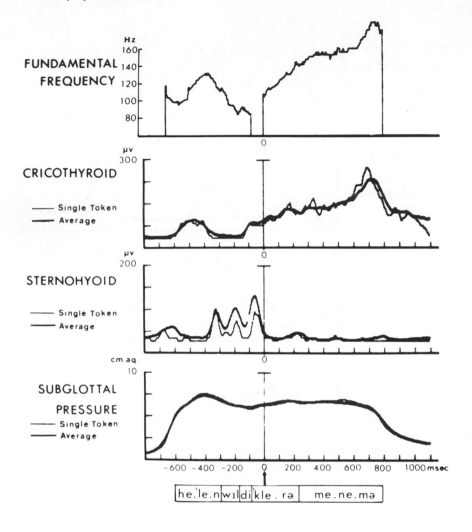

CONTOUR 10

4.7 Contour 10: see caption to figure 4.5

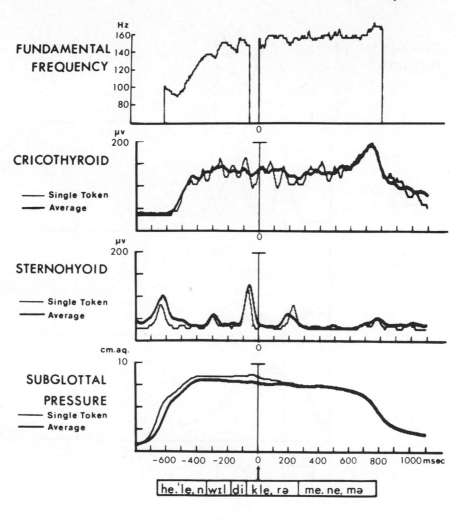

CONTOUR 13

4.8 Contour 13: see caption to figure 4.5

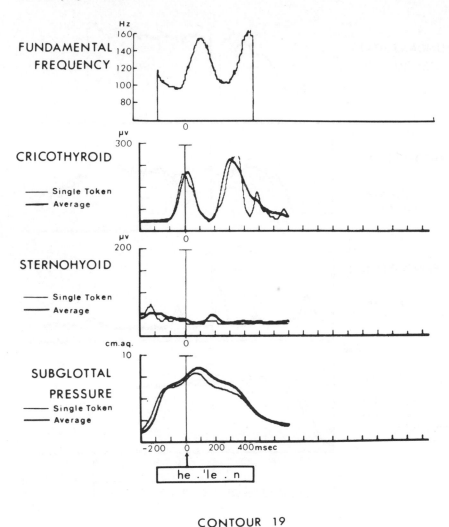

CONTOUR 19

4.9 Contour 19: see caption to figure 4.5

whenever F_0 is rising or high. However, the contraction of SH does not really explain the F_0 falls. For one thing, we observe SH peaks during portions of high F_0, and some of the SH peaks that do occur in the vicinity of F_0 falls are timed too late to be responsible for the initiation of the pitch movement. Also, there is sometimes little or no SH activity at all when F_0 is suddenly lowered over a large interval (see contour 19). On the other hand, the observable F_0 falls correlate well with the pattern of CT relaxation.

As far as P_s is concerned, it can be observed that its time course varies very little from one contour to the next. Basically, P_s rises at the onset of phonation and gradually decreases over the entire duration of the utterance, to suddenly drop at the end. Some pressure curves appear to be modulated with small peaks that co-occur with rise–falls in F_0. However, these local pressure changes are far too small to account for the observed F_0 change. They may well be the mere passive consequence of the increased glottal resistance caused by the action of the laryngeal muscles that raise F_0. However, as will be explained in chapter 5, the gradual decrease of P_s may be held responsible to a large extent for the phenomenon of declination.

The content of proposition 6 emphasizes the role of the laryngeal muscles in F_0 control, and minimizes the influence of P_s on the production of salient F_0 changes. This statement does not imply, of course, that the laryngeal muscles only have an intonational function. Some of them are equally involved in segmental articulation, for instance in producing the voiced–voiceless distinction in obstruents. In fact, a single laryngeal muscle such as the cricothyroid may have a double function: its contraction increases the extrinsic tension of the vocal cords, making them vibrate more rapidly; but CT can also contribute to making an obstruent voiceless, presumably by 'stiffening' the cords. The same is true of the sternohyoid muscle; its activity may play a role in F_0 lowering and in the production of open vowels such as /a/. In the latter case, SH contraction stabilizes the hyoid bone in support of the muscles that lower the jaw. This state of affairs implies that EMG recordings of the laryngeal muscles are difficult to interpret, unless one knows which intonation pattern the speaker intended to produce. As we have argued before, this knowledge cannot be inferred from a direct inspection of the F_0 curve. The latter has first to be interpreted in perceptual terms. Such an interpretation brings to light that there is a strong correspondence between perceptually relevant F_0 changes and moments of salient activity in the laryngeal muscles. This correspondence lends support to our basic assumption, stated as proposition 1.

Proposition 7: Intonation takes precedence over accentuation in determining the shape of a pitch contour

In the introductory chapter we referred to 'prosody' as a cover term for at least three non-segmental phenomena: pitch variation, prominence and prosodic duration. These phenomena can be studied independently of one another, especially if the level of abstraction is sufficiently high, as is the case in formal linguistic analysis. Indeed, in the linguistic tradition, distinct descriptive frameworks have been set up for the assignment of accentual and intonational features. Both in the American structuralist school (Pike, 1945; Trager and Smith, 1951) and in contemporary prosodic studies (Pierrehumbert, 1980; Ladd, 1983a: 728; Ladd, 1983b) 'sentence stress levels' and 'pitch levels' are distinct units of description.

In our own phonetic analysis of prosody we have attempted, too, to deal with pitch without reference to prominence. This has appeared to be feasible, but only to the extent that the melodic analysis and description, as presented in preceding chapters, has not necessitated any discussion in depth of accentual matters. Indeed, our dealing with prosodic matters has confronted us with the interaction of intonation and accentuation, especially at the phonetic level of description.

The stylization and standardization procedures that we apply have brought to our attention the fact that some (types of) pitch movements coincide with accented syllables, while others never do. For instance, rise '1' and fall 'A' are always associated with accented syllables; with isolated rise '2' and fall 'B' this is never the case. With regard to the relation between intonation and accentuation, it may suffice to state the observed 'coincidence' or 'co-occurrence', as Ladd, Pierrehumbert and others prefer to do. However, following Bolinger, we adhere to the concept of 'pitch accentuation': some kinds of pitch movements *cause* the impression of prominence. This causal relationship is demonstrated by the fact that any displacement of a prominence-lending pitch movement immediately has consequences for the perception of the accent, which either shifts to another syllable or disappears altogether. Conversely, the addition of a properly timed rise or fall to an existing contour will automatically increase the number of perceived accents. This interaction of pitch and prominence at the phonetic level is a matter of fact, but it is still open to two alternative interpretations, to be paraphrased as two competing hypotheses.

Hypothesis 1: Those pitch movements that occur on prominent syllables are entirely and exclusively caused by the accentuation demands of the utterance; the remaining pitch movements (and declination) result from the requirements of intonation proper.

This hypothesis states that a pitch contour is a sequence of pitch movements that are caused either by the accentual or by the intonational demands of the utterance, but never by both requirements simultaneously. This viewpoint is adhered to by, for instance, Vanderslice and Ladefoged (1971). In their analysis, accent demands result in momentary pitch obtrusions (rise–falls). Intonational requirements only affect the terminal portion of a contour, where the following alternatives are possible: Cadence (falling), Endglide (rising) or a combination of both. In other words, the overall pitch contour is a linear addition of accentual and intonational features. As a consequence of this view, rise–fall combinations in the non-terminal portion of a contour are purely accent-related, whereas the last rise–fall receives a different interpretation: the rising part is the manifestation of [+ accent], whereas the falling part is the implementation of Cadence.

A similar view is espoused by Thorsen (1980). In her analysis of Danish intonation, she relates the rises and falls to the realization of successive pitch accents; they are not considered as intonational phenomena. Intonation proper is limited to the features of the line that connects the F_0 values measured in (the middle of) stressed syllables.

In 't Hart and Collier (1979) we have argued against this functional separation of pitch phenomena. If rises and falls can provoke the impression of prominence, either singly or in combination, it should be immaterial which type of pitch change or combination of changes is selected to produce a pitch accent. In actual fact, this freedom of choice does not exist. In Dutch, for instance, two successive pitch accents can be implemented either by two rise–falls or by a rise on the first and a fall on the second syllable to be stressed. All the other logical possibilities are excluded (e.g. a succession of fall–rises, two successive rises, or a fall followed by a rise). There is nothing in the nature of the accents that would predict this restriction: contours that violate this restriction do, in fact, produce the required pitch-accent impression, but they sound ill-formed. So, we suggest that the choice of the kind of accent-lending pitch movements is subordinate to the kind of intonation pattern that is to be implemented. This primacy of intonation over accentuation can be formulated as:

Hypothesis 2: (a) The melodical and sequential properties of all the pitch movements in a contour are solely determined by the intonation pattern that has been selected.

(b) Among the pitch movements of any contour there may be one or more with such phonetic properties as are necessary to induce the perception of a pitch accent.

(c) The location of the accent-lending pitch movement(s) is determined by the position of the words that have to be accented.

According to this hypothesis *all* the pitch movements that make up a contour constitute the speech melody of an utterance. It is not the case that some pitch movements are entirely and exclusively related to accentuation requirements, whereas others implement intonational features. Rather, some pitch movements have the capacity to lend prominence to the syllable on which they occur and, consequently, their position in a contour is flexibly adjusted so as to coincide with words or syllables that require a pitch accent (Van Katwijk and Govaert, 1967; Collier, 1970; Van Katwijk, 1974).

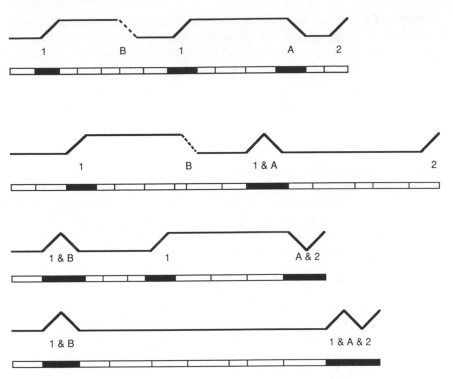

4.10 The 'elasticity principle' allows the same sequence of pitch movements to be distributed differently over an utterance, depending on the number and the position of the accented syllables (black rectangles)

Take, for example, the sequence of pitch movements [1B1A2]. The order of these movements in the contour is strictly determined by the grammar of intonation, but their distribution over a spoken message is governed by some sort of 'elasticity principle', to the effect that the movements '1' and 'A' will coincide with accented syllables. The same sequence of pitch movements, hence the same contour, can therefore be realized on a great variety of utterances as long as they contain two or three syllables to be accented. Figure 4.10 illustrates a number of cases.

In other words, intonation takes precedence over accentuation in determining the shape of the pitch contour, but it allows the actual distribution and timing of the pitch movements to follow the accentual demands.

The greater explanatory power of hypothesis 2 can be demonstrated by means of the following observations. (See fig. 4.11.) Contours (a), (b) and (c) are three possible variants of the hat pattern. For all their difference in melodic

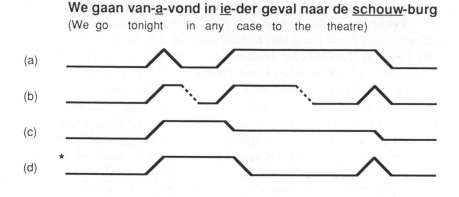

We gaan van-a̲-vond in ie̲-der geval naar de schouw̲-burg
(We go   tonight   in any case to the   theatre)

(a)

(b)

(c)

(d)

We gaan van-a̲-vond in ie-der geval naar de schouw̲-burg

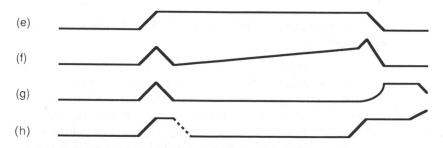

(e)

(f)

(g)

(h)

4.11 Eight different pitch contours (of which one is ill-formed: see*) to go with an utterance with three (contours (a)–(d)) or two pitch accents (contours (e)–(h))

detail, they share the property that their prominence-lending pitch movements are located on the same accentuated syllables. Contour (d), which is very similar to (a), is nevertheless impossible, not because it fails to produce the required three pitch accents, but because it is not a permissible variant of any known intonation pattern. In contour (e) only two pitch accents are realized. To this effect a single rise is combined with a single fall. This is exactly the same melodic configuration as in the second half of contour (a), with only a shift in the location of the rise. Hypothesis 1 can only account for contours (a) to (e) by listing the possible types of prominence-lending pitch movements. But it cannot explain the structure of the contours, e.g. the impossibility of contour (d), which, after all, does not contain any unlawful ingredients. Moreover, hypothesis 1 cannot account for the fact that (a), (b) and (c) are melodically dissimilar while remaining accentually identical, nor for the fact that (a) and (e) are melodically similar, but accentually dissimilar. Hypothesis 2, on the other hand, states that the intonational requirements can be met in such a flexible way that the accentual demands are satisfied at the same time.

A stronger test for hypotheses 1 and 2 is the interpretation of contours (e), (f), (g) and (h). Here we have manifestations of four basically different intonation patterns. Yet in these four cases exactly the same words are rendered prominent. Hypothesis 1 cannot explain why these accents are implemented in so many different, mutually exclusive ways. Hypothesis 2, on the other hand, relates these differences in pitch to the choice of different intonation patterns and explains the accentual similarity by the fact that the prominence-lending components of the various patterns are flexibly moved to the same locations.

In summary, one cannot predict for every single accent which type of pitch movement should be used to implement it, unless one derives this choice from the prior decision as to which intonation pattern is to be implemented.

Proposition 8: The correspondence between intonation and syntax is neither obligatory nor unique

One of the linguistic functions of intonation may be to highlight certain syntactic properties of an utterance. For instance, it is conceivable that the terminal portion of a contour may mark the end of the clause and, by the same token, be a cue for the continuation of the utterance. It is equally possible that minor syntactic boundaries within the same clause (e.g. between phrases) are marked by some particular melodic features. Finally, it is not excluded that a pitch contour is used to disambiguate syntactically homonymous surface structures. This interaction between intonation and syntax has often been a major research topic in many linguistic studies of prosody, and the linguistic literature provides numerous examples of this 'syntactic' function of intonation (e.g. O'Shaughnessy, 1976, 1979).

A good example is the one presented by Bolinger (1986: 26–7):

$$\text{If you don't} \quad \text{st}^{\text{o}\text{p}} \quad \text{as soon as I sign}^{\text{a}\text{l}} \quad \text{you'll receive a sho}_{\text{ck}}$$

$$\text{If you don't st}^{\text{o}\text{p}} \quad \text{as soon as I} \quad \text{sign}^{\text{a}\text{l}} \quad \text{you'll receive a sho}_{\text{ck}}$$

However, with regard to such a demonstrable relation between syntax and intonation, we want to emphasize two points: first, the observable correspondence is not obligatory; and second, there are no melodic features that are

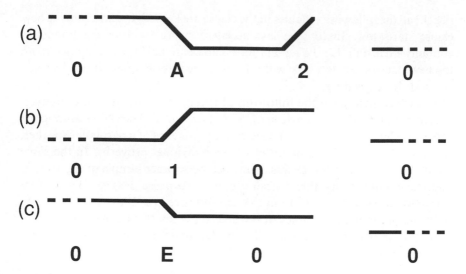

4.12 Three possible configurations to mark a boundary

uniquely and exclusively used for the purpose of marking aspects of syntactic structure. We will substantiate these two claims with some data on Dutch. It must be kept in mind that we limit ourselves to purely melodic features, and refrain from taking the functional contribution of other prosodic factors into account (in particular pause and preboundary lengthening).

Optional correspondence

If an utterance consists of two or more clauses, the syntactic boundary can be marked by intonational means. However, the speaker always has the option not to do so. 't Hart and Cohen (1973) report an experiment in which six subjects had to read aloud a series of Dutch proverbs, fourteen of which contained a clause boundary. In nine of these fourteen proverbs the boundary was marked intonationally by at least four of the six subjects. This means that only in two-thirds of the material was the boundary highlighted by the majority of the readers; in many cases the readers felt no need to do so.

Whenever subjects chose to produce a melodic continuation cue, they selected one of three possible configurations, shown as (a), (b) or (c) in figure 4.12. In (a), the last accent before the clause boundary is brought about by means of fall 'A'; the last syllable before the boundary contains the late rise '2', which serves as a continuation rise; and the new clause begins at a low pitch (in most cases). In (b), the last accented syllable before the boundary contains a rise '1'; all the following syllables in the clause are kept high; and again the new clause starts low. In (c), the last accented syllable before the boundary contains a half-fall 'E'; the remaining syllables are half-high; and once more the new clause starts low. We will refer to these three configurations by 'A2', '1', and 'E' respectively.

The experiment gave the following distribution of the three alternatives: twelve instances of 'A2', nineteen of '1' and five of 'E'. The choice among the three possibilities did not correlate with the preference of a particular speaker, nor with the syntactic peculiarities of the individual proverbs. In the same study this freedom of choice was confirmed by another sample of eighty-four melodic continuations, taken from a connected prose passage. There were forty-two cases of 'A2', thirty-five of '1' and seven of 'E'.

In summary, the free choice of the speaker is double: he may or may not mark the syntactic boundary, and if he prefers to do so, can select one of three possible configurations.

Non-unique correspondence

The three different configurations that have been observed to co-occur with syntactic boundaries in Dutch are not uniquely related to that function. Indeed, exactly the same pitch-movement configurations can be found in other than clause-final positions. For instance, Collier (1972) collected more than 400 instances of rise '2' in a large corpus of quasi-spontaneous Dutch utterances. In 66 per cent of the cases this pitch movement formed part of configuration 'A2' found at the end of a complete utterance, i.e. not of a clause followed by yet another clause, so that its presence was not related to the function of signalling syntactic continuation. Likewise, there were more than 200 configurations of type (b) with '1' as last accent, of which 45 per cent occurred in utterance-final position; and of the 112 tokens of the half-fall 'E', 55 per cent were found in the last syllable of a complete utterance, and only 26 per cent were in clause-final (but not utterance-final) position; the remaining 19 per cent occurred in terrace-shaped contours, between movements '1' and 'A'. Evidently, then, the correspondence between syntax and intonation is not deterministic: clause boundaries need not be marked melodically, and if they are, they are accompanied by pitch configurations that also occur in other syntactic environments.

A hypothesis, and experimental evidence

If syntactic continuation is marked by means of a rise (as in cases (a) and (b) of fig. 4.12), the pitch has to be lowered at the clause boundary before the next

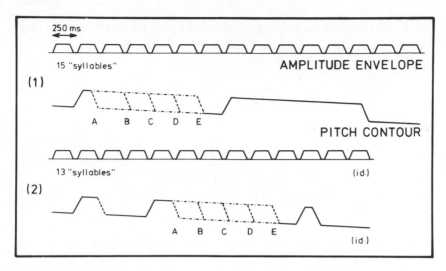

4.13 Stylized representation of an experiment with hummed syllables to which subjects were required to make adequate sentences

contour can start from the lower declination line. A comparable type of sudden pitch lowering occurs between successive accent-lending rises. This movement is called the non-final fall 'B', as opposed to the final fall 'A'. The latter is accent lending, whereas the former is not. Fall 'B' may be found on the same syllable that also contains the preceding rise, or on the next one, but in many cases its occurrence is delayed. The stylization procedure reveals that there is no objective difference between the sudden switch from high to low pitch at a clause boundary on the one hand, and in between accent-lending rises within a clause, on the other. This leads to the supposition that fall 'B' may be involved in the melodic marking of clause-internal phrase boundaries. The distribution of fall 'B' is then as follows: either it is combined with a preceding rise on the same syllable; or it is delayed so as to coincide with the next phrase boundary. Consequently, the prediction is that a delayed and therefore isolated fall 'B' can only co-occur with a phrase boundary. A fall 'B' combined with a preceding rise on one syllable or on two adjacent syllables does not mark a boundary (except incidentally, when the rise coincides with the boundary). As already mentioned, a fall 'B' within a clause and the pitch lowering at a clause boundary are phonetically identical. Therefore, both types of lowering can be labelled fall 'B', and a hypothesis can be formulated to the effect that, unless 'B' occurs in the syllable that also contains rise '1', or one syllable later but still in the same word, it has to be delayed until the next syntactic boundary: 'B' is either executed during the pause or occurs early in the first syllable after the boundary if there is no pause.

Table 4.4 *Correspondence between 'B' and boundary (explanation in the text)*

		Number of syllables between rise '1' and boundary (N_W)				
		0	1	2	3	4
Number of	0	4	10	9	3	3
syllables	1	1	27	0	0	0
between	2	0	3	25	0	0
rise '1' and	3	1	2	1	22	0
fall 'B' (N_H)	4	2	3	1	2	25

This hypothetical syntactic constraint on the implementation of 'B' was examined in the following experiment (Collier and 't Hart, 1975). We constructed a series of stylized pitch contours that were superimposed on 'hummed', isochronous syllables. In these hummed utterances the position of the non-final fall 'B' was varied systematically, as shown in figure 4.13. We presented five listeners with these contours and instructed them to think of syntactically coherent sentences for which the hummed contours would constitute a suitable course of the pitch (also taking the location of the pitch accents into account). The hummed contours were played back from a tape loop and were repeated as long as necessary for the subjects to write down at least two possible sentences for each contour. On the answer sheets the number of syllables was indicated with dashes and the position of the pitch accents was marked with arrows. The subjects wrote down a total of 144 sentences. Of these, twenty-nine went with the contours 1A and 2A of figure 4.13, in which the fall is not delayed; hence they are not directly relevant to our hypothesis. Of the other 115 (relevant) sentences there were ninety-nine of which the surface syntactic structures were in accordance with our hypothesis: they had a clause or a phrase boundary that coincided with the location of the delayed fall. Table 4.4 presents an overview of the results. Notice the high figures on the main diagonal, where the number of written syllables between the accented syllable and the syntactic boundary (N_W) equals the number of hummed syllables between rise '1' and fall 'B' (N_H). On the whole, the hypothesis was confirmed in 86 per cent of the cases in which $N_H \geqslant 1$.

The data in the top row of table 4.4 (where $N_H = 0$) are indirectly relevant to our hypothesis as well. Indeed, they concern those contours in which the fall was not delayed. In such a case, the listener does not feel constrained by the properties of the pitch contour in thinking of a suitable sentence, and the length of the syntactic constituent containing rise '1' may vary freely.

This experiment was followed by one in which ten (other) subjects were instructed to read aloud thirty sentences, selected from among those produced by the listeners in the first experiment. They read the sentences twice. The thirty sentences differed in the length of their syntactic constituents, so that there was potential variation in the number of syllables over which the non-final fall 'B' could be delayed. The analysis was made by two of the authors. The first question was whether or not intonational marking of the boundaries aimed at had taken place. Since, as we have seen, there is no obligation to mark syntactic boundaries melodically, only 360 of the 600 utterances turned out to be relevant to our hypothesis. The second question was to decide which of the three possible kinds of boundary marking had been used (see fig. 4.12). We were only interested in cases with the delayed fall 'B' after rise '1' ((b) in fig. 4.12), since these are fully comparable to the situation in the first experiment. Thus, the only thing needed for making the decision was to establish whether the last pitch accent before the boundary was a rise, or a (half-)fall. It turned out that of the 360 relevant cases, the marking was done by using 'A2' or 'E' ((a) and (c), respectively, in fig. 4.12) together 156 times. The remaining 204 cases had the delayed non-final fall 'B'.

In 192 of these 204 cases the delayed fall coincided with a syntactic boundary, as predicted. In other words, in the great majority of the cases, there was complete agreement between the listeners and the readers as far as the coincidence of syntactic and melodic features is concerned. Apparently, the interaction of intonation and syntax is such that if the speaker chooses to delay the fall 'B', he has to take syntactic structure into consideration.

One may ask whether a contour with a delayed fall 'B' that does not coincide with a syntactic boundary will sound ill-formed; in other words, is there still an acceptable alternative with respect to the location of 'B'? In table 4.4 we see a striking asymmetry: for $N_H \geq 1$ all the sixteen exceptions to the main trend lie on that side of the diagonal where the fall occurs later than the boundary. Apparently, our subjects consider that kind of 'mismatch' less disturbing than if a delayed fall precedes the boundary. If we try to look for an explanation of this asymmetry, we may put forward the following considerations:

1. If a delayed 'B' occurs later than the boundary, the listener has already been able to notice other prosodic cues, such as pre-boundary lengthening, to indicate the location of the boundary. And although, according to De Rooij (1979: 103), the effect of such a temporal marker may be weakened by the presence of the later non-final fall, it is by no means overruled.
2. If, however, a delayed 'B' occurs prior to the boundary, the listener has not yet had the opportunity to receive the alternative cue, and thus may be led astray by the assumption that 'B' signals the boundary.

A *post hoc* check in our corpus (which had been transcribed five years before these experiments) showed that among the many hundreds of delayed falls 'B', only 6.5 per cent could lead to a misinterpretation of the location of a boundary.

From what precedes, one may conclude that there is truth in Bolinger's (1957/8: 36) statement: 'Intonation operates in its own sphere, and the uses that grammar makes of it are catch-as-catch-can': the two do not necessarily go separate ways, but they do not cling together all the time, either.

The rather loose ties between intonation and syntax suggest that one should not overrate the role of speech melody as a major cue for the listener who attempts to parse the incoming message. For one thing, a monotonous utterance remains understandable, showing that syntactic parsing can be based on surface-structure information, without additional prosodic cues. Contemporary psycholinguistic models of this parsing often assume that the incoming message is processed as soon as possible: as successive words are being recognized, the listener immediately attempts to organize them into possible syntactically coherent structures, such as NP, PP, etc. (Wanner and Maratsos, 1978). This process implies that the listener continuously generates hypotheses about potential syntactic boundaries. In some cases, intonation may provide a direct cue concerning the presence of such a boundary. In Dutch, for instance, the occurrence of rise '2' is invariably coupled to the last syllable of a syntactic constituent. When the listener perceives this rise, he knows that the preceding words should be integrated into one syntactic unit. In other cases, intonational cues can only confirm the presence of a syntactic boundary that was hypothesized on other grounds. For instance, the half-fall 'E' may coincide with the last syllable of a clause, and thus lend support to a tentative syntactic segmentation at that place. The same holds for the delayed fall 'B'. As we have seen, this movement is located typically in the first syllable after a syntactic boundary and may thus confirm, in retrospect, that such a break has indeed occurred.

The limited correspondence between intonation and syntactic structure makes it possible that, on a rare occasion, speech melody may constrain the syntactic hypothesis-formation in the presence of surface-structure ambiguity.

In an utterance such as *The queen said the knight is a monster*, the listener is likely to integrate *the* and *queen* as a noun phrase and to consider the verb *said* as the beginning of the verb phrase of one and the same clause. An audible fall–rise on *queen*, however, may set this constituent so clearly apart that the listener may hesitate to integrate the next word *said* with it and prefer to hypothesize that the NP phrase boundary is at the same time a clause boundary: *The queen, said the knight, . . .* In other words, the melodic cue here

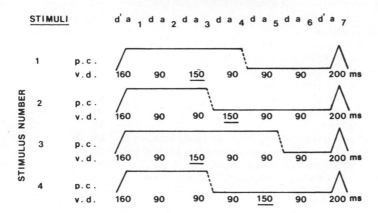

CONFLICTING BOUNDARY MARKERS
TEMPORAL AND NON-FINAL FALL

4.14 Stimuli with conflicting boundary markers: syllable lengthening (duration underlined) at location different from that of intonational cue (a non-final fall)

has an exceptional admonishing value: it blocks in time the application of the most common parsing strategy and prevents later backtracking of the parser.

With regard to the syntactic disambiguation of speech melody, some further comments are in order.

First, there are numerous syntactic-surface ambiguities that cannot be resolved by intonational means. In Dutch, for instance, utterances such as *De gevangenen waren uitgehongerd* have two interpretations: 'The prisoners were starving' and 'The prisoners had been starved'. In the first case *uitgehongerd* has adjectival value and is a nominal part of the predicate ('starving'); in the second case it has participial value and is a verbal part of the predicate ('starved'). The syntactic difference has interpretative consequences: the prisoners are either still alive but very hungry; or they have been starved to death. This double interpretation cannot be disambiguated by intonational means.

Second, sentences may contain local ambiguities that go unnoticed and cause comprehension difficulties later on in the sentence. This is the case with so-called 'garden-path' sentences. In Dutch, for instance, a severe comprehension problem can arise from the local ambiguity of *het* + noun. The straightforward interpretation of this word combination is article + noun, i.e. NP, as in *het vlees* ('the meat'). But *het* can also be the neuter pronoun ('it'). If it happens to be followed by a noun, then the syntactic interpretation has to be NP + NP. This state of affairs leads to garden-path sentences such as *Het jongetje merkte dat het vlees lekker vond*, in which *het vlees* is not to be

107

Table 4.5 *The effectiveness of temporal and intonational boundary markers*

Set	Stimulus condition	Percentage of correct responses
B	temporal marker (180 ms) + continuation rise	90
C	temporal marker (150 ms) + non-final fall	86
D	temporal marker (180 ms) alone	84
E	temporal marker (150 ms) alone	86
F	continuation rise alone	30
G	non-final fall alone	36
H	temporal marker (180 ms), conflicting with continuation rise;	82
	continuation rise, conflicting with temporal marker (180 ms)	29
I	temporal marker (150 ms), conflicting with non-final fall;	88
	non-final fall, conflicting with temporal marker (150 ms)	30

integrated as one NP. Rather, the meaning is: *The little boy noticed that it* (= *the boy*) *liked meat*. Again, intonation cannot differentiate between the two syntactic interpretations.

Third, some ambiguities may be resolved by prosodic means other than intonational. The number and location of sentence accents, the temporal structure of the words, the presence of pauses, etc., may be other (and better) cues for the syntactic organization of an utterance.

De Rooij (1979) has investigated the relative importance of temporal and melodic cues for the perception of prosodic boundaries, which in turn may be cues for the existence of a clause boundary. He used nonsense utterances (viz. a sequence of seven /da/ syllables) and provided them with temporal markers (syllable lengthening) and pitch markers (end rise '2' or delayed non-final fall 'B') in various positions. The two types of markers could occur singly or in combination on the same syllable, and there were also stimuli with conflicting cues, i.e. a temporal cue on one syllable and a melodic cue on another (see fig. 4.14).

His main results are summarized in table 4.5. It can be seen that the presence of a temporal marker induces the perception of a prosodic boundary in the great majority of the cases, whether or not it is accompanied by a pitch marker. Pitch markers alone are far less effective cues than temporal markers alone: only in about one-third of the cases does a pitch marker by itself lead to the perception of a prosodic boundary. In cases of conflict, the temporal marker always overrules the effect of the pitch marker.

In a second experiment, with meaningful syntactically ambiguous utterances, similar results were obtained, although the effect of temporal markers

No	Simplified pitch contour	Judgment (%), N = 140		
	"Hij wil een weduwe met charme verleiden"	(A)adj.	(B)adv.	(C)
1		48	42	10
2		61	29	10
3		63	22	15
4		31	53	16
5		28	60	12
6		28	59	13

4.15 Outcome of an experiment with six pitch contours for an ambiguous sentence (A = adjectival, B = adverbial, C = ambiguous)

was less dominant here. But with conflicting cues, the temporal markers were once again more powerful than the pitch markers in determining the perception of the prosodic boundary.

Let us now examine how another prosodic feature, viz. sentence accentuation, can determine the interpretation of a syntactic-surface structure.

't Hart (1976b) reports on an experiment in which subjects had to decide on the interpretation of syntactically ambiguous utterances in which the number and the location of the accents were varied. One of the utterances was *Hij wil een weduwe met charme verleiden*: (a) 'He wants to seduce a charming widow'; or (b) 'He wants to seduce a widow by his charm.' Figure 4.15 shows the six different pitch contours that were used to produce (partially) different accent patterns. The right-hand part of figure 4.15 presents the judgements of seventy listeners who had to choose among three response alternatives: adjectival ('charming'); adverbial ('by his charm'); or ambiguous. All the stimuli were presented twice in random order.

Contours 2 and 3, with two accents, neither of which is on the verb *verleiden*, receive a predominantly adjectival interpretation. Contours 4, 5 and 6, which produce two or three accents, one of which is on the verb *verleiden*, lead to a majority of adverbial interpretations. Notice, however, that the differences in interpretation are not very marked: there is always a substantial number of dissenting votes, so that no single response category ever attracts an overwhelming majority. Clearly, the accent structure of the utterance can resolve its syntactic ambiguity to some extent. But even if prosody may be helpful in such cases, it is accentuation, not intonation, that does the work.

Interestingly, contour 1 with only one accent (on *charme*) is totally ambiguous, but this conclusion can only be inferred from the bi-modality of the responses in the first two columns; only few listeners are definitely aware of the ambiguity, even after they have been warned that the test utterances could be subject to a double interpretation. This makes one wonder whether a speaker is ever able to foresee that a particular syntactic structure he is about to use is ambiguous, then to consider alternative accent or intonation patterns that could go with that structure and finally to select the prosodic form that is most likely to resolve that ambiguity for the listener. The psychological implausibility of such a strategy leads to the conclusion that 'prosodic disambiguation' is only a marginal issue.

Proposition 9: Intonation features have no intrinsic meaning

It is a widely accepted view that intonation may affect the semantic interpretation of an utterance. This interpretation is determined by, among other things, the meaning of its words and the syntactic relations among its phrasal constituents. To the extent that intonation can differentiate between alternative syntactic interpretations of the same surface structure, it may be said to serve a semantic purpose, if only indirectly: it influences the syntactic analysis, which in turn affects the semantic interpretation.

More commonly, however, the semantic function of intonation is looked for in the paralinguistic domain of 'attitude'. The so-called 'tone of voice' is considered a means of vocal expression by which the speaker can add certain shades of meaning to an utterance: surprise, boredom, disbelief, anger, etc.

The term 'tone of voice' is ambiguous: it suggests that 'tone', i.e. pitch inflection, can be a cue to attitude, but that some other feature, 'voice quality', may also be involved. In fact, almost any conceivable sound attribute of an utterance can take a value that departs from what is considered normal or neutral, and this markedness may have some expressive function. Crystal and Quirk (1964) and Crystal (1969, 1975) are good examples of an attempt to devise a multidimensional framework for the description of the linguistic and paralinguistic features of non-segmental speech properties in English. According to these authors, at least nine variables enter into play: pitch direction, pitch range, pause, loudness, tempo, rhythm, tension, voice quality and voice qualification. Each of these dimensions exhibits a number of binary or multivalued contrasts. Clearly, the complex interaction between so many variables makes it extremely difficult to come to experimental grips with the attitudinal function of prosody. For this reason we ourselves have not been very eager to tackle this problem; moreover, we have been discouraged by the meagre results obtained by others in a number of experimental approaches to this issue.

Admittedly, in some experiments with F_0 as the only independent variable, high scores for correct identification have been obtained (e.g. Hadding-Koch and Studdert-Kennedy, 1964). However, in these studies the number of forced-choice alternatives was very small, often only two, viz. statement vs question. It is conceivable that subjects become easily aware of the simple dichotomy in the F_0 variation of the stimuli (which either have rising or falling pitch at the end), and that they adopt a strategy in which they concentrate analytically on the utterance-final pitch: if the interval covered by the final rise is large enough, they anticipate that the expected response should be 'question'. This strategy and its success may not be very representative of the everyday communication situation.

The encouraging results of experiments in which the simple opposition of statement vs question is at stake seems to have led to the assumption that, more generally, there is a strong correspondence between intonational and interpretative categories. This may have inspired Gussenhoven (1984) to attempt an experiment with nine intonational categories. The results are far from random, but clearly less clean than those obtained with only two categories. If we try to understand why this is so, we might envisage that attitudinal considerations dictate the choice of a particular intonation pattern. But for all we know, the number of basic intonation patterns per language is very limited, whereas the variety of shades of meaning and attitudes is nearly infinite. Of course, the concrete realization of one and the same intonation pattern allows for some freedom in overall register, pitch range, etc. This variation may not be entirely free, but may be linked with attitudinal expression, to the effect that, for instance, a relatively wide pitch range corresponds to an attitude of 'excitement' (Van Bezooijen, 1984). But again, neither the speaker nor the listener can consistently distinguish so many different values along the dimensions of pitch range, register and the like as would be required to have a one-to-one correspondence between intonation and attitude. Rather, the relation between intonational and attitudinal features must be one-to-many, possibly even many-to-many.

Crystal (1969) ran an experiment in which he instructed six subjects to read three sentences with the 'tone of voice' suggested by twenty attitudinal labels (excited, dismayed, puzzled, etc.). From this corpus he selected twenty utterances that were judged to be good renderings of these attitudes. The same six subjects were then asked to assign the twenty attitudinal labels to the utterances. No subject obtained a score of more than 60 per cent correct identification. There was little agreement among the listeners: no two subjects made the same set of identifications or misidentifications. A few weeks later the same subjects were once more presented with the twenty test utterances. This time they were asked to assign any attitudinal label of their choice to each of them. 'Correct' identification now dropped to 20 per cent and the total number of different labels rose to nearly one hundred.

Apparently, there are two major problems with experiments of this type. First, irrespective of the number of labels used, it is virtually impossible to interpret their meaning consistently: the same label may have partially different meanings for each of the subjects as well as for the experimenter; some labels may be considered synonymous; some may be hyponyms of others, etc. The second problem is that, if use is made of natural speech, prosodic cues other than intonational are present in the stimuli, and one cannot tell apart their relative effects. Consequently, in Crystal's study, the independent contribution of intonation is likely to have been smaller than the maximum of 60 per cent correct identification suggests.

If the relation between intonational and attitudinal features is taken to be many-to-many, then the attitudinal interpretation of any given pitch contour becomes impossible unless it is severely constrained by situational factors in the broadest sense. How exactly a message such as *You darling* or *You bastard* is to be understood, cannot be inferred from the meaning of the words only, but even the accompanying prosodic features will not help to determine the interpretation unless some amount of situational knowledge is brought into play.

Such a pragmatic approach to intonational meaning is evidently a big challenge to the experimental linguist, who faces the task of independently varying the content of the message, one or more of its prosodic features (including intonation) and the situation in which it is produced. And if he manages to do so, he remains confronted with the problem that the dependent variable to be 'measured' is the attitude, which must either be captured directly in troublesome labels or inferred by means of an indirect procedure (e.g. the semantic-differential technique). In order to simplify the experimental design, one may attempt to build some aspect of contextual variation into the test utterances themselves. Take, for instance, an utterance such as *You feel ill*. Since one cannot easily make a statement about the inaccessible internal state of another person, this utterance is 'question-prone', i.e. it is likely to be used with an interrogative intent. Conversely, an utterance such as *I feel ill* is 'statement-prone': it is rather unlikely for a speaker to ask a question about an inner state he is exclusively supposed to know, viz. his own. Finally, an utterance such as *He is ill* is not communicatively biased to the same extent: it can be used as a statement or as a 'declarative question'. In these three cases the use of a different grammatical person as the subject can be considered as an utterance-internal pragmatic variable: it constrains the contexts in which the utterance can be produced. Reasoning along such lines, Geluykens (1985, 1987) formulated the hypothesis that question-prone utterances would be more likely to be interpreted as actual questions if provided with a final pitch-rise than statement-prone utterances, which would resist an interrogative interpretation because of their pragmatic bias. In order to test this hypothesis, Geluykens chose four declarative utterances, varied the personal pronouns (*I, you, he*) and provided each of the twelve utterances with four different types of rising intonation and one type of falling intonation. The artificial pitch contours were stylized versions of Halliday's (1970) 'primary tones', as generated by the synthesis rules of De Pijper (1983). Fifteen British subjects evaluated the question or statement status of the sixty stimuli on a four-point scale, to the effect that the score for each of the stimuli, taken over all subjects, could range between 0 and 60. The general picture of the results was as follows.

The *I*-utterances got a unanimous 'statement' response with a falling pitch contour; with a rising contour the proportion of 'question' responses varied between 7/60 and 11/60, depending on the type of rise used (but these differences were not significant). The *he*-utterances got unanimous 'statement' responses when the pitch was falling; and with rising pitch the proportion of 'question' interpretations ranged from 10/60 to 20/60. On the one hand, this result confirms the predicted difference in sensitivity to rising pitch for *I*- and *he*-utterances; on the other, it shows that the rising pitch contour cannot induce more than one-third of 'question' responses in the pragmatically unbiased *he*-utterances. In the *you*-utterances, the proportion of 'question' responses to rising pitch rose to about 50 per cent. Again, this is in accordance with the predictions, but the cue value of the rising pitch contour remains unexpectedly low in these question-prone utterances. Even more surprisingly, the same 50 per cent proportion of 'question' responses was obtained with the falling pitch contour. In other words, the *you*-utterances appear to be inherently ambiguous as far as their communicative value is concerned and this ambiguity cannot be resolved by manipulating the pitch contour.

Evidently, a rising pitch contour can turn a statement into a question, but the extent to which this can be done is determined by the lexico-pragmatic characteristics of the utterance itself, and even under the best of pragmatic circumstances the effect of the intonational cue remains limited. Meanwhile, the outcome of this experiment demonstrates that even a dichotomy as simple as the one used in Hadding-Koch's and Studdert-Kennedy's experiment may lead to considerable difficulties.

In conclusion, we believe that the questions regarding the communicative, attitudinal meaning of intonation are interesting and legitimate. For one thing, our own melodic approach to intonation has produced an inventory of basic intonation patterns in Dutch and English, but we still cannot answer the question how a speaker makes a selection among these basic alternatives nor how he makes a choice among the many different contours that are realizations of the same pattern (except in terms of syntactic and accentual requirements). We speculate that these choices are influenced by the attitudinal meaning that a speaker wants to add to the literal meaning of his utterances. But the actual encoding of this attitudinal meaning into an individual pitch contour is evidently governed by so many pragmatic and situational factors that we are still looking for a manageable experimental paradigm in which to tackle this complicated issue.

Proposition 10: The successful programming of a pitch contour requires only a limited 'look-head' strategy that integrates intonational, accentual and surface-syntactic information

Under proposition 4 we presented a formal statement of the melodic possibilities of Dutch, cast in a 'grammar' of intonation, and under propositions 8 and 9 we discussed the influence of accentuation and syntax on the actual distribution of the pitch movements in a contour. The resulting general picture is that the observable properties of a pitch contour do not exclusively depend on the intonation pattern that is realized, but also on non-intonational factors. The interaction of intonation with accentuation and syntax, described in propositions 8 and 9, implies that, in the process of programming a pitch contour, the speaker has to consult at least three sources of knowledge. The question then is: at which point(s) in time does which sort of knowledge become important?

Introspectively, one has the impression that, prior to the act of speaking, one does not know exactly what formal properties the message is going to have (in terms of chosen lexical items and their syntactic arrangement). It is equally improbable that a speaker has to decide from the very outset which intonation pattern he is going to use. Indeed, the choice of an intonation pattern mainly affects the Root of the contour, which is the final or the near-final portion of it. The earlier part of the contour is the domain of the Prefixes, which can to a large extent be selected independently from the Root. This state of affairs suggests as a possible programming model one in which the relevant decisions are taken *sequentially*, as one goes along through the utterance that is being developed.

The simplest 'sequential' model is one in which the choice of a particular pitch movement is made syllable after syllable on the basis of *strictly local* information, i.e. solely depending on information that is associated with that syllable. Using Ladd's (1983a) terminology, we may call this a Tone-Sequence (TS) model. It describes the generation of a pitch contour as the realization of a sequence of pitch movements whose order of appearance is determined by the sequential constraints of the intonation grammar, and whose actual distribution over the utterance is a function of local syntactic and/or accentual features that are attached to the syllable. The locality principle implies that no 'look ahead' is necessary.

Let us examine now what sorts of Dutch pitch contours can be programmed with such a TS model.

Suppose we have to provide the utterance in (10) with an acceptable contour that also takes care of the prominences on [+accent] syllables.

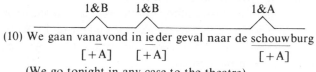

(10) We gaan vanavond in ieder geval naar de schouwburg
     [+A]   [+A]   [+A]
    (We go tonight in any case to the theatre)

According to the grammar of intonation we can select a contour that consists of a sequence of rise–falls. The interaction of intonation and accentuation is such that a rise–fall has to be associated with an accented syllable. One can easily see that the TS model is capable of accounting for the contour in question: for each successive syllable, it is decided whether it is [+accent]; if so, a rise–fall is assigned to it.

The TS model can also take care of the melodic marking of a clause boundary by means of an 'end rise', which is associated with any syllable marked [\$]. For instance,

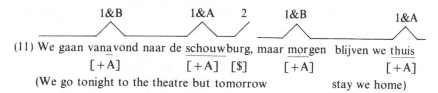

(11) We gaan vanavond naar de schouwburg, maar morgen blijven we thuis
    [+A]   [+A] [\$]   [+A]   [+A]
    (We go tonight to the theatre but tomorrow   stay we home)

In this example the appropriate course of the pitch can once more be programmed on a strictly local basis, i.e. by looking at the features of successive syllables through a window that is just one syllable wide.

The two examples above are variants of the 'hat pattern', which in these cases takes a Root in the form of a rise–fall and is preceded by one or more Prefixes which happen to take the same rise–fall form. If we replace the 'hat pattern' /1A/ with another pattern, e.g. /4A/, this will have melodic consequences for the Root, not for the Prefixes. For example,

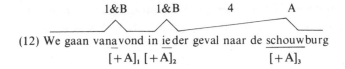

(12) We gaan vana vond in ie der geval naar de schouw burg
$\qquad$ [+A]₁ [+A]₂ $\qquad$ [+A]₃

The melodic difference between (12) and (10) is fairly small, but the TS model already fails to account for the programming of the contour in (12). Indeed, as a Root, pattern /4A/ has to be associated with the *last* accented syllable of the clause, [+A]₃, in such a way that fall 'A' occurs on that [+accent] syllable, while rise '4' leads up to that syllable, starting after the *preceding* accented syllable, [+A]₂. This means that the choice of the intonation pattern has to be made at the right time. In particular, the speaker should know that [+A]₂ is the *penultimate* accented syllable. If the choice were delayed until [+A]₃, the gradual rise could no longer be implemented.

The same advance knowledge about whether a given accented syllable is the penultimate one is necessary for the programming of another variant of the 'hat pattern': viz. the one in which the rise and the fall occur on separate syllables, as in (13).

(13) We gaan vana vond in ie der geval naar de schouw burg

In comparison with (10), a sequence of two 'pointed hats' has now been replaced by one 'flat hat'. But this substitution is only permitted if the pointed hats occur on the *last two* accented syllables of the clause, i.e. if the first pointed hat is a Prefix and the second is a Root.

Both the examples (12) and (13) indicate that the successful generation of their contours necessitates a 'look-ahead' strategy. The speaker has to check at each accented syllable whether there is a following [+accent] syllable. If there is one, he has to decide whether that will at the same time be the last one in the clause. Only in the latter case can the speaker embark upon producing the rising or high sustained pitch between the penultimate and the final stressed syllable.

Indirect evidence for the 'look-ahead' component in the speaker's strategy comes from observable intonation errors. Such errors often occur in reading aloud, when the speaker literally fails to look ahead far enough. Two types of error are then observed, illustrated in (14) and (15):

116

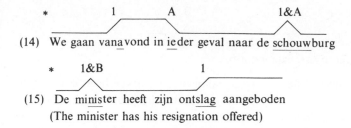

(14) We gaan vanavond in ieder geval naar de schouwburg

(15) De minister heeft zijn ontslag aangeboden
(The minister has his resignation offered)

The error in (14) results from the fact that the speaker did not anticipate on *schouw-*, therefore treated the accent on *ie-* as the last one and started to realize a 'flat hat' on the syllable *-a-*. Later in the utterance, he did not want to leave *schouw-* unaccented, and had no choice but to make an additional rise–fall, thus violating the rule that a 'flat hat' can only be contour-final. The error in (15) is caused by the fact that the speaker expected the accent on *-slag* to be followed by just one more, and therefore started to make a 'flat hat', only to discover that there was no following accent on which to implement the fall. The resulting contour is not ill-formed *per se*, but the intonation pattern does not match the content of the message. In a situation like this, a newsreader was once heard to round off the utterance with the exclamation 'Period!', indicating his awareness of the error.

In conclusion, there are types of Roots in Dutch contours that cannot be programmed successfully on the basis of strictly local information concerning the accentuated nature of a syllable. The same is true for the choice of a particular type of Prefix: viz. one in which the falling pitch movement ('B') is delayed until the next (clause-internal) syntactic boundary. For example,

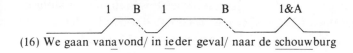

(16) We gaan vanavond/ in ieder geval/ naar de schouwburg

Notice that the delaying of the fall is an option that is strictly limited to the Prefix; it does not apply to the rise–fall Root on *schouw-*. Now, since every contour has to end in a Root, mostly associated with the *last* accented syllable, the Prefix status of a rise–fall depends on the speaker's knowledge that the current accented syllable is *not* the last one. Therefore, an option that essentially serves a *syntactic* purpose appears to be also determined by advance knowledge of the accentual structure of the rest of the utterance. Indeed, if the speaker were to decide to delay the fall on purely syntactic grounds, viz. in anticipation of a clause-internal boundary, he might produce ill-formed contours such as (17):

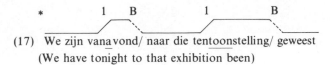

(17) We zijn vana vond/ naar die tentoonstelling/ geweest
      (We have tonight to that exhibition been)

In this example the end of the prepositional phrase is marked by a delayed fall, but this is wrong because -*toon*- turns out to be the last syllable that can possibly be accentuated, hence it should have carried the Root of the contour, not a Prefix. If, however, there had been one more accentuated syllable to carry the Root, the delay of the fall would have been perfectly acceptable, as in (18):

(18) We zijn vana vond/ naar de tentoonstelling/ gefietst!
      (We have tonight to the exhibition cycled)

In summary, the examples (16) to (18) provide additional support for the view that the programming of a pitch contour requires the anticipation of at least two sorts of non-intonational information, viz. the presence of a next accent, specified as [± last], and the occurrence of a clause-internal phrase boundary.

As far as strictly intonational knowledge is concerned, we have already seen that the choice of the pattern, which determines the shape of the Root, sometimes has to be made at the time the *penultimate* accent is implemented. One reason for this was given with the examples (12) and (14): the Root of these contours starts at or after that syllable. But there is a second reason: the choice of pattern /4A/ or /3C/ blocks the option to delay the fall in the immediately preceding Prefix. Consequently, when this Prefix comes along on the penultimate accented syllable, the type of Root that will follow has already to be known, even if in the case of /3C/ (as opposed to /4A/) the Root is only implemented starting from the last accented syllable, as in (19):

(19) We gaan vana vond in ie der geval naar die tentoonstelling
      (We go tonight in any case to that exhibition)

The constraint that Roots /3C/ and /4A/ exert on the shape of the preceding Prefix is a form of strictly melodic interaction. The other examples above illustrate the interaction of intonation with accentuation and syntax. The important conclusion is that these two types of interaction cannot be accounted for on a syllable-by-syllable basis, as the Tone-Sequence model would have it. The latter model, in fact, just exemplifies one strategy on the part of the speaker: viz. that in which he behaves like a Finite-State Machine that produces a rise–fall on each accentuated syllable.

Conclusion

It does not take a great deal of imagination to think of a dozen questions regarding the form and function of pitch variation in speech. These questions can hardly be ranked according to their intrinsic relevance or theoretical importance, since each of them reflects in its own way the justifiable research interests of the individual investigator. Yet some questions may take extrinsic priority over others, if only because they relate to matters of phonetic substance and thus acquire logical precedence over issues of phonological form or of functional interpretation. One should not hurriedly venture into theorizing about phenomena that have not been properly observed and described.

At the outset of our investigations, in the early sixties, we were faced with the observational and descriptive problems that we mentioned at the beginning of chapter 3, and a great deal of our research effort was directed towards solving difficulties of a phenomenological and methodological nature. As a consequence, the resulting theory that we have presented in this chapter, has a strong experimental-phonetic inclination. It purports to explain how the melodic features of utterances are perceived and how they relate to the physical and physiological counterparts of pitch contours. It also intends to clarify the relation between pitch contours and intonation patterns, and between the melodic organization of an utterance and its accentual and syntactic structure. Thus, the theory also has a linguistic component.

In its essential parts, our theory is well supported by empirical evidence that was gathered under controlled conditions, in experiments of a predominantly novel design. Originally the theory and methodology were applied to Dutch, but in recent years the approach has been duplicated and refined in the analysis of English, German and Russian intonation. The application of our analytic and interpretative framework to languages other than Dutch has produced insightful results on each of these occasions. Besides being extendible to different languages, our approach has shown further merits in allowing for linguistic generalization (ch. 6) and technological application (ch. 7).

To conclude this chapter we try to highlight some major features of our theory by capturing them under a number of familiar labels that refer to well-known dichotomies.

Our theory is based on a *bottom-up* approach that is concerned with the *concrete* manifestation of intonation in the form of speech melody. We attempt to elucidate primarily how the listener deals with pitch variations in speech and, secondarily, we pay attention to the physical and physiological correlates of intonation. Our theory also addresses issues that relate to the *abstract* properties of intonation in so far as they have a plausible basis in phonetic *substance* as revealed through experimental observation. Abstract properties are thus not posited on *a priori* phonological considerations. The same is true of the *functional* properties of intonation. We do not start from the assumption that intonation has a communicative function and then set out to look for those pitch features that have a particular signalling capacity. Rather, we prefer a phonetic approach that lays bare the melodic properties of the language and subsequently looks for their possible functional value, e.g. in terms of boundary marking or prominence lending. Our concern with phonetic substance implies that we see no need to postulate the existence of *pitch levels*, but emphasize the observable *pitch movements* as elementary descriptive units. These atomistic and local units enter into sequences, or *configurations*, which in turn build up complete *pitch contours*. Contours extend over a domain that corresponds roughly to the syntactic *clause*, a unit that is formally better defined than alternatives such as *sense group, breath group* or *information unit*. Contours are concrete melodic structures that relate to corresponding abstract *intonation patterns*. The latter determine the nature and the order of the pitch movements in a contour, which are therefore not selected on a strictly local basis. Because we advocate the hierarchical supremacy of the intonation patterns, our views belong in the class of '*Contour-Interaction*' models, not in that of '*Tone-Sequence*' theories, to use Ladd's (1983a) terminology. Contour interaction means that the listener's perception of speech melody is constrained by *top-down* information: he makes use of knowledge concerning the structural properties of contours, expressed in the intonation grammar. On the speaker's side, contour interaction implies that the successful production of a pitch contour requires a limited 'look-ahead' strategy that allows the integration of melodic and textual information.

5

Declination

5.0 Introduction

It has now become common usage to make a distinction between local and global attributes in intonational matters. Local attributes comprise characteristics of F_0 relating to only a few syllables, whereas global attributes extend over longer stretches of speech, such as an entire clause or utterance. If we apply this dichotomy here, it follows that in the preceding chapters, we have mainly dealt with local attributes. Admittedly, the gradual movements ('4' and 'D') may extend over quite a number of syllables, but they do not cover an entire clause or utterance.

In languages like Dutch and English, the most important global attribute is the observed tendency of F_0 to decrease slowly from beginning to end of an utterance. This phenomenon has already been reported by Pike (1945: 77): 'The general tendency of the voice is to begin on a moderate pitch and lower the medium pitch line during the sentence.'

One way of demonstrating this tendency is to make histograms of (log-converted) F_0 values taken every 10 ms for initial, medial and final parts of utterances; unless the utterance contains a very unbalanced distribution of local events, this procedure will show a gradual shift of the peak of the distribution from higher to lower as the sample is taken later in the utterance (see fig. 5.1).

But in quite a number of cases, the effect is already observable by visual inspection of an F_0 curve. Once we started our own analysis of F_0 in utterances of some considerable length, we tried to relate the local rises and falls to some kind of reference line, for which we first chose a horizontal line through the overall average of F_0 in the utterance. This turned out to be not very helpful, mainly because the values of F_0 were almost consistently higher than that line in the first half of the recording, and lower in the second half. When we subsequently tried a slightly downward tilted line through local F_0 minima, it gave rise to a far more natural visual interpretation of the local events as being superimposed on the reference line. Thus, in the belief of having corroborated Pike's auditory impression through acoustical measurement, we decided to

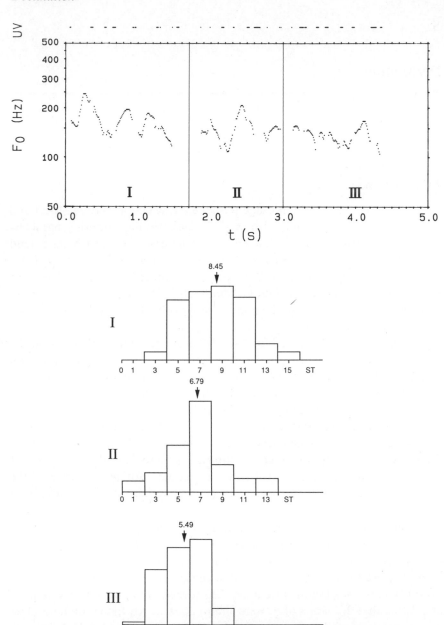

5.1 F_0 curve and histograms for initial, medial and final parts, showing lower average F_0 values (in semitones with respect to 100 Hz) towards the end. The sentence had a duration of 5.65 s and was read out from text by a professional speaker

name the phenomenon: declination (Cohen and 't Hart, 1965). Already on that occasion (the Fifth International Congress of Acoustics), we were able to demonstrate, by means of making audible some short sentences provided with artificial intonation contours with and without declination, that declination was not only a convenient construct enabling the investigator to better interpret an F_0 recording, but also a perceptually relevant attribute: it simply sounded more natural whenever declination was added.

The perceptual relevance of declination brings us back to the basic assumption, formulated in chapter 3, that movements considered relevant by the listener should be related to certain activities on the part of the speaker, characterized as discrete commands to the vocal cords, and should be recoverable as so many discrete events in the F_0 recording. The assumption was meant to be applicable to local events in the first place; and with respect to such local events, it has been confirmed in the measurements by Ohala (1970), Collier (1975a), Atkinson (1978) and Gelfer *et al.* (1985): during local changes of F_0 there is activity in the cricothyroid muscle (CT), but in stretches with mere declination, such activity is almost always entirely absent.

The basic assumption was put forward in an attempt to bring about a distinction between programmed, voluntary F_0 changes, on the one hand, and physiologically determined, involuntary fluctuations, on the other. If the assumption were valid unreservedly for declination too, the perceptual relevance should imply that declination is a programmed and voluntary F_0 change. But, since there is generally no pitch-related laryngeal activity in stretches with mere declination, the assumption can only be maintained for global effects in a modifed version. In such a modified version, we could still assume that there is corresponding activity on the part of the speaker, but not necessarily in the form of commands to the vocal cords, let alone in the form of discrete commands. The corresponding activity may be considered, for instance, to take place in the respiratory system.

Another consequence of the perceptual relevance of declination is that it might be linguistically relevant. This need not be dependent on the question whether or not declination is produced voluntarily. The act of speaking contains many involuntary products that nevertheless convey linguistic information, e.g. in coarticulation. In Cohen, Collier and 't Hart (1982), we expressed some doubts about the validity of various claims put forward in the literature on the (psycho)linguistic relevance of declination. However, in the same paper we stated that we had found reasons to attach greater psycho-linguistic importance to declination than we used to do. And we gave suggestions for new experiments on this topic, some of which have meanwhile been executed, and will be reported in this chapter.

The outline of this chapter is as follows. In section 5.1, we will deal with acoustic and perceptual aspects of declination, and with a technique to establish its form of appearance in a reliable way. In 5.1.1, we will concentrate on some general properties of the slope, and in 5.1.2, on the phenomenon of baseline resets.

In section 5.2, the production of declination (5.2.1) and of declination resets (5.2.2) will be examined. After a review of the respiratory activity in speech (5.2.1.1), an attempt will be made (5.2.1.2) to answer the question whether declination is speaker-controlled or automatic. It will be shown that, on quantitative grounds, it is implausible to assume that it is under voluntary control of the speaker; instead, a model will be proposed in which a control mechanism, meant to compensate for the loss of air during speech, and hence of air pressure, gives rise to declination as an inevitable by-product. The production of resets will be shown to be connected to laryngeal activity in 5.2.2.

Section 5.3 deals with communicative aspects, with 5.3.1.1 about perceived peak height as a function of position in the utterance, and 5.3.1.2 about the possibility that a listener can build up an expectation as to utterance duration on the basis of declination-related cues. Finally, in 5.3.2, an account will be given of the relation between declination resets and syntactic structure as found in a corpus; and an experiment will be described in which the communicative relevance of resets has been tested.

5.1 Acoustic and perceptual aspects

Despite the optimistic statement in the introduction to this chapter, viz. that the effect of declination is often observable by mere visual inspection of an F_0 curve, the acoustic manifestation of declination is not always without problems. In many cases, there are quite a number of local perturbations, to the effect that the global trend is hardly visible, or at least that it is difficult to decide how to draw the (lower) declination line (the baseline, as it is called by Maeda, 1976). One complication is, for instance, the rather consistent occurrence of extra-low F_0 values preceding the first prominence-lending rise (this was called the 'anticipatory dip' by Cohen and 't Hart, 1967, and was also observed by Maeda, 1976). If in such cases one draws the baseline by connecting the lowest points at beginning and end, the result is not very satisfactory, since intermediate valleys are missed.

As an alternative, one could try to draw the so-called topline, connecting the peaks. This is, of course, impossible if there is only one peak, but there is a more general drawback. Peaks are usually associated with accented syllables, and it is reasonable to expect that possible differences in the strength of the accents are reflected in different peak heights (e.g. Rietveld and Gussenhoven, 1985). This would make the slope of the topline dependent on the strengths of the accents relative to each other. More particularly, in American English the first peak is consistently exceptionally high, making it preferable to exclude it from a line that connects the other peak values (see e.g. W.E. Cooper and Sorensen, 1981).

Apart from practical inconveniences, there is also a theoretical issue in that, as Ladd rightly observes (1984: 56), 'it makes sense to model trend lines only if the points to which the trend lines are fitted are known to be phonologically equivalent'. In other words, it may be risky to connect successive peaks or valleys if one is not sure that these are the results of F_0 changes that belong to the same category. In British English, for instance, full rises are to be distinguished from half rises, which in turn fall into low and high rises. To connect two peaks, the first of which is attained by a low half rise and the second by a full rise, would be meaningless (see fig. 5.2). Consequently, such trend lines cannot be drawn unless phonological equivalence can be established independently. Fortunately, there are already, on phonetic grounds, several reasons to consider this theoretical issue a more serious threat to the adequacy of the topline than to that of the baseline. One is that while raising F_0 requires muscular contraction, which can be applied in various degrees, its lowering is mostly the product of muscular relaxation, thus making the valleys phonetically more equivalent than the peaks. Another is that in utterances with few pitch accents the baseline will show up without any interpretative inference being necessary.

In order to circumvent the difficulties with fitting the baseline by eye as mentioned above, it is often helpful to first make a close-copy stylization, and then to try to find out if the lower stretches can be replaced by pieces of one straight line, without serious perceptual consequences. In principle, this method gives more reliable results than a mere visual fit, since the drawn baseline is audibly indistinguishable from the 'genuine' baseline.

The intermediate step of making a close copy together with a perceptual check may sometimes reveal that the baseline is interrupted by a 'declination reset': in many longer utterances, a rapid jump upwards of the baseline is observed at one or more places. The phenomenon of baseline resetting has already been mentioned by Maeda (1976). W.E. Cooper and Sorenson (1977) measured topline resets with varying success (Sorensen and Cooper, 1980; W.E. Cooper and Sorensen, 1981); since they used relative peak height as a criterion, special measures had to be taken in order to separate resetting from local stress-heightening. Thorsen (1985, 1986), inspired by the findings reported by Lehiste (1975) at sentence boundaries, has studied, for Danish,

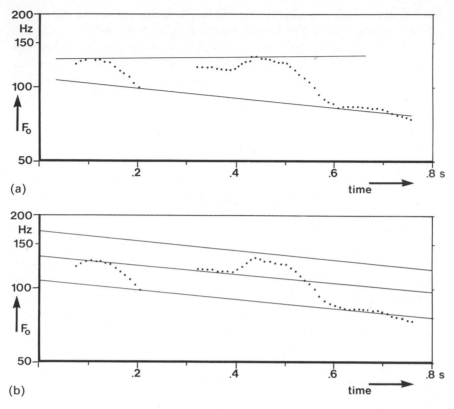

5.2 An arbitrary (a), and a more revealing way (b) of fitting declination trend-lines to the F_0 curve of the short English utterance Yes, you will *(spontaneous speech)*

the courses of both 'lower lines' (connecting the lowest points in first and last accented syllables) and 'upper lines' (connecting the highest points in first and last post-tonic syllables) in successions of declarative terminal sentences and in corresponding strings of co-ordinate main clauses. She found resetting between sentences, but also between clauses; the latter were smaller than the former, reflecting the closer relation between co-ordinate structures.

In reporting on our own occupations with declination in Dutch and British English, we will maintain a dichotomy between aspects of the slope of declination, on one hand, and of resets, on the other.

5.1.1 Slope

Given that declination is perceptually relevant, does that mean that it should be literally present as a tilted line whenever there are no local events, or may it

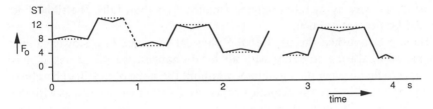

5.3 An attempt to simulate declination by making falls larger than rises in a stylized pitch-contour results in unacceptable, monotonous stretches (dotted lines). Attempts to remedy this by means of the introduction of kink points (solid lines) are equally unsuccessful

just as well be present in a more implicit way, e.g. as the consequence of F_0 falls being larger than rises? The question has to do with a suggestion by Vaissière (1983), inspired by the work of Ohala and Ewan (1973) on the speed of pitch change. The latter two found that it is more difficult to produce a rise than a fall. 'This asymmetry, together with a "laziness principle" means that speakers should tend to produce smaller rises than falls', as Ladd (1984) explains Vaissière's suggestion.

Part of an answer to this question was found experimentally. For a small number of utterances, we made standard stylizations in two different ways: one with genuine declination, and rises and falls of equal size; the other one with falls larger than rises and no further declination, but such that the utterance-initial and -final frequencies were the same as in the former versions. When presented with these contours, listeners largely agreed that the second versions were entirely unnatural. We assume that the reason is that in actual speech strict monotony is so rare that its occurrence (even in relatively short stretches) in the second versions is very conspicuously different from what listeners are used to hear in natural speech, whereas the first versions, with genuine declination, are experienced as fair approximations to natural speech. Admittedly, since the monotonous stretches are caused by the straight horizontal lines in the second versions with the 'implicit' declination, the need for genuine declination is only demonstrated for straight-line stylizations in such an experiment. Therefore, we replaced each horizontal segment by two segments, with a kink in the middle, below the horizontal line for the topline, and above it for the baseline (see fig. 5.3). The effect was that as soon as the distances of the kinkpoints to the originally horizontal lines were large enough to make the stretches audibly different from monotony, spurious pitch movements became audible, which gave rise to yet another kind of unnaturalness, or at least to a loss of perceptual equivalence with the original version.

We concluded that the effect of declination cannot be brought about in a satisfactory way by merely applying smaller rises than falls; the tilted line should be present as such.

Having established the need of the physical presence of a slowly falling course of F_0 during stretches without local changes, we might ask if it is possible to make generalizing statements about the slope of the tilted baseline, on the basis of observed systematic properties. In other words, just as with the other perceptually relevant pitch movements, we are in need of some kind of standardization.

One regularity, which has already been observed by Maeda, is that the end frequencies of utterances spoken by an individual speaker show relatively little variation (unless, of course, a final rise is at stake). Our experience is that this variation is mostly less than a semitone. For practical purposes this implies that we can assume a fixed endpoint for the baseline.

Maeda found reasons to believe that the total amount of declination, the difference between start and finish, also showed only a small variation within a given speaker. As a result, his initial frequency is fixed as well, irrespective of the duration of the utterance. The effect is that the slope of the declination line decreases as the duration increases. Contrary to Maeda, we found that the initial frequency is higher in longer than in shorter utterances (others have observed the same tendency, e.g. W.E. Cooper and Sorensen, 1981). On the other hand, we could corroborate his finding of less steep slopes in longer utterances. On the basis of the analysis of a restricted corpus of utterances produced by various speakers (male and female), we found the following formula to satisfy: $D = (-1)/(0.13 + 0.09t)$, in which D is the slope in semitones per second (ST/s), and t the duration in seconds. Later, this expression was replaced by

(1) $D = (-11)/(t + 1.5)$

for the sake of simplicity. This formula covers the two effects observed: viz. the higher start and less steep slope with increasing duration. For example, if $t = 2$, $D = (-11)/3.5 = -3.14$ ST/s, and with end frequency $= 75$ Hz, the initial frequency becomes 108 Hz; and if $t = 4$, $D = (-11)/5.5 = -2$ ST/s, the amount is 8 ST, and the initial frequency is 119 Hz (again with end frequency $= 75$ Hz).

In a perceptual evaluation, the application of the formula gave satisfactory results, except for rather long utterances: especially if there happened to be an early pitch accent, the high initial frequency combined with the accent-lending rise led to an unnatural-sounding high pitch in the peak. Therefore, it was decided to skip the effect of higher initial frequency for the longer durations, by using a different formula, which accounts for a fixed amount of declination of 8.5 ST. We end up with:

(1) $D = (-11)/(t+1.5)$ for $t \leqslant 5$ s
(2) $D' = (-8.5)/t$ for $t > 5$ s

At this point, two questions may arise. The first one is related to the fact that the baseline is represented by a straight line of constant slope (in the logarithmic F_0 domain). The question is whether this is a valid approximation, from both an acoustic and a perceptual point of view. Indeed, one could think of at least two alternative courses of the baseline: viz. convex (less steep in the beginning, steeper towards the end); or concave (steeper in the beginning). The convex shape has been proposed, in an extreme form, by Lieberman (1967), but it has not been confirmed by other authors. This is, of course, dependent on how easily the baseline can be seen at all; but, for instance, in the very robust procedure with which Thorsen is able to cope with declination for Danish (by simply connecting the lowest points in the accented syllables), such a tendency should have been clearly visible.

Some evidence in favour of a concave shape has been provided by Gelfer *et al.* (1985): declination was steeper in the beginning in five out of six cases studied. Their results are presented in Hz/s, but remain valid if recalculated in ST/s: on average, the slope during the first second is 1.5 ST/s steeper than the overall slope.

We feel no reason to reject the straight-line approximation, mainly because the concaveness just mentioned is, in view of the relatively low sensitivity of the human auditory system for differences in slope, as was mentioned in chapter 2, section 2.3.2.4, not perceptible.

The second question has to do with the topline. It has already been mentioned that it is generally more difficult to draw one line through the peaks than through the valleys. Nevertheless, it is not very difficult to see that, in general, the topline declines more steeply than the baseline, also in log-converted recordings. In our practice of making standardized stylizations, we make the topline (and the middle line in British English) parallel to the baseline, thus violating the acoustic reality. However, although highly trained listeners are capable of hearing the difference between parallel and converging toplines, contours with parallel toplines are not judged less natural than those with convergence.

5.1.2 Baseline resets

As was mentioned before (p. 125), in longer utterances the baseline has a fair chance to be interrupted by one or more declination resets. In such cases, the formulae for the declination slope as a function of duration do not apply for the slopes in the parts divided by a reset. The general situation can be

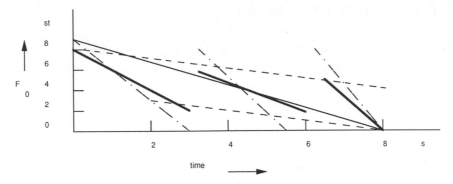

5.4 Schematic representation of the baseline for a long (8s) utterance: (a) one uninterrupted baseline, according to formula (2) (solid line); (b) baseline fragments as would have been predicted by formula (1) (interrupted lines . __ . __ . __ . __ .); (c) the situation usually found (bold solid lines): steeper than (a), less steep than (b), with lower start frequency, and with gradually lowering start and end frequencies for successive fragments (dotted lines). Ordinate: semitones relative to mean end frequency of an individual speaker

characterized as follows (see fig. 5.4): the slopes in the parts are steeper than the one in an uninterrupted baseline, but less steep than would be predicted on the basis of the partial durations; the start frequency is lower than that for an uninterrupted baseline, and after a reset, the new start frequency is generally lower than that of the previous stretch; non-terminal end frequencies tend to be somewhat higher than the end frequency of the last part. These properties make for a kind of superordinate declination effect (Thorsen, 1985, 1986), to which we will return at the end of this section.

The first quantitative data on resets in Dutch have been collected by Collier (1985, 1987). He produced utterances consisting of either main clause plus subclause or subclause plus main clause, each with four different pitch contours. During the brief pause at the syntactic boundary there was an inhalation in half of the cases. The expectation was that at the clause boundaries resets would occur. In order to examine this, F_0 values at beginnings of second clauses (B_2) were compared to those at the beginnings of first clauses (B_1), and to those of their endings (E_1). These comparisons were made for the cases in which, in terms of our stylized description, the pitch was at baseline level at either side of the boundary. In case both E_1 and B_2 were at topline level, only E_1 and B_2 were compared; a comparison between B_2 and B_1 was left out, since B_1 was always low. Comparisons of E_1–B_2 were meant to'see if there was at least partial resetting (in the sense of Sorensen and Cooper, 1980); those of B_1–B_2 should check the occurrence of complete resetting. It is important to note that the syllables in which B_1, E_1 and B_2 were measured were always unaccented.

B_2 appeared to be systematically higher than E_1, the average difference being 1.7 ST if averaged F_0 values (over an entire syllable), and 2.7 ST if extreme values are compared. The former value corresponds remarkably well with a measure that, having been proposed in 1979, has become common practice in our synthesis-by-rule programmes: in case of a pause (operationally defined as 250 ms or more of silence) declination is interrupted, and the non-final fall 'B', or the 'resumption of low pitch' after a continuation rise '2' is made 1 ST less than standard. This measure was necessary for perceptual reasons: if not applied, the pitch after the pause was so low as to give the impression that the utterance was taken over by a different speaker.

The B_1–B_2 comparisons did not give rise to systematic differences. The difference between the two subsets (with and without inhalation) was small enough to allow pooling of the data. From this it turns out that B_2 is, on average, only slightly lower than B_1. Therefore, it is likely that, perceptually, B_1 and B_2 have equal pitch, thus giving the impression of complete resetting.

The expectation about the occurrence of resets at clause boundaries was verified in this experiment. Although the resets as observed here are not large, their omission had earlier been shown to sound unacceptable for reasons that were at that time not well understood. Their systematic occurrence at certain clause boundaries has clarified this matter.

A second study on resetting in Dutch is reported on in Appels (1985). It started from an accidental observation of a particular kind of ambiguity. In a radio broadcast, the news-reader said the following sentence: *The generals met together with their colleague X who is in jail in order to study the strategic possibilities* in such a way that it seemed as if X was the syntactic subject of the infinitive clause, suggesting that X was in jail with the purpose of studying the strategic possibilities. Since no recording of this utterance was available, an experienced reader was asked to speak the sentence twice, once with the implication as given above, and a second time with the implication that the generals are the syntactic subject of the infinitive clause, and that it was the meeting of the generals that should serve the purpose of studying the strategic possibilities. An acoustic analysis suggested that, apart from a difference in timing, there was a declination reset after *who is in jail* in the second, correct version which was absent in the incorrect version. It was decided to study this phenomenon systematically in a larger sample. To this end, a corpus of fifty-one long sentences was collected. They were recorded from radio newsreels presented by four different male speakers, who read their texts from paper (as was checked in a telephone call), but who make the impression of speaking spontaneously, if only by their high speech-rate (of six to seven syllables per second, or around 200 words per minute).

Through the technique of making close-copy stylizations, the baselines in these long sentences (most of which were rather long: average duration 7.8 s, standard deviation 2.4 s) were checked for declination resets. In addition, audible inhalations within sentences were noted down.

In all, seventy resets were found (and 129 declination-line fragments). Averaged over the four speakers, the size of the resets turned out to be 4.9 ST (standard deviation 1.3 ST). This value is much larger than the 1.7 (or 2.7) found by Collier for the kind of boundaries used in his material. This may be related to the much longer durations of these sentences than those used by Collier. An alternative suggestion is that if a possible ambiguity is at stake, experienced speakers tend to make easily perceivable resets in order to cue the aimed at interpretation. We will come back to this suggestion in section 5.3.2.

The slopes of the declination-line fragments did not obey the formulae for uninterrupted declination lines, as was mentioned earlier. For this material, they appeared to be systematically less steep than would be calculated on the basis of the individual durations. On average, the difference turned out to be about 1 ST/s (with a standard deviation of 0.7 ST/s).

The acoustic analysis further showed that for three of the four speakers (forty-five sentences altogether), the end frequencies of the successive partial declination lines had a small, gradual decline; the resulting difference between the end frequencies of the first and the last partial declination line was 1 ST on average. One speaker (six sentences) had a very small tendency to make higher end frequencies in later parts. A perceptual test gave an indication that if the end frequency of a non-final declination fragment is notably lower than the end frequency of the sentence-final declination fragment, it is experienced as less acceptable than if it is higher. These results corroborate Thorsen's (1985, 1986) observation about a 'superordinate F_0 declination'.

5.2 Production

This part of the chapter will deal with production aspects of declination slope and of declination resets.

5.2.1 Slope

In this section, we first want to examine whether there is a physiological mechanism that can be held responsible for declination in general. As will be shown in 5.2.1.1, a serious candidate for the explanation of declination is the slow decrease of the subglottal pressure (P_s), although several additional effects are conceivable.

Secondly, in 5.2.1.2, we want to try to find an answer to the question whether the mechanism responsible for the decreasing P_s is under voluntary control of the speaker, or must be considered an automatism.

132

5.2.1.1 Respiratory activity in speech

It is generally accepted that for speech it is often necessary to prolong the duration of exhalation (as compared to normal breathing). This is made possible by the activity of the external intercostal muscles such that the rather quick decrease of the volume of the thoracic cavity in normal breathing is slowed down (Ladefoged, 1967: 14). However, the expenditure of air causes the subglottal pressure to decrease, to the effect that the pressure drop over the glottis will soon fall below a minimum value needed for phonation, if no countermeasure is taken. This countermeasure consists in reducing the volume of the thoracic cavity by gradually relaxing the external intercostal muscles (and later, if necessary, activating the internal intercostal and other muscles). From the measurements by Ohala (1970), Collier (1975a) and Atkinson (1978) it becomes apparent, however, that the effect of this countermeasure is such that there remains a slow decrease of P_S, and this may well cause F_0 to fall gradually.

In a number of cases, it is found that the ratio between the change of F_0 and that of P_S is substantially larger than the generally accepted 3 to 7 Hz/cm H_2O (e.g. Baer, 1979), or 0.03 to 0.07 Hz/Pa (Pa stands for 'pascal'; 1 Pa is 1 newton per square metre). Such cases indicate that sometimes the decrease of P_S is not sufficient to explain the observed declination slope. Apparently, an additional pitch-lowering mechanism may be involved.

Irrespective of such a possible additional mechanism, it seems justified to consider the decreasing subglottal pressure to be the primary source for declination. This conclusion has found indirect support in later measurements by Collier (1987) on speech utterances that were deliberately produced on a monotone; in such cases, P_S was observed to remain constant.

The conclusion just arrived at does not mean to say that it is always and exclusively the subglottal pressure that causes declination. For one thing, there is the possibility of an additional mechanism; for another, Gelfer *et al.* (1985) have found instances of concave courses of the declination line, as was mentioned in section 2.1. The EMG tracings showed that the cricothyroid muscle was active in order to produce the extra-high onset of F_0, whereas a gradual relaxation of CT-activity could be held responsible for the steeper initial part of the declination line.

A possible reservation one could make with respect to the systematic declination phenomena found in acoustic analysis is that the speech materials on which the measurements have been performed consisted of read-out sentences. As yet, however, we see no reason to assume that in spontaneous speech the mechanism responsible for declination would be radically different from that in read-out speech. This can be illustrated by Willem's (1983) successful attempt to test the formulae for the declination slope as a function of the duration (which were originally derived from read-out Dutch sentences) for British English. Using the technique of close-copy stylization, he measured the declination slope in thirty-five British English utterances as read out by five speakers, and in thirty-five spontaneous utterances by ten different speakers. Durations varied between 0.6 and 6.3 seconds. Each time, the measured slope was compared with the calculated slope, and two histograms were made of the differences, one for the read-out sentences, and one for the spontaneous material. The averaged differences were -0.51 ST/s for loud reading, and -0.30 for spontaneous speech. The standard deviations were 0.79 and 2.05 ST/s respectively. The greater deviations did not typically originate from the longer utterances. The mean deviation of only -0.30 ST/s for spontaneous speech shows that speakers have a remarkably accurate general idea how to manipulate their initial F_0 and declination slope. On the other hand, the rather large standard deviation of more than 2 ST/s indicates that speakers' accuracy in individual cases is rather poor.

This outcome seems to suggest that speakers apply a certain amount of preplanning: if the duration of the utterance they are about to produce is known in advance, they can choose a start frequency and a slope suitable to finish at their individual end frequency. Estimating the duration can, understandably, be done fairly accurately if the speaker is reading from text. The fact that such a preprogramming is less successful in individual cases of spontaneous speech does not entirely rule out its occurrence.

5.2.1.2 Speaker-controlled or automatic?

The observation at the end of the previous section may suggest that declination is a programmed and voluntary phenomenon, just like the local perceptually relevant pitch movements are. However, it is highly unlikely that a speaker always knows in advance the utterance duration accurately enough to make the required calculations. On the other hand, it is equally implausible that he would be capable of producing voluntarily, in a stretch with mere declination, every next syllable at an average pitch of less than 1 Hz lower than the previous one; or, for that matter, control P_s syllable by syllable.

Thus it seems that, if we want to maintain the position that declination is voluntarily programmed, we will have to make a choice between two mechanisms, neither of which seems very likely. In order to find out whether an alternative view is at all possible, let us try to examine the process of the respiratory activity in speech in some more detail, namely in a quantitative way. To that end, we might, each time for a short interval of time, first calculate the decrease of P_s due to the loss of air, and subsequently the compensating effect of the reduction of the volume of the thoracic cavity. Both calculations could, in principle, be done using Boyle's law:

(3) $P_1V_1 = P_2V_2$, (where P = pressure, and V = volume)

but this law is not valid for a mixture of gases, one of which can condensate and evaporate in the condition under consideration (air with water vapour). In Schutte (1980) we found that the following expression holds:

(4) $(P_1 - P_V)^2{}_*V_1/P_1 = (P_2 - P_V)^2{}_*V_2/P_2$

in which P_V is the saturated vapour pressure at the given temperature. At 37°C, this pressure is 6.3 kPa (kilopascal). We will include this correction, which is very small compared to P_1 and P_2, in our calculation in order to avoid the possibility that the final result could be attributed to an artefact introduced by its omission.

We take the original lung volume to be 3,000 cm³. For P_S we can use data from measurements by Collier (1984; also in Gelfer, Harris and Baer, 1987) on a sentence with a duration of three seconds: 0.709 kPa in the beginning, 0.392 kPa at the end (the atmospheric pressure = 101.325 kPa, so the actual pressure below the glottis is 102.034 kPa and 101.717 respectively). Let the short time interval be 50 ms. An acceptable value for the air expenditure is 200 cm³/s. This amounts to 10 cm³ in 50 ms.

It might be necessary to remark here that, in this chapter, we are only dealing with global effects. Since P_S not only depends on pulmonic force, but also on glottal resistance, which varies substantially with the segmental content of the utterance, it may be expected that the actual course of P_S between these successive short time intervals will show a great amount of variation. Dealing with global effects only implies that this kind of variation is not taken into account. As will be shown at the end of this section, a recent experiment by Gelfer, Harris and Baer (1987) has demonstrated that neglecting short-term variation of glottal resistance is fully justified.

In order to calculate what would be the pressure below the glottis before compensation has taken place, we represent the system by a cylinder of 3,000 cm³ with a piston containing a valve through which the air can go only from inside to outside. (Such a model may be used irrespective of the physiological mechanism responsible for it.) We push the piston so far that 10 cm³ of air streams out, and next pull it back into its original position. Now, formula (4) applies in the following way:

(5) $(102.034 - 6.3)^2{}_*2,990/102.034 = (P_2 - 6.3)^2{}_*3,000/P_2$

from which P_2, the pressure after the loss of 10 cm³ of air but before the thoracic-cavity volume has been diminished, can be calculated to be 101.763 kPa, 0.271 kPa less than beforehand.

Despite the compensation measure, there is a small drop in P_s. From Collier's measurements we calculated a rate of change of P_s during the first 50 ms of 0.007 kPa, and during the last 50 ms of 0.004 kPa. With this knowledge, we can use formula (4) once more in order to calculate the volume of the thoracic cavity V_n after compensation:

(6) $(101.763 - 6.3)^2 * 3,000/101.763 = (102.027 - 6.3)^2 * V_n/102.027$

from (6) it follows that $V_n = 2,991.2$. Thus, whereas 10 cm³ of air has been used, the compensation corresponds to a decrease of thoracic-cavity volume of only 8.8 cm³, and this is, of course, in agreement with the decrease of P_s. For the situation at the end of the utterance, we have an initial P_s of $0.392 + 101.325$ kPa $= 101.717$ kPa and an initial volume of 2,400 cm³. P_2 becomes 101.372 kPa, V_n becomes 2,390.9 cm³, the decrease of volume being 9.1 cm³.

In terms of pressure, the incomplete compensation during the first 50 ms can be seen to be $(0.271 - 0.007)/0.271$ or 97.42 per cent, and during the last 50 ms $(0.345 - 0.004)/0.345$ or 98.84 per cent, instead of 100 per cent in case P_s would not have decreased.

This is a surprising result. It has been reported earlier (e.g. Mead, Bouhuys and Proctor, 1968; Collier, 1987) that P_s can be kept constant with remarkable accuracy in sustained phonations of constant amplitudes, showing that a complete compensation for the loss of air is possible in some conditions. That performance was already considered quite an achievement by Mead, Bouhuys and Proctor, in view of the fact that, at different lung volumes, a different pattern of muscular action is demanded for a particular P_s. What we have found above, for a more dynamic, speech-like situation (reiterant speech), constitutes an even more delicate balance: a compensation which is very close to, but consistently below 100 per cent. It is hardly conceivable that the speaker is able to perform this voluntarily. Rather, we must presume that the muscular activity involved is subject to an automatic control system.

In order to examine this possibility more closely, a differential equation was formulated for the behaviour of air pressure in a cylinder with a narrow, tube-shaped opening at one end and a piston at the other. If $p(t)$ is the change of pressure by the air expenditure, as compared to a certain reference pressure P_r, and $v(t)$ is the change of volume by the action of the piston, the differential equation takes the form of (7):

(7) $dp/dt + A.dv/dt + B(P_r + p(t)) = 0$

as can be derived on the basis of elementary physical laws. A and B are constants containing initial volume, atmospheric pressure, temperature, resistance of the tube-shaped opening, etc.

The action of the piston is controlled by a regulator, which uses a comparison between the actual pressure in the cylinder and the reference pressure P_r as its criterion. We have examined several kinds of regulators, two of which have appeared relevant for our purposes.

The first one performs a proportional control, to the effect that the change of volume is directly proportional to the difference between the actual pressure (at moment t) and the reference pressure:

(8) $v(t) = k.p(t)$, and hence, $dv/dt = k.dp/dt$

The differential equation then takes the form in (9):

(9) $dp/dt + A.k.dp/dt + B(P_r + p(t)) = 0$

and its general solution becomes:

(10) $p(t) + P_r.(\exp(-a_1 t) - 1),$

in which a_1 contains all the physical entities referred to before; it contains also k, in such a way that a higher value of k results in a slower exponential decay of the subglottal pressure (P_s).

Since $(-a_1 t)$ is always negative (both a_1 and t are positive), $\exp(-a_1 t)$ is smaller than 1, and hence $p(t)$ is increasingly negative, and the resulting P_s ($= P_r + p(t)$) is always lower than P_r (except for $t = 0$), and will fall off continuously, with an asymptote, for $t = \infty$, at $p(t) = P_r$.

The inevitable loss of pressure can be seen to originate from a combination of two facts: controlling the volume of necessity lags behind an initial drop of pressure, and in this action only the momentary value of $p(t)$ is used as a criterion. Furthermore, since the course of $p(t)$ is exponential, its first derivative dp/dt decreases; and since dv/dt is proportional to dp/dt, the speed at which the volume is reduced also decreases over time. Therefore, the continuing loss of pressure can never be retrieved.

An alternative regulator consists of an integrator: in this system, the change of volume is proportional to the integral of $p(t)$ over the elapsed time. This makes

(11) $dv/dt = k.p(t)$

and equation (7) will be rewritten as:

(12) $dp/dt + A.k.p(t) + B(P_r + p(t)) = 0,$

with the general solution:

(13) $p(t) = b.P_r.(\exp(-a_2 t) - 1)/a_2,$

with, again, a_2 containing the physical entities mentioned before, and also the factor k. Seemingly, formula (13) is similar to formula (10); however, for the same value of k, a_2 is about a hundred times greater than a_1. This is caused by

137

the fact that, whereas the expression for a_1 has the structure $a_1 = c/(d + k.e)$, in which k.e is large with respect to c and d, the expression for a_2 becomes $a_2 = (c + k.e)/d$. The high value of a_2 results in a very rapid decay of $\exp(-a_2 t)$, which is soon negligible with respect to the value 1 in formula (13). Therefore, after somewhat more than 100 ms, p(t) will remain constant.

This regulator also takes into account the loss of pressure suffered in the past, and since, in the beginning of the process, p(t) increases, dv/dt, the speed at which the volume is reduced, also increases. This leads to an equilibrium. If k is chosen large enough, the resulting P_S is only slightly lower than the reference value.

Clearly, the integrating control system is adequate for the situation in singing or in speaking on a monotone, for which it has been reported that P_S can be held constant very accurately. But it cannot account for normal speech, with its slow but nevertheless consistent decay of P_S.

Since the model with the proportional control does appear to show this behaviour, it seemed worth trying whether the parameter k (the amplification factor) could be given such values that the exponentially decaying P_S and F_0 curves could be made to fit the measurements made by Collier on reiterant /ma/-utterances. It turned out that if the value of k is chosen dependent on utterance duration, satisfactory agreement between model and experiment can be obtained. For instance, utterance duration in Collier's experiment varied between somewhat less than 1 and about 3.5 seconds, and good fits with the curves of P_S were obtained with $k = 0.5$ cm³/Pa for the short utterances, and 1.7 cm³/Pa for the longest utterance.

Further calculations by means of the model showed that, irrespective of utterance duration, the mean air expenditure should be about 200 cm³/s (slightly more in the beginning, and less towards the end), a value which is in agreement with the literature (Schutte, 1980). On the basis of the measured amount of decrease of P_S, which fluctuated around 400 Pa, about the same value can be deduced from the measurements.

Understandably, the slow decrease of P_S inherent in the model with the proportional control gives rise to a gradually falling F_0, and as can be seen from the dependence of k on utterance duration, the model will predict a less steep slope for the declination in longer utterances.

The possible validity of the model presented above does not necessarily exclude the possibility of an additional cause for declination, such as, for instance, the 'tracheal-pull' mechanism, as proposed by Maeda (1976). However, it does not compel us to change our view that declination is largely an automatic by-product of properties of the respiratory system, since it is very unlikely that the tracheal-pull mechanism is under voluntary control of the speaker, either.

Gelfer, Harris and Baer (1987), too, have asked themselves if the time course of the drop in P_s during speech is a controlled variable or the passive consequence of lung deflation. They are, of course, aware of the already existing evidence indicating that lung deflation during speech is not a purely passive phenomenon. But this evidence is based on measurements on sustained phonations of constant amplitudes. And the varying air-flow resistance at the glottis gives rise to e.g. higher air-flow rates for utterances containing the reiterant syllable /fa/ than for those with reiterant /ma/.

An examination of the behaviour of P_s in such utterances, with different air-flow requirements, could, in principle, answer the question whether the variation in pressure over time is the natural by-product of unchecked expiratory forces, or whether it reflects ongoing control of the respiratory musculature in order to produce dynamically stable pressures.

As was expected, the air-flow rate for the /fa/ utterances turned out to be greater than for the /ma/ utterances. But the curves for P_s were not different in the two conditions. Now, if lung deflation were passive in nature, P_s would decrease more rapidly for utterances using greater rates of air flow. The authors therefore conclude that their data suggest that P_s is a controlled variable.

With the aid of our model, we can easily show that the only measure needed to be taken in order to maintain the observed course of P_s in case of a reduced air-flow resistance is to apply a higher value of the amplification factor k. As we have seen, a suitable value of k should be chosen anyway: viz. in connection with the expected utterance duration. Therefore, we may expect that speakers have ample experience in selecting adequate values for this parameter. It does not seem to constitute an insuperable extra requirement, then, to also take into account the difference between air-flow resistance in /fa/ utterances and that in /ma/ utterances in this particular experimental task.

We think that we have made plausible in this section that the model of a proportional control system is at least a possible one for normal speech. Once it has been 'switched on', declination follows automatically. In other words, it is not necessary to assume that the speaker controls the declining pitch syllable by syllable. On the contrary, he only needs to give a suitable value to one parameter for each fragment of speech which he plans to produce on one uninterrupted baseline. And in as far as the speaker has knowledge in advance about the duration of that fragment, he must be considered to be a match for this task.

5.2.2 Production of resets

The experiments by Collier (1985, 1987) on declination resets were not restricted to the measurement of F_0: they also comprised simultaneous recordings of the electromyographic activity in the cricothyroid muscles and of the subglottal air-pressure. These measurements revealed that P_s alone could not be held responsible for the observed amount of resetting, but that some laryngeal activity is involved as well. In one subset of the data, without inhalation and with a resetting of 15 Hz on average, the increase of P_s fluctuated around a value of less than 1 cm H_2O; in the other, with inhalation, the average P_s increase was about 1 cm H_2O, but F_0 at the onset of the second clause was 5 Hz lower than at the end of the first clause. Furthermore, in spite of its increase after the pause, P_s was systematically lower at the start of the second clause than at the onset of the first, and yet, there was often almost complete resetting of F_0 (on average, B_2 was only 4 Hz, or less than 1 ST, lower than B_1). In general, the limited increase of P_s did not correlate with the amount of F_0 resetting in either of the subsets, let alone in the ensemble of the data. From these observations, it became apparent that P_s primarily provides the driving force for phonation, and cannot explain the clause-initial F_0 values in any detail.

On the other hand, the difference in F_0 for each pair of clause onsets correlated significantly with the difference in CT activity in the corresponding first syllables. This strongly supports the hypothesis that the onset frequency of the declination line in general, and of the newly started declination line after a reset in particular, is dependent on the level of CT activity.

As was mentioned earlier (pp. 131–2), in the corpus of fifty-one long utterances collected by Appels (1985), not only the occurrence of declination resets was examined, but also inhalations within sentences were auditorily determined. The aim was to find out if there would be a coincidence of resets and inhalations. It turned out that of the seventy resets found, only thirty co-occurred with an (audible) inhalation. In five cases, there was inhalation but no reset. These figures are indicative of the following:

(a) making a reset does not require inhalation as a means to increase the subglottal pressure;
(b) taking a new breath does not necessarily cause the fundamental frequency to rise.

Both (a) and (b) are in agreement with the findings of Collier mentioned above (p. 139), from which it was concluded that sets (at utterance beginnings) and resets are under laryngeal control.

The question about the possible co-occurrence of resets and inhalations can also be viewed from the side of the inhalations: in the corpus, thirty-five inhalations within sentences were counted. Of these, thirty coincided with resets. This high proportion is related to the fact that, as will be explained in section 5.3.2, resets are preferably made at syntactic boundaries of such a strength that taking time for breathing is in concord with marking the boundary by means of a pause as a temporal cue.

5.3 Communicative aspects

In dealing with communicative aspects of declination, we will continue to use the subdivision into 'slope' and 'resets' as applied in the previous sections.

5.3.1 Slope

Given the declining baseline, it is no wonder that, at least in standard stylizations, the peaks are lower as they occur later in the utterance, and the high portions between successive isolated rises and falls show declination as well. This is the inevitable consequence of the choice of standard sizes for the rises and falls in such stylizations. Since the peaks are unequal in absolute height, but equal by virtue of their distances relative to the baseline, one may be interested in the question how peak height is experienced by the listener. Two experiments, to be dealt with in section 5.3.1.1, have been done in an attempt to find an answer to this question.

Given the dependence of declination slope on utterance duration, it is to be expected that the slope may serve to enable the listener to predict, before the utterance has actually ended, for how long it is still going to be continued. This possibility is examined in an experiment to be reported on in section 5.3.1.2.

5.3.1.1 Peak height

In an unpublished paper, Breckenridge and Liberman (1977) (see also Breckenridge 1977) report a number of experiments on this issue, some of which were published two years later by the first author (see Pierrehumbert 1979). Of two peaks, superimposed on a declining baseline, the height of the second was varied, and for each stimulus subjects were asked to indicate whether the second peak was higher or lower than the first one. In this way the experimenters were able to determine a second peak height that is perceptually as high as the first one. Now, if the listeners were to straightforwardly compare the absolute pitches in the two peaks, the point of subjective equality (PSE) would be reached when F_0 is equal in both peaks. If, however, listeners were to judge the peak heights relative to the baseline, the PSE would correspond to a situation in which F_0 in the second peak would be somewhat lower than in the first. Pierrehumbert (1979) found that the two stressed syllables sounded equal in pitch when the second was, objectively, 9.2 Hz lower. In a second set of stimuli in this experiment, she narrowed the pitch range (from 71 to 41 Hz), and in this condition, the PSE was reached with the second peak 5.6 Hz higher. According to the author, it seems unlikely that the subjects expected a pitch updrift in the narrow-range stimuli. Rather, a response bias might have shifted both curves to the right: since the number of physically higher second peaks was equal to that of the lower second peaks, the number of subjectively higher second peaks increases as the PSE is situated more to the left; but the experiment elicited 51 per cent 'second peak higher' responses, which suggests that the subjects had balanced their answer sheets.

This rather dissatisfying result called for a second attempt. Leroy (1984) reports a repetition of this kind of experiment, putting it into the wider framework of the psychological reality of declination. The general hypothesis was that 'listeners perceptually compensate for the declination effect when evaluating the relative height of successive peaks in an utterance' (p. 39). From this, four more specific predictions were derived:

1. If we give the stimuli a standard slope of declination (one that is appropriate to the length of the utterance) then the second peak will be considered to be as high as the first one when it is objectively lower, and to be higher than the first peak when it is objectively equal to it.
2. When the stimuli are given a declination slope that is steeper than standard, the compensation will be proportionally greater; in other words, the overestimation of the relative height of the second peak will be stronger.
3. When the two peaks are superimposed on a monotonous (not declining) baseline, the overestimation of the height of the second peak will be reduced to zero.
4. When the stimuli consist of two syllables, each with a F_0 peak, but separated by silence, likewise no compensation will take place.

Leroy adds that 'it is implicitly understood in these predictions that the listener will compensate for *perceived* declination, not for an *expected*, possibly mentally computed, declination slope' (1984: 40; Leroy's italics).

Four series of stimuli were constructed, in accordance with the four predictions given above. In view of the response bias as observed by Pierrehumbert, the second peak values were (on the basis of a pilot test) taken such that there would be a subjective rather than an objective balance between higher and lower. Objectively, 58 per cent of the second peaks were lower, 16 per cent were equal, and 26 per cent were higher than the first peak. The conditions were named N (normal baseline), S (steep baseline), M (monotonous baseline) and IS (isolated peaks).

In condition N, the slope of the declining baseline was appropriate to the duration of the utterance, as calculated by means of formula (1), viz. -3.35 ST/s; in condition S, it was -5.78 ST/s. Stimuli for conditions N, S and M were repeated three times and randomly mixed together before being tape recorded. Stimuli of condition IS were repeated five times, tape recorded in random order, and presented in a separate stimulus block. The segmental information was reiterant /ma/, seven 'syllables', with F_0 peaks on the second

Table 5.1 *Amounts of declination in the time interval between first and second peak, and points of subjective equality of peak height (with standard error, in semitones) in the four different conditions (Normal and Steep baseline, Monotonous baseline, and ISolated peaks)*

Condition	Amount of declination between P_1 and P_2	PSE	Standard error
N	-3.21	-1.81	0.89
S	-5.54	-2.08	0.55
M	0	-1.03	0.41
IS	(0)	-0.32	0.58

and the penultimate syllable. Listeners were asked to decide whether the second peak was higher than $(+)$, lower than $(-)$, or equal to $(=)$ the first peak. In condition IS there were just the two syllables /ma/, but the instruction was the same as for conditions N, S and M.

The relevant stimulus data and results are given in Table 5.1. Taking the four conditions together we see that the PSE is always negative, indicating that, in general, there is compensation. In condition IS, the value of -0.32 is too low to be significantly different from zero (in line with prediction 4); but in condition M it is -1.03, which suggests that listeners are not guided solely by perceived declination. This is further illustrated by the fact that the PSEs for condition N and S are considerably lower than the actual amounts of declination, and that their mutual difference is negligibly small with respect to the difference present in the stimuli. The alternative, that the listeners evaluate on the basis of mere expected declination, is refuted by the fact that, although in conditions N and S compensation is smaller than the expected amount of declination (of -3.21 ST or thereabouts), these conditions show a larger effect than does condition M. Thus, the conclusion must be that listeners are sensitive to perceived amount, but besides are influenced by expected amount of declination.

5.3.1.2 Slope as a predictor of total duration?
If a speaker intends to say a long sentence, but for some reason stops at a point at which the word content could suggest that the sentence is finished, can a listener then nevertheless decide, on the basis of phenomena connected with declination alone, that the sentence is not yet finished? In such a case, three different cues may be present: viz. a higher start frequency, a less steep slope, and a higher end frequency than if the actually produced short utterance were said intentionally.

This was studied in a second experiment by Leroy (in the same thesis). Using diphone synthesis, the following utterances were constructed:

short   Pas jij even op de kleren (1)
intermediate Pas jij even op de kleren van de vrouwen (2)
long   Pas jij even op de kleren van de vrouwen bij de molen (3).
(Would you mind the clothes | of the women | at the mill)

Each of these can still be followed by another constituent, but can also be considered a complete sentence. The utterances had durations of 1.78, 2.74 and 3.62 seconds respectively.

According to formula (1) for the declination slope, appropriate rates of declination are -3.35, -2.59 and -2.15 ST/s. With an end frequency of 75 Hz, the declination lines start at 106, 113 and 118 Hz respectively. In the experiment, the long sentence was truncated after the second constituent (version 3-2), and after the first one (version 3-1); likewise, the intermediate sentence was truncated after the first constituent (version 2-1). The end frequencies of the truncated versions were 84 Hz for 3-2, 94 Hz for 3-1 and 87 Hz for 2-1. The truncated versions were mixed randomly with versions 1-1, 2-2 and 3-3, which had appropriate declination conditions.

In synthesizing the utterances, no use was made of rules for the temporal organization in connection with utterance length, or place (of a word or syllable) in the utterance. In particular, preboundary lengthening was absent.

Twenty-eight listeners were told that there would be four possible sentences in the experiment: *Pas jij even op de kleren/ van de vrouwen/ bij de molen/ langs het water*, and they were informed about the truncations. In this way, the possibility remained that the longest sentence was obtained from an even longer one by deleting the last constituent. Subjects were asked to indicate for each of the stimuli whether they thought the utterance was 'finished' or 'not finished' (forced choice). The expectation was that utterances with appropriate declination would sound 'finished', whereas with 'less' or 'much less' declination, they would sound 'unfinished'.

In a pilot experiment, the same sentences were also used, but without declination, in order to examine possible bias effects that had nothing to do with declination. Two such bias effects were: if no pitch accent occurred (the presence or absence of pitch accents was one of the experimental variables), there was a bias towards 'not finished'; the longest sentence tended to be judged 'finished' more often than chance.

Taking into account these two biases, the predictions for the main experiment were: (a) if the declination rate in a given utterance is appropriate for its length, the number of subjects who consider it to be 'finished' will be significantly greater than if there is no declination; (b) if the declination rate is less than appropriate, the number of listeners who consider the utterance 'finished' will be significantly smaller than if there is no declination.

The predictions were verified in a comparison of the results of the main experiment with those of the pilot experiment.

1. For utterances of short and intermediate duration, the prediction was confirmed; long utterances tend to be considered 'finished' anyway: their scores suffered from a ceiling effect.

2. A distinction should be made between a 'less' and a 'much less' than appropriate declination rate (long sentence truncated to intermediate sentence, or intermediate to short, versus long sentence truncated to short sentence). There was no major difference in 'finished' responses for utterances with 'less' than appropriate declination and those without declination. But the difference between 'much less' and 'no' declination was highly significant. It appeared that a significant majority of the subjects had considered an utterance to be 'not finished' when its declination slope was at least 1.2 ST/s less than would have been appropriate to its length; a possible extra cue may have been that in the truncated versions both the initial and the final frequencies were higher than might be expected in versions with normal declination.

Further observations were: (a) exactly as in the pilot experiments, for utterances with less or much less than appropriate declination the absence of pitch accents increased the number of 'not finished' responses. But for utterances with appropriate declination slopes the presence or absence of pitch accents did not make a difference; (b) the bias towards 'finished' in long utterances was still present in contours without pitch accents, but it disappeared in contours with pitch accents (and declination).

From what we have seen in chapter 2 about the poor discriminability of the rate of change of fundamental frequency, we could already have expected that the detectability of finishedness and unfinishedness on the basis of declination slope alone would be limited. Moreover, the absence of temporal cues constitutes an extra complication for the listener. However, an audible effect has been shown to exist with sentences of which the declination slopes differed by at least 1.2 ST/s; therefore, it may be expected to play a part in everyday speech, in which larger differences in declination slope tend to occur.

5.3.2 Communicative aspects of declination resets

The second study on resetting in Dutch (Appels, 1985) was not only meant to examine the acoustic manifestation of this phenomenon. Another aim was to try to find out if there is a systematic relationship between the place of a declination reset and the syntactic structure of the sentence. This will be dealt with in section 5.3.2.1.

As has already been mentioned towards the end of section 5.1.2, the large size of the resets in that corpus suggested that the speakers wanted to provide easily perceivable cues in order to avoid misinterpretations in ambiguous situations. So, a third aim was to find out whether the presence or absence of a reset can influence the interpretation of particular ambiguous sentences. This will be reported on in section 5.3.2.2.

5.3.2.1. Relation with syntactic structure

The general tendency in the corpus is that the part of the sentence after the reset does not link up with the constituent immediately preceding it, but with an earlier constituent. This regularity can take a number of widely varying forms.

In the sentence that triggered this study (see section 5.1.2), the absence of a reset between . . . *in jail* and *in order to* . . . would suggest that general X's stay in jail is aimed at studying the strategic possibilities, because of the strong link between these two parts. A reset would connect studying the strategic possibilities with the meeting of the other generals with their colleague X.

Many sentences in this corpus contained a rather long initial part before the finite verb, in most cases the subject, which may consist of a noun phrase and a prepositional phrase. For example: *President Reagan of the United States of America has* . . . with a reset between 'America' and has', to indicate that President Reagan, and not America, has . . . The subject may also consist of a noun phrase and a relative clause: *Egypt, which lives in an undercooled kind of peace with Israel, has* . . . It is often supposed that the entire relative clause would be situated on a lower baseline, and that the parts of the main clause are on the same, higher baseline. What we found to occur consistently is that (in terms of this example) the subject and the relative clause are on one baseline and, with a reset after the relative clause, the remainder of the main clause on a new one. Likewise, in an example of British English (in Halliday's (1970) course), we found (declination reset at '/'): *And if you go in spring, when the gorse is out, or in summer, when the heather is out,/ it is really one of the most delightful areas in the whole country*, whereas the impression is that *or in summer, when the heather is out* is on a lower baseline than the parts before and after.

One might also have expected a reset in this example between . . . *gorse is out* and *or in summer* . . ., in line with the general tendency, to indicate that *or in summer* links up with *if you go*, rather than with the immediately preceding subclause. Instances of this kind have been found in this corpus, at least with two main clauses with a common subject (which is deleted in the second

146

clause): *Israel is much benefited with the removal of the mines in the Red Sea,/ and welcomes the arrival of the international naval forces.*

Having a common subject is not a necessary condition, however; we have also observed resetting at co-ordinative S_1–S_2 boundaries with two different subjects. Moreover, it is not only in the case of a common subject that a reset is found: also a common finite verb may call for a reset: *Iraq says to have destroyed five hostile vessels / and to have shot down an Iranian fighter.*

Also in line with the general tendency is the following sentence: *They write this to the international peace office in Geneva,/ namely in letters in which...* And: *He says that trade-unionism manages better the government's policy to reduce unemployment / than (do) the employers.*

A last example (translated in English using the Dutch word order): *The chairman... Georg Leber / reported that the most important change a shortening of working-time to 38.5 hours concerns,/ which will be compensated by means of a rise in wages.* The first reset suggests that the speaker conceived *the chairman* as the real subject rather than the name of the chairman. The second reset might not have been necessary in English, which would place *concerns* before *shortening*. Perhaps, in this particular case, with two prepositional phrases after *shortening*, also in English a reset would be appropriate; but in general, the Dutch word order makes it more necessary.

Even these professional speakers made some spurious resets, to the effect that the sentence can be interpreted differently from what obviously is intended: *Egypt, which... Israel / has not yet applied to that country / in order to come to a solution together.* The second reset wrongly suggests that Egypt's aim of not making contact with Israel is to come to a solution.

5.3.2.2 Influence of resets on interpretation
As was mentioned in the beginning of section 5.1.2, the slopes in the parts of a baseline that is interrupted by one or more resets are steeper than the slope in an uninterrupted baseline. This implies that a reset can be introduced in an uninterrupted baseline by rotating clockwise the baseline parts on either side of the point where the reset is wanted, the left side round its starting point, the right side round its endpoint. Likewise, a reset can be removed by rotating the parts in the other direction until they have become collinear. In order to do the experiment to be described below, a program was written with which it is possible to do just these manipulations, i.e. leaving intact the remaining original variations of F_0 as produced by the speaker. In this way, in a subset of the sentences of the corpus, resets were introduced or removed to see if, in the first instance, listeners could hear the difference. The results were rather disappointing, probably due to the long durations and complicated structures of the sentences.

Therefore, a set of twelve much simpler ambiguous sentences was constructed. Eight of these contained a prepositional phrase that could have either an adverbial or an adjectival function (the classical example for English is: *They decorated the girl with the flowers*). Three other sentences contained the infinitive-clause construction (*in order to*) with two possible implicit subjects (as was the case in the sentence with the generals). One sentence had a relative clause with two potential antecedents: viz. the head noun of a complex nominal phrase, or the noun in its prepositional modifier (*The daughter of the shopkeeper, who...*). This kind of construction had not been observed in the corpus, but it was expected that, in agreement with the general tendency, a reset after the second noun would favour the link of the relative clause with the head noun. For all sentences, care was taken to avoid bias effects due to word content.

Eight subjects did a pilot experiment with the sentences read by an experienced speaker in such a way that they were optimally ambiguous. On the basis of the reactions of these subjects, ten sentences were selected for the main experiment, seven with the adverbial–adjectival distinction, two with infinitive clauses and the one sentence with two potential antecedents. The manipulations were applied in such a way as to give rise to no reset, a rather small reset (of 4 ST) and a large reset (of 8 ST). The outcome was as follows: for the seven adverbial–adjectival sentences, there was a consistent tendency towards an increase of adverbial interpretations with increasing size of the reset, as expected; for both sentences with infinitive clauses, the number of interpretations in which the implicit subject of the subclause corresponds to the explicit subject of the main clause, increased with increasing size of the reset, as was also expected; the result for the sentence with two potential antecedents was contrary to the expectation, for reasons which are not well understood.

The outcome of these experiments could lead to the generalizing view that it is local events only that have a communicative function, since, of course, resets are local events. But an alternative way of reasoning is also possible. The fundamental frequency of a speaker is bound to a lowest limit. It is by virtue of this limit that the global phenomenon of declination must inevitably every now and then be interrupted by a reset. In other words, if the declination slope were nil, resetting would not be necessary. In that sense, not only to declination resets, but also to declination, a communicative function can be attributed.

5.4 Concluding remarks

In this chapter, we have looked at the phenomenon of declination from a number of angles, and we were able to gain some new insights, bringing us closer to the answers to a number of important fundamental and practical questions. Without being exhaustive, we would like to pass some of these new insights in review.

By means of the application of the close-copy technique, it has become possible to determine the slope of the baseline more reliably, since it can be done not only on the basis of mere visual criteria, but also with the aid of the required perceptual equality between close-copy and resynthesized original. Moreover, with this technique the presence of baseline resets is detected more easily than was possible in the past. The systematic occurrence of resets at certain clause boundaries has answered the question why in some cases their absence in artificial contours led to unacceptable results, even if the apparently necessary resets could be relatively small in size. Larger resets, as found in the much longer and more complicated sentences in Appels's corpus, may be (and have been found to be) helpful to avoid possible ambiguities.

As for the production of declination, evidence already existed in favour of a relationship with the decreasing subglottal pressure. The possibility of an additional mechanism is not excluded. Furthermore, the hypothesis that laryngeal activity is exclusively responsible for local events, and the subglottal pressure for declination, cannot be entirely upheld. Nevertheless, it does not prevent us from considering the decrease of P_s as the primary source for declination. In the framework of the question whether declination is voluntarily controlled or takes place automatically, indications have been obtained in favour of an automatic declination by means of a control system. For resets, on the other hand, there is substantial evidence that these are voluntarily controlled by the speaker, witness the laryngeal activity involved in their production.

This puts the question about preprogramming in a new light. For relatively short utterances, the speaker may in most cases well know in advance their duration. This would enable him to make a suitable choice for the value of the only parameter needed according to the model, in order to, at least on average, satisfy the formulae that had been derived for the baseline slopes in read-out sentences. Longer utterances are more difficult to preprogram as a whole, but, since the probability of the occurrence of resets increases with utterance length, knowing in advance their entire duration becomes a far less important issue.

As we have stated on an earlier occasion (Cohen, Collier and 't Hart, 1982), we have welcomed the possibility that declination may be interpreted as more than a mere theoretical construct, by means of which the structure of an F_0 curve can more easily be understood. In the same paper, we concluded that some of the then recent claims about the psycholinguistic importance of declination lacked conclusive evidence. It seems as if there is now increasing evidence against a possible look-ahead strategy. Moreover, the signalling function of declination appears to be restricted, since its possible acoustic attributes, in as far as they are systematically present, are only just above the threshold of perception in most cases.

On the other hand, in the paper mentioned above, we proposed a number of experiments which seemed to be promising. One of them should concentrate on the question of whether the mental projection of the baseline can be interfered with when different declination slopes are applied to the stimulus material. Leroy's experiment on peak height has given an affirmative answer to that question. A second experiment was intended to examine whether listeners' interpretations can be influenced by manipulating the location of resetting. The outcome of Appels's experiment was clear enough, but different from what was expected. Taking the sentence *They decorated the girl with the flowers* as the example, the expectation was that a reset between *girl* and *with* would favour an adverbial interpretation, which indeed happened. But the other part of the expectation was that a shift of the reset to another location, viz. between *decorated* and *the girl*, would be necessary for the alternative, adjectival interpretation. This experiment showed that the absence of a reset can do the job already.

Finally, the fact that the presence or absence of resets has been shown to be linguistically relevant within the constraints of this experiment, can be seen in connection with the direct measurement of laryngeal activity in (setting and) resetting of the baseline: this is entirely in line with one of the main implications of our basic assumption.

6

Linguistic generalizations

6.0 Introduction

Our study of Dutch intonation has resulted in a melodic description of (nearly) all possible pitch contours of that language. The inventory of permissible contours is explicitly defined by the 'grammar of intonation', presented in chapter 4 (propositions 4, 4.1, 4.2, 4.3). Contours are global melodic entities that tend to coincide with clauses or complete utterances. They can be broken down into the structural units that we labelled Prefix, Root and Suffix configurations, each of which consists of one or more discrete pitch movements. The atomistic pitch movements are the elementary descriptive units of our melodic model. We have supplemented their perceptual characterization with an acoustic definition that can be used to control the F_0 parameter of synthetically produced speech. We have also established a link between perceptually relevant pitch changes and the voluntary manoeuvres that a speaker executes in order to produce variations in the course of F_0. Finally, we have gained some insights as to how the infinite variety of pitch contours relates to a restricted set of more abstract melodic categories or intonation patterns.

Generally speaking, different contours belong to the same intonation pattern if they share a common Root configuration, even if they differ as to the number or type of their Prefixes, or with regard to the presence or absence of a Suffix. Such fundamental differences and correspondences are not clearly reflected in the 'grammar of intonation', which is primarily a generative device that produces well-formed strings of pitch movements without much internal structure. In particular, the grammar fails to explain how different Prefixes relate to each other and how the same Root can manifest itself in more than one melodic shape. Clearly, a number of further generalizations are in order. It may be attempted to express melodic regularities in terms of basic forms, which then enter a set of rules that derive all possible alternative representations.

This chapter presents our efforts to make the structure of Dutch intonation more insightful. In the first part of this chapter we will introduce and define a number of descriptive units and categories and will show how they apply to abstract intonational structures. Secondly, we will present a set of derivation rules that convert underlying intonation patterns into more elaborate and concrete melodic entities. Finally, we will show how melodic structures and textual (sentential and segmental) elements can be mapped onto each other. As a whole, our generalized and systematic description stays fairly close to phonetic reality, even if it borrows descriptive devices from phonology. In the second part of the chapter we will compare our approach to a more orthodox phonological treatment of Dutch intonation and examine whether our own generalizations can profitably be pushed one step further by introducing even higher levels of abstraction.

6.1 A systematic-phonetic treatment of Dutch intonation

Since the individual pitch movements each have an established perceptual identity, we will start with a definition of the various rises and falls in terms of a set of distinctive features (6.1.1). Next we will elaborate on the basic structure of contours (6.1.2 and 6.1.3). Then we will propose a set of rules that elucidate the relation between basic forms and their surface manifestation (6.1.4). In the next section (6.1.5) we will express some views on Tune and Text association. Section 6.1.6 will deal with phonetic implementation. The first part of the chapter ends with an evaluation (6.1.7).

6.1.1 The feature decomposition of pitch movements

Basically, Dutch intonation can be modelled at the phonetic level as a sequence of pitch rises and falls. Pitch variation, however, is not limited to a contrast in direction of change. Rises and falls have to be further differentiated according to variables such as position in the syllable, size and slope. The identity of each pitch movement and the extent to which it differs from all the others can be expressed with a notation in terms of binary distinctive features. Such features have to meet the following requirements:

(a) they should allow for a unique specification of the pitch movements that enter into the definition of all the distinct intonation patterns;
(b) they should allow for the specification of all the pitch movements that make up the contours that are variants of these patterns;
(c) they should allow for a straightforward interpretation at the phonetic level.

Table 6.1 *Pitch movements and their feature composition*

	/1/	/2/	/3/	/4/	/5/	/A/	/B/	/C/	/D/	/E/
RISE	+	+	+	+	+	−	−	−	−	−
EARLY	+	−	−	−	+	−	+	−	−	+
LATE	−	+	−	+	−	−	−	+	+	−
SPREAD	−	−	−	+	−	−	−	−	+	−
FULL	+	+	+	+	−	+	+	+	+	−

It appears to be necessary to distinguish five features for the specification of the pitch movements of Dutch:

[RISE]:　　[+rise] indicates that the pitch movement is a rise;
　　　　　　[−rise] indicates that the pitch movement is a fall.

[EARLY] and [LATE]: [+early] indicates that the offset of the pitch movement is located near the beginning of the voiced part of the syllable; [+late] indicates that the offset is located near the end of the voiced part of the syllable. A pitch movement cannot be both [+early] and [+late], but it can be both [−early] and [−late], in which case its offset is located near the middle of the syllable.

[SPREAD]: a [+spread] pitch movement is associated with two or more successive syllables, so as to reach its end point in the last of these syllables;
　　　　　　a [−spread] movement is confined to one syllable.

[FULL]:　　[+full] indicates that the pitch movement actually covers the full distance between the lower and upper declination lines (standard size);
　　　　　　[−full] indicates that the movement is smaller than the standard size.

With the features listed above we can uniquely characterize all the perceptually distinct pitch movements in Dutch. The inventory of rises and falls is listed in table 6.1, together with the short-hand of alphanumeric symbols that were introduced in chapter 4. It should be emphasized that these pitch movements are not the basic intonation patterns of the language, but the building blocks of such patterns as well as of their variants. The matrix of table 6.1 serves a classificatory purpose: the definition of the features refers to phonetic reality, but the features do not describe that reality in any detail; they will have to be phonetically interpreted at a later stage (see 6.1.6).

6.1.2 Configurations and contours

We will now introduce some more descriptive units and their definitions.

6.1.2.1 Configurations

Some pitch movements combine with others into close-knit units that we call configurations. A configuration may also consist of only one movement. We distinguish three types of configurations: Prefix (P), Root (R) and Suffix (S). The distinction is useful because it allows us to highlight the internal structure of the contours (see 6.1.2.2). As the analogy with morphology suggests, a Root configuration can occur all by itself, whereas the other two types of configuration are of necessity attached to a Root. The morphological analogy only concerns the formal properties of these higher-order constructs, and does not imply that pitch morphemes have some meaning of their own.

6.1.2.2 Contours

A contour is the largest descriptive unit in our intonational system. Its domain of application is operationally limited to one clause (or a one-clause sentence). A contour is a sequence of configurations, or it may consist of just one configuration, which then has to be a Root.

A contour has the following general structure:

$$\text{Contour} = (\text{Prefix})^n \text{ Root (Suffix)}$$

Prefix and Suffix are optional. The Prefix is recursive (^{n}): it can be preceded by another Prefix. A Suffix cannot be followed by another Suffix. Since a contour is a sequence of pitch movements, grouped in configurations, it may be considered as the *systematic-phonetic* representation of the melodic plan that a speaker wants to execute during the production of his speech melody. At the same time it is the perceptual structure that the listener has to recognize during his melodic interpretation of an F_0 curve.

We will now present in detail which pitch movements make up the Prefix, Root and Suffix configurations.

6.1.3 The structure of configurations

In this section we define the basic form of the various configurations. In the next section we will explain how their variants can be derived.

6.1.3.1 Root configurations

Since a Root is the only obligatory element at the core of a contour, this configuration will determine the melodic identity of the utterance: it will

Table 6.2 *Root configurations*

Short-hand	Movements		Stylized F_0 curve
/1A/	+ rise + early − late − spread + full	− rise − early − late − spread + full	
/4A/	+ rise − early + late + spread + full	− rise − early − late − spread + full	
/3C/	+ rise − early − late − spread + full	− rise − early + late − spread + full	
/1E/	+ rise + early − late − spread + full	− rise + early − late − spread − full	
/1/	+ rise + early − late − spread + full		
/2/	+ rise − early + late − spread + full		

Table 6.3 *The Prefix configuration*

Short-hand	Movements		Stylized F_0 curve
/1B/	+ rise	− rise	
	+ early	+ early	
	− late	− late	
	− spread	− spread	
	+ full	+ full	

indicate which intonation pattern is being realized. Therefore, we must distinguish as many Roots as there are basic patterns. In chapter 4 we gave a survey of the six Dutch intonation patterns. In table 6.2 we list the corresponding six Roots, represented in terms of the pitch movements they are composed of. The table also includes the short-hand notation that we used in the preceding chapters, and a stylized representation of the corresponding F_0 contour. Evidently, some of the Roots differ only minimally from one another. It may therefore be tempting to reduce them in number (possibly even to just one), and to derive the other Root configurations by rule. We object to this solution on the grounds that such a derivation would imply that the derived configurations are merely variants of a common underlying form, which they are not: native listeners consider them as categorically distinct basic patterns (see chapter 4, proposition 5).

6.1.3.2 The Prefix configuration
We assume that there is only one Prefix configuration in the basic form of a contour. It is presented in table 6.3. The various alternatives of the Prefix are derived by rule (see 6.1.4).

6.1.3.3 The Suffix configuration
We also assume that there is only one basic form for the Suffix. It is represented in table 6.4.

Some configurations consist of two pitch movements, others have only one. At the basic level of representation, each movement is associated with a different syllable, so that a configuration is mapped onto either one of two syllables, depending on the number of movements it contains. The selection of the appropriate syllable(s) is an aspect of Text and Tune association, to be discussed in a later section (6.1.5). On the other hand, the occurrence of two or more movements on the same syllable is considered a variation on the basic structure and it is derived by rule (see 6.1.4).

Table 6.4 *The Suffix configuration*

Short-hand	Movement	Stylized F_0 curve
/2/	$\begin{bmatrix} +\,\text{rise} \\ -\,\text{early} \\ +\,\text{late} \\ -\,\text{spread} \\ +\,\text{full} \end{bmatrix}$	

6.1.4 A grammar of Dutch intonation

In chapter 4 (proposition 4.3) we presented a grammar that generates the surface-phonetic pitch contours of Dutch directly, i.e. as trajectories through a transition network. Here we introduce a generative scheme that accounts for the same contours in a different way: first, the basic representation of a contour is generated with a rewrite rule; next, the possible variants are derived by modification rules. The two types of rules operate on the pitch movements and configurations, defined in sections 6.1.1 and 6.1.2. The grammar does not take into account any formal property of a particular or possible sentence. It generates all and only the permissable pitch contours 'blindly', i.e. irrespective of how these contours are to be associated with lexical, syntactic or semantic structures. The association of Text and Tune is dealt with by a separate set of conventions (see 6.1.5).

1. The first rule of the grammar (R1) states the possible basic forms of a contour by specifying the sequence of pitch movements and their organization in terms of Prefix, Root and Suffix constituents. For the sake of convenience, the rule makes use of the short-hand notation rather than the feature specification of the movements. For their conversion tables 6.1 to 6.4 are to be used.

$$(\text{R1}) \ \ \text{Contour} \Rightarrow (/1\text{B}/)^n \left\{ \begin{matrix} \left\{ \begin{matrix} /1\text{A}/ \\ /4\text{A}/ \\ /1/ \end{matrix} \right\} \ (/2/) \\ \left\{ \begin{matrix} /1\text{E}/ \\ /3\text{C}/ \\ /2/ \end{matrix} \right\} \end{matrix} \right\}$$

$$\quad\quad\quad\quad\quad\quad |\,\text{P}\,| \quad\quad\quad |\,\text{R}\,| \quad\quad |\,\text{S}\,|$$

157

where ^{n} indicates the recursiveness of the P configuration. It appears from the formulation of (R1) that, whichever contour is generated, the first movement always has the feature [+rise]. It follows that, in its basic form, a pitch contour always starts at a low pitch level. Since the domain of the contour is the clause, it also follows that after a clause boundary the pitch is automatically lowered.

2. Some contours generated by (R1) have a variant in which the [−rise] of the Prefix or of a Root is made to extend over several syllables. Rule (R2) takes care of this change.

(R2) A [−rise, −late, +full] pitch movement may become [+spread]

This rule accounts for the fact that /D/ is a variant of /B/ or /A/.

3. In some contours two (or three) pitch movements may combine on one and the same syllable. This contraction only applies to two movements that are part of the same configuration, or to the last movement of a Root and the single movement of the Suffix. In the limiting case then, two movements of a Root and the rise of the Suffix can co-occur on the same syllable. Rule (R3) states this possibility.

(R3) Two successive pitch movements that constitute a Prefix or a Root can be joined on the same syllable. This contraction is obligatory in the Prefix if it is followed by either Root /3C/ or /4A/. The Suffix rise can also co-occur on the same syllable with a complete Root or with the second pitch movement of a Root.

For instance, (R3) combines the sequence /1A/ into /1&A/, or the sequence /1A2/ into either /1&A2/, or /1A&2/, or /1&A&2/. (The combined movements are linked by means of '&'.) Rule (R3) also accounts for the obligatory combination of /1B/ to /1&B/ when preceding /3C/ or /4A/.

4. When two pitch movements are combined on one syllable, two kinds of conflict may arise with regard to their timing features [early] and [late]. The first regards the contraction of /1B/ to /1&B/, where both the [+rise] and the [−rise] are [+early, −late]. In such a case, the [−rise] is positioned later in the syllable, i.e. becomes [−early]. The second conflict concerns the combination of /1E/ on one syllable. In this case the [−rise] retains its [+early] feature, but it is moved to the following syllable. These conflicts can be resolved by rule (R4).

(R4) If two pitch movements occur on the same syllable and both are [+ early], the second movement becomes [− early] if it is [+ full], or shifts to the next syllable if it is [− full]. If there is no next syllable, the current (i.e. last) syllable is reduplicated.

The reduplication mentioned in (R4) concerns cases like *New York* or *Jan*, which – if provided with a /1E/ contour – are pronounced as *New Yo-ork* or *Ja-an*.

5. So-called terrace-shaped contours can occur as variants of the Root configurations /1A/ and /1E/. The derivation is taken care of by rule (R5).

(R5) Between the pitch movements [+ rise, + early, − late, − spread, + full] and [− rise] of a Root, a [− rise, − full] movement may be inserted, either once or repeatedly.

Rule (R5) changes /1A/ to /1EA/, /1EEA/, etc., or converts /1E/ to /1EE/, /1EEE/, and so on.

6. Following the introduction of (R1), we have stated that in its basic form, a contour always starts at low pitch. To account for contours that, in their surface-phonetic shapes, start at a high pitch level, we need a rule that derives them from the basic forms generated by (R1), by deleting the initial [+ rise].

(R6) A contour initial [+ rise, + early, − spread] movement may be deleted if followed by a [− rise].

Thus, for instance, a contour can start with the pitch movements /A/, /B/ or /E/ rather than with /1A/, /1B/ or /1E/. The onset pitch of the contour is then high.

7. Another instance of insertion concerns the addition of a half-sized rise /5/ between the two pitch movements of Roots /1A/ and /4A/.

(R7) A [+ rise, − full] movement may be inserted between either the [+ rise], or the [+ rise, + spread], and the [− rise] movements of a Root. The inserted rise occurs on the same syllable as the [− rise] movement.

Rule (R7) causes /1A/ or /4A/ to become /15&A/ or /45&A/ respectively. Since the inserted /5/ is [+ early] and /A/ is [− early], there is no timing conflict and no need to apply Rule (R4).

8. Finally, a rule is needed that may change the Prefix /1B/ into its variants /3B/ or /4B/.

(R8) The [+rise] of the Prefix may receive either the feature [−early] or the feature [+spread].

We conclude this section with a number of sample derivations. The effect of the successive application of the rules is indicated in short-hand notation. In the three examples below, the first contour is always the one that results from the application of (R1). In that sense it is the 'basic' contour. All the other, 'alternative' contours are derived from the basic one by means of optional rules. Notice that all the contours in a derivation are possible phonetic manifestations of speech melody in Dutch. It is *not* the case that only the last contour is the surface-phonetic form, while the others would represent intermediate (impossible or unattested) melodic shapes. The only exception occurs after the application of (R3), whose output may be ungrammatical unless (R4) is applied (as in (example 2)).

Example 1	/1B/	/1B/	/1A/
(R6)	/ B/	/1B/	/1A/
(R8)	/B/	/3B/	/1A/
(R5)	/B/	/3B/	/1EA/

Example 2	/1B/	/1B/	/4A/
(R2)	/1D/	/1B/	/4A/
(R3)	/1D/	/1&B/	/4A/
(R4)	/1D/	/1&B/ [−early]	/4A/
(R7)	/1D/	/1&B/ [−early]	/45&A/

Example 3	/1B/	/1A/	/2/
(R3)	/1B/	/1A&2/	
(R8)	/4B/	/1A&2/	

6.1.5 Tune and Text association

Syntactic structure and accentuation (or sentence stress) are two linguistic variables that play a role in the association of Tune and Text. Assume that we have two sets of linguistic objects: one contains all possible pitch contours in their systematic-phonetic form; the other contains all possible phrase markers, with their surface syntactic bracketing and their accentual structure. Tune and Text association then amounts to specifying which objects in one set are compatible with which elements in the other. To this end we need a body of rules that specify for any given pitch contour which sentences can be associated with it, given their syntactic and accentual structure. Conversely, the rules also specify for any given sentence that has specific syntactic and accentual features, which possible pitch contours it can be associated with. Evidently, there is not a one-to-one, but rather a many-to-many relationship between the objects in both sets, the Texts and the Tunes. It may be expected that a number of factors determine this relationship, and that pragmatic factors will be the most prominent among them. In the framework that we elaborate here, we assume that pragmatic factors already have exerted their influence *prior* to the level of Text and Tune association: they have already influenced the choice among alternative basic forms (i.e. intonation patterns); they have already played their part in deciding on the number and the location of sentence accents; and they have already influenced the shaping of the syntactic surface form of the sentence. In other words, we think that Text and Tune association is nearly exclusively determined by syntax and accentuation, and that it operates at the level of surface representation for the three variables involved: syntax, accentuation and speech melody. The mapping rules are sensitive only to features of these surface forms.

For the formulation of Text and Tune association we assume that we have at our disposal the systematic-phonetic specification of a pitch contour on the one hand, and the surface-structure information concerning syntax and accentuation on the other. As to the former, we make use of phrase markers with labelled brackets that indicate the nature of the syntactic constituents (phrase, clause and sentence) and their boundaries; furthermore, we assume that a feature [+stress] has been assigned to at least one syllable (unless [+rise, −early, +late] is the only movement).

6.1.5.1 Accentuation

Some of the pitch movements in a contour are to be associated with [+stress] syllables. To mark these movements as such, we apply rule (A1).

(A1) Assign the feature [+prominence lending] (henceforth [+PL]) to a pitch movement that has one of the following feature combinations: [+rise, −late, −spread], or [−rise, −late, −early, −spread], or [−rise, −full].

This rule adds the feature [+PL] to the movements /1/, /3/, /A/ and /E/. These movements now become associated with syllables that are marked as [+stress].

Some configurations whose pitch movements have been contracted on one syllable, through the application of (R3), may have two [+PL] features in the same location. Rule (A2) takes care of the necessary simplification.

161

(A2) If a syllable contains two pitch movements with the feature [+PL], this feature is deleted for the second movement.

Thus only one [+PL] feature is assigned to the combinations /1&A/ and /1&E/. The [+PL] feature that is assigned to some pitch movements plays a role in the process of Tune and Text association to the extent that a given contour and a given sentence are compatible only if they agree in the number of their accentual features.

6.1.5.2 Syntactic bracketing

Some pitch movements are to be associated with elements of clause structure, in particular with a clause boundary (CB) or with a clause-internal phrase boundary (PB). The following rules express this co-occurrence.

(S1) If the [−rise] pitch movement of the prefix is not combined with the preceding [+rise] on one syllable, it receives the feature [+PB].

The assignment of the feature [+PB] is interpreted by the phonetic-implementation rules in such a way that the pitch movement concerned coincides with the first syllable after the PB, or with the pause – if present – at the PB.

(S2) The [+rise] pitch movement of the Suffix or of Root /2/ and the [−rise, −early, +late] movement of Root /3C/ receive the feature [+CB].

The assignment of [+PL], [+PB] and [+CB] features to the appropriate movements constrains the association of Text and Tune in the following way. A given contour and a given clause are compatible only if they agree as to the number of their accentual features. Any mismatch will result in too many or too few prominent syllables. Furthermore, for a given contour to be compatible with a clause, the number of its phrase boundary features (PB) should be equal to or smaller than that of the clause. The contour need not contain a clause boundary feature (CB), although a clause always has one.

For example, the contour in (1) is compatible with the utterance in (2).

(1)   / 1   B / / 1   A   2/
       +PL +PB   +PL +PL +CB

(2)   X   Y   Z   X   Y   Z
                 PB   CB
    +stress   +stress +stress

A concrete instance may be the following:

(3)   1   B   1   A   2

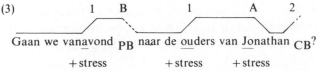

Gaan we vanavond $_{PB}$ naar de ouders van Jonathan $_{CB}$?

     +stress   +stress   +stress

In this instance the agreement between (1) and (2) is maximal. A contour such as in (4) is also compatible with the clause in (2) even if it lacks the $[+PB]$ feature.

(4)   / 1&B /   / 1   A   2/
         +PL   +PL +PL +CB

With a contour of this type the PB boundary in (2) will not be marked melodically. However, as we have argued in chapter 4 under proposition 8, the melodic highlighting of syntactic boundaries is not obligatory. Therefore, a contour such as (5) is also compatible with clause (2), even if it lacks both a $[+PB]$ and a $[+CB]$ feature.

(5)   / 1&B /   / 1   A   /
        +PL   +PL +PL

From the point of view of the clause, it follows that a given clause is compatible with a contour if it has the same number of accentual features and if the number of its syntactic boundary features is equal to or larger than that of the contour.

6.1.6 Phonetic implementation

The features with which the essential properties of the pitch movements are defined have so far been used as classificatory labels. Now they will be given phonetic content. In the preceding sections we have introduced the features [rise, early, late, full, spread] and we have shown how they enter into the definition of ten distinct pitch movements. Since the pitch movements are explicitly defined in terms of standardized physical values (F_0 over time), it follows that the features themselves can be interpreted in the same concrete terms. For instance, $[+rise]$ implies a positive rate of change of F_0, which should be of the order of 50 ST/s if $[-spread]$. If $[+full]$ is interpreted as an excursion size of six semitones, it follows that in its phonetic implementation a pitch movement has a duration of 120 ms. If the $[+rise]$ movement is $[+early, -late]$ the peak of the F_0 rise will be situated at 50 ms beyond the vowel onset of the syllable. Thus it becomes possible to actually simulate the operation of the grammar in an algorithm that computes an acceptable-sounding pitch contour for an arbitrary input sentence.

Such an algorithm was designed for Dutch by H.W. Zelle (Zelle, de Pijper and 't Hart, 1984), and for British English by N.J. Willems (Willems, Collier and 't Hart, 1988). The Dutch algorithm mirrors rather closely the generative process of the grammar and it implements the principles of Text and Tune association. It offers the user a selection of 'basic patterns', roughly corresponding to the inventory of Root configurations, with or without the Suffix. The program asks questions about the number and the locations of the sentence stresses and about the nature and the site of syntactic boundaries. It then suggests variants for the basic forms: a gradual instead of a steep change; a high instead of a low contour onset; a 'flat' hat instead of two 'pointed' hats, etc. For the sake of convenience, the program operates with the short-hand symbols for the pitch movements, but it could be made to work with feature constellations.

6.1.7 Evaluation

The grammar of Dutch intonation that we presented in chapter 4 is essentially a device that produces well-formed strings of pitch movements. Its output is a phonetic transcription or short-hand notation for all possible pitch contours. It may be considered as *observationally adequate*. Its chief merit resides in the fact that it reduces the overall perceptual impression of speech melody to a sequence of discrete, local pitch events. It also clarifies the internal structure of a contour in terms of configurations (Prefix, Root and Suffix); and it accounts for our intuition that there are families of contours that relate to the same intonation pattern by highlighting their common Root. However, it generates different sorts of Prefixes and several variants of the same Root in mere juxtaposition and does not formally define what they have in common. In this respect it is not *descriptively adequate*.

The preceding sections of this chapter have introduced an alternative analysis that attempts to remedy these shortcomings. The most prominent feature of this alternative is that it introduces a systematic distinction between basic and derived forms. Thus, for instance, some dozen different Prefixes are reduced to just one basic representation, $/1B/$, and all the observable variation is derived by rule. Another illustration is the treatment of the hat-pattern Root. The earlier version of the grammar simply listed all the possible variants as:

$$/(1)(E)^n(5) \left\{ \begin{array}{c} A \\ D \end{array} \right\} /$$

The present description postulates only one basic form, $/1A/$, and provides a set of rules by which all the variants can be derived. In this way formal expression is given to the intuition that such variants are essentially similar.

The new version of the grammar is also more explicit as to how the melodic layer of an utterance may interact with other levels of linguistic organization, i.e. accentuation and syntax.

These improvements go some way towards making our analysis descriptively more adequate. Yet it could be objected that our phonetic description does not really advance our understanding of intonation as a linguistic phenomenon. What is still lacking is a phonological description of the melodic facts. Indeed, phonologists such as Ladd (1983a) and Gussenhoven (1988), who have taken an interest in our melodic description of Dutch, have criticized it for 'its excessive concern with perceptual and acoustic details' and for 'its inability to express many phonological and functional generalisations' (Ladd, 1983a: 721). In a similar way, Gussenhoven (1988) tries to show that his phonological approach is better equipped to explain intonational phenomena than a description which is based on the categorization of surface phonetic forms. In principle, the phonologists could be right: intonation may exhibit deep structural properties that do not overtly manifest themselves acoustically nor perceptually and can only be brought to light through linguistic analysis. Indeed, ever since the early days of structuralism we have witnessed numerous examples of how a phonological analysis can unravel interesting facts about language that are hidden under the facts of speech.

6.2 Ladd's analysis of the 'hat pattern'

In the second part of this chapter we present a brief critical assessment of Ladd's phonological analysis of the Dutch 'hat pattern'.

Ladd's (1983a) article is an attempt to design a set of phonological features for the phonetic-linguistic description of intonational contrasts. In order to demonstrate both the necessity and the usefulness of his taxonomy, he applies his framework to the analysis of a sample of pitch contours in English, Dutch and standard Hungarian (as well as the Transylvanian variety of that language). As far as Dutch is concerned, Ladd wants to demonstrate how a great number of different pitch contours that are derived from the 'hat pattern', can be described in such general terms that their membership of the same intonational category (i.e. 'neutral declarative') receives a natural explanation.

According to Ladd, the basic phonological structure of the hat pattern is /H_0 HL/: a sequence of two tonal targets with the features *H*(igh) and *L*(ow), which can be preceded by any number of *H*s. Thus, for example, a 'flat-hat' contour such as (contour 1) exhibits the structure /H HL/. It ends in a low boundary tone (L%).

(contour 1)   '1'   'A'

Dat huis is te koop   (p. 747)

H   HL   L%

(That house is for sale)

On the other hand, a 'pointed-hat' contour for the same utterance (with two accents) is analysed as the sequence /HL HL/, as in (contour 2).

(contour 2)

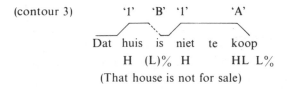

Notice that the sequence /HL HL/ in (contour 2) is not an *expansion* of the basic structure /H_0 HL/, but a *repetition* of the minimal combination /HL/. This is to say that (contour 1) contains one 'hat pattern', while (contour 2) consists of two. Although both contours are perfectly interchangeable in most cases, they are analysed differently, so that a generalization is being missed.

Ladd discusses two other variants of the hat pattern that do result from an expansion of the basic /H_0 HL/ structure. One is a contour with a delayed fall 'B', as in (contour 3); the other is a terrace-shaped contour containing the half-fall 'E', as in (contour 4).

(contour 3)   '1' 'B' '1'   'A'

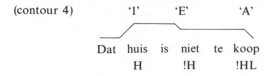

Ladd argues that his analysis 'expresses the fundamental similarity between this pattern and the "flat hat"' (p. 747). This generalization is achieved by inserting a prosodic boundary (%) between the first two Hs, thus making fall 'B' superfluous and eliminating by the same token an irrelevant phonetic detail. Ladd wonders, however, whether the prosodic boundary should be accompanied by a low boundary tone (L%), to ensure low pitch after it. Such a measure is indeed necessary, since the pitch is allowed to be high or low after a boundary and hence has to be specified. In our view, then, the addition of L% is nothing more than a relabelling of fall 'B': in the phonetic analysis fall 'B' is a pitch movement that marks the boundary, while in the phonological analysis L% is a boundary that results in pitch lowering.

The terrace-shaped (contour 4) is accounted for as a variant of the hat pattern by assigning it the basic structure /H_0 HL/, 'with the added feature [downstep] throughout the utterance domain' (p. 748).

(contour 4)   '1'   'E'   'A'

Dat huis is niet te koop
      H   !H   !HL

166

'Downstep' is a feature of peak scaling: it indicates that the H target has to be lowered (transcribed as '!H'). The problem with Ladd's analysis of (contour 4) is that it does not agree with the domain of application of 'downstep' as stated above. The first H must indeed not be downstepped, but it is hard to see why this target should fall outside the utterance domain. On the other hand, the last H (in !HL) must not be downstepped either. The final fall may phonetically be small-sized, but it lowers the pitch to the level of the lower declination line, and therefore it sounds like a genuine 'A', not 'E'. It is the endpoint of the pitch movement, not its onset-peak value that determines its perceptual identity as either 'A' or 'E'. In other words, the commendable attempt at generalization fails because it overlooks a fundamental phonetic difference.

A more extensive critical appraisal of Ladd's proposals is given in Collier (1989), who also discusses a number of similar shortcomings in Gussenhoven's analysis. For our present purpose it is sufficient to notice that the proposed reanalysis is defective in more than one respect. Possibly, these shortcomings are only errors of analysis, and do not undermine the principle that a phonological analysis is both necessary and possible. But they do show that a 'top-down' approach, going from underlying forms to systematic-phonetic representations, should never lose sight of the phonetic reality at the bottom end of the derivational process. Therefore, in working out an alternative analysis of our own, we have proceeded in a 'bottom-up' fashion, and have avoided positing underlying representations that depart from surface phonetic forms.

6.3 General discussion

In this chapter we have presented two attempts to insightfully describe the melodical features of Dutch. Our own proposal (section 6.1) purports to express a number of generalizations in terms of basic contours from which alternative contours are derived by rule. What constitutes a 'basic contour' is defined by the grammar: it is any sequence of pitch movements that can be generated by its first rule, (R1).

Basic contours minimally consist of an obligatory Root, which can be preceded by a Prefix and – in certain cases – be followed by a Suffix. Their maximum expansion is obtained by multiplying the number of Prefixes. A first generalization expressed by the grammar is that there is only one basic Prefix, /1B/, while other Prefix configurations are derived by rule. A second generalization is that each Root is represented by just one basic form, whereas alternative shapes result from the application of optional rules. A third generalization is that the number of Roots corresponds to the number of intonation patterns. The basic form of the Prefix and the Roots is chosen on the basis of two criteria: (a) they contain the minimum number of pitch movements; and (b) they correspond to the most common form of appearance. Because of these criteria of simplicity and frequency it can be said that the basic shape of a contour represents its 'canonical form'. Many other generalizations concern operations of substitution, combination, deletion, insertion and the like, which appear to hold for more than one pitch movement or in more than one melodic context. It should be borne in mind, however, that the most drastic generalizations have been achieved at an earlier stage, where the infinite variety of physical changes in F_0 are reduced to just ten perceptually relevant pitch rises and falls (ch. 3 and 4). The perceptual criterion leads to such a high degree of data reduction that the resulting descriptive units, the pitch movements, can hardly be simplified any further. It can only be attempted to systematize their combinatory possibilities, and that is exactly what the intonation grammar does. This grammar, already presented in chapter 4, was further refined in this chapter by introducing a distinction between 'basic' and 'alternative' contour shapes.

In section 6.2 we presented Ladd's attempt to carry the generalizations one step further, to what may be called a 'phonological' level of intonation analysis. One major difference between his phonological and our phonetic description resides in the choice of descriptive units. Ladd and other phonologists (e.g. Gussenhoven, Liberman, Pierrehumbert) replace pitch movements by stationary pitch targets: H (high) and L (low). These two basic units, especially the H target, have inherent properties that can be modified by rule. Thus, for instance, the pitch peak inherent in H can become [+ delayed], or the high pitch level of H can be 'downstepped', which results in a small local fall. Essentially, the inventory of melodically important units is reduced to just two pitch targets, which are scaled in frequency (position in the speaker's pitch range) and in time (position in the syllable). This scaling is indispensible in order to establish a link with observable phonetic variation.

Our major point of criticism against Ladd's approach to Dutch intonation is that the reduction of perceptually distinct pitch movements to just two abstract pitch targets undermines the identity of the intonation patterns. The latter differ categorically from each other because their Roots consist of essentially different pitch movements. If such distinct movements are derived from invariably the same underlying Hs or Ls they can only be variants of each other, and so must be the contours that are composed of them.

Notwithstanding present shortcomings, the phonological strive for melodic simplification and generalization deserves further attention, since it can – in principle – reveal insights that are still lacking. An important measure for the success of the phonological enterprise will be whether the proposed solutions are psycholinguistically and phonetically plausible.

7

Applications

7.0 Introduction

In the preceding chapters we described how an analysis was made of the melodic properties of Dutch and British English intonation, and gave the results in terms of 'intonation grammars'. We explained what these grammars are claimed to do.

In this chapter we will concentrate on applications. It will become apparent that these should not be thought to lie exclusively in the domain of speech technology.

We will make a dichotomy between already existing and implemented applications, on the one hand (7.1), and potential applications, on the other (7.2). With respect to the first, we will deal with a course of Dutch intonation, to be used by, among others, people who want to study Dutch as a second language (7.1.1). Subsequently, we will present some promising results obtained in investigations on the use of an intonable electrolarynx by laryngectomees (7.1.2). Section 7.1.3 will deal with the incorporation of some rules for Dutch intonation in aids for otherwise vocally handicapped people. In section 7.1.4 we will illustrate how the experimental phonetic analysis may help to focus on a number of specific intonation-related linguistic problems.

With respect to potential applications, we will briefly discuss (section 7.2.1) why we expect that Dutch students of foreign languages will benefit from the explicit description of the melodic possibilities as obtained in the analysis of intonation in languages other than Dutch. Next, in section 7.2.2, we will deal with the possibilities of automatic stylization of F_0 curves to be applied in visual feedback in favour of learners of a second language, or of congenitally deaf children. In section 7.2.3, we will try to illustrate how an attempt to develop full synthesis by rule of intonation, in e.g. a text-to-speech system, may not only constitute a goal in itself, but may also have a heuristic value, since it confronts us with the limits of our knowledge. Section 7.2.4 discusses the possibilities of applying prosodic analysis to automatic speech-recognition. In a final section (7.3) we will try to formulate some conclusions.

7.1 Existing applications

7.1.1 Acquisition of intonation

The acquisition of the intonation of a foreign language was until recently dependent on 'listen-and-repeat' drills. The disappointing result, as it was often felt, was that students talented in imitation, who would have been able to learn it anyhow, even without these drills, could profit from them, but the others would not.

Now that explicit descriptions have become available, it has become possible to choose a different approach: viz. one in which the student is told explicitly what the rules are, in order to have them internalized. Such a strategy could be called a cognitive approach. One may have good hopes that, thanks to this new dimension, the other students can also be taught the essentials of the intonation of the target language.

The results of our investigation do not merely consist of a description of the physical events: it has also been our aim to give an account of the perceptual structure in F_0 curves. Consequently, we thought it possible to provide the student with explicitly described perceptual targets. We have therefore tried to devise a teaching method that would make the student conscious of the same features of intonation as those that are relevant to the native ear.

A possible objection to such a method could be, that, in general, too much concentration on isolated events in a training programme might prevent the student from learning to produce the aimed-at activity in an integrated way, the problem being that the overall result cannot be obtained by simply gluing together the various isolated movements one after the other. This may be true for the acquisition of the techniques for quite a number of human skills. However, our investigations on intonation have revealed that the perceptually relevant pitch movements do constitute recombinable elements, to the effect that, within the sequential constraints of a pattern, fully acceptable pitch contours are obtained. In writing the 'Cursus Nederlandse Intonatie' (Collier and 't Hart, 1981) we therefore concentrated on what we expected to be essential for the student: to be able to hear these elements so analytically that their perceptual targets could be established.

It is interesting to mention here an experiment by De Bot (1982), in which sixty-seven students of Dutch or education had to imitate the intonation of fifty English sentences as spoken by a native speaker. The aim was to investigate the influence of three conditions: (a) an instruction of a quarter of an hour in which subjects were made aware of the phenomenon of intonation by means of a number of auditorily and visually presented demonstrations; (b) the same instruction plus auditory and visual presentation of the intonation of the sentences that served as examples to be imitated, as well as auditory and visual feedback of the subjects' imitations during the task itself; (c) the same instruction plus presentation of the examples and feedback of their own productions, but only auditory, not visual. The subjects' performance during two tests, one before and one after the 'treatment' was judged by a panel of trained listeners by means of scores on a five-point scale. A control group received no treatment between pretest and post-test.

The outcome was that the control group gave no significant difference between the tests, whereas conditions (a), (b) and (c) all gave significant, although small improvements. Interestingly, condition (a), mere instruction, resulted in larger improvement than what was achieved additionally by means of the feedback techniques.

No data are available of formal tests of how helpful the use of our course of Dutch intonation is for foreign students of Dutch, but on the basis of De Bot's outcome for condition (a), it may be expected that giving a full course rather than making the student aware of intonation during a quarter of an hour will lead to further improvements.

The fact that feedback had only a relatively small additional effect in this experiment may be due to the circumstance that the displayed F_0 curves were obtained from the raw data by only applying a slight median-smoothing, to eliminate obvious outlying values. We expect that a confrontation with stylized pitch contours in a visual-feedback condition will turn out to give larger effects, since in that case, the student will immediately see the perceptually relevant movements as discrete events. We will take up this point later, in section 7.2.2.

7.1.2 An intonable electrolarynx (for Dutch)

An encouraging result has been obtained in an examination of the possibility of teaching laryngectomees to control an intonable electrolarynx. To this end, the circuitry of a commercially available (monotonous) electrolarynx (EL) has been modified in such a way as to automatically take care of as much of the F_0 variation as possible. EL users are taught to keep the apparatus switched on only while actually speaking, and to switch it off at pauses, also within sentences. When switched on, the EL automatically produces declination, and each time it is switched off, a declination reset is made. Of the abrupt changes of F_0, the sizes and the durations are built in to match the standard values for Dutch. The only parameter left to be controlled by the user is the timing of the abrupt movements. Yet another parameter is under the control of the user, but in an implicit way: the declination resets are not abrupt, but are brought

171

about by means of an exponential function with a decay time of about one second. The effect is that the amount of the reset is dependent on the duration of the pause, and this results in a welcome variation in the starting frequencies of the stretches between pauses within an utterance; only with pauses of more than a second is the reset complete.

The apparatus is devised in such a way that it is possible to make variants of the hat pattern in the first place. In principle, it can generate specimina of some other basic patterns as well. But the training concentrates on controlling the movements '1' and 'A' for accentuation, and '2' and 'B' for boundary marking. As we have shown earlier (table 4.1), the crucial differences are in the timing. Not only does the user have to execute in a conscious way, with his fingers, what he used to do unconsciously with his laryngeal muscles, he should also have enough insight into the analytic detail of the intonation planned by himself to know precisely where and when to press or release the buttons.

This implies that the user should run through an abbreviated version of the Dutch intonation course before practical training can begin. Van Geel (1983) describes the first attempts to find out whether the rather complicated task can be mastered at all. He developed a systematic training programme with three EL speakers, and did some tests to evaluate the naturalness and the intelligibility of the resulting speech. One participant was eighty-six years old and moderately hard of hearing. Despite these handicaps, he managed to produce fairly well intonated EL speech after thirty training sessions of about seventy-five minutes each (including theory lessons, pitch-perception training and learning to speak with the EL as such, i.e. without pitch control). Another participant (fifty-seven years old, with no hearing deficiency) became a brilliant example of what can be achieved under the best circumstances; after forty sessions his performance was almost perfect. The third participant (aged seventy-six) nearly attained correctly intonated spontaneous EL speech in twenty-one lessons, but had to discontinue the sessions due to illness.

One of the remarks Van Geel makes is that in EL speech the use of discrete pitch movements is to be preferred to a continuous inflection control. It has appeared that it is virtually impossible to learn to manipulate an EL with continuous control, like the one produced in the US (Gandour and Weinberg, 1982). Van Geel's success has provided additional evidence for the validity of our approach by showing the psychological legitimacy of the descriptive units, i.e. the perceptually relevant pitch movements. This implies that the applicability of an EL with pitch control requires an analysis of the intonation system of the language at issue in terms of standardized and discrete perceptually relevant pitch movements, and an intonation grammar that combines them. Next, an appropriate subset of movements and their combination possibilities should be chosen, mainly on the basis of their frequency of occurrence. For British English the set of movements and the grammar are now available, and a comparable analysis of German intonation is under way. However, more (technical) research is still necessary in view of the complicating factor that British English, and most probably German too, uses three declination levels instead of two, as does Dutch. This means that maintaining the important principle that what can be done automatically must be done automatically requires a more sophisticated implementation of these levels than was necessary for a Dutch EL.

7.1.3 An aid for the vocally handicapped

In the Netherlands there are several tens of thousands of people, who, some temporarily, some permanently, lack the ability to speak in a normal way. In view of the importance of spoken communication for human functioning, it seemed worth while to investigate to what extent at least some of these people might profit from an apparatus that can do the speaking for them. At IPO, prototypes of a keyboard-to-speech system have been built on the basis of diphone synthesis, and as a matter of course, these devices had to allow the user to enrich the speech output with melodic variation (Deliege and Waterham, 1986; Deliege, Speth-Lemmens and Waterham, 1988; Deliege, 1989).

Again, the principle of maximum automation applies, be it only because the user is preoccupied with the need to type his messages in a quasi-phonetic spelling (a grapheme-to-phoneme converter was not yet available at the time the first prototype was built). A second principle is that the user, contrary to the EL speaker, need not know explicitly which F_0 variations have to be executed: these must be derived from higher-level notions, and, as was explained in chapter 4, these are intra-utterance clause boundaries, intra-clause phrase boundaries and locations of pitch accents.

It was decided that the apparatus would speak as soon as the complete message had been typed in. To signal 'end of message', a full stop is typed, or a question mark, if a final rise is wanted (irrespective of the utterance being a question or not). In longer utterances, the user is encouraged to type a comma at one or more appropriate places. The hope is, of course, that the commas will coincide with clause boundaries, but this will not always come about. The system will in any case interpret them as clause boundaries, and will provide the melodic line each time with an intonational marker appropriate to a clause boundary. The desired variation in the various possible ways of marking clause boundaries can, in principle, be obtained either by choosing randomly among the alternatives, or having this choice be dependent on some variable property of the input string. We opted for the latter, and decided to take into account the distance, in number of syllables, between the last pitch accent before the boundary and the boundary itself. A further option consists of having the system speak the beginning of the message while the user types in the next clause: in such a case a declination reset is made between the two clauses.

We cannot expect the user to mark clause-internal phrase boundaries, let alone to decide whether or not these should be marked intonationally. This could have posed a problem, but, fortunately, the Dutch intonation system has free variation between the use of the abrupt fall 'B' (in which case its location should be known), and of the gradual fall 'D', which extends itself over all the syllables between two accent-lending rises. Thus, by choosing the gradual falls in the keyboard-to-speech system, although introducing a simplification, we still comply with the rules, and therefore, the resulting contours are fully acceptable. These contours have a sawtooth-like shape: for each pitch accent an abrupt rise, followed by a gradual fall till the next pitch accent occurs. An exception is formed by the last two accents: after the penultimate accent, with rise '1', F_0 follows the high declination line, and makes a final fall 'A' for the last pitch accent. If a question mark is added to the input string – the decision is up to the user – the contour will end in a final rise '2'.

The third kind of information needed is the location of the pitch accents. This time we must ask the user to select for himself which words he wants to be accented, and whenever it is a polysyllabic word, to indicate which syllable bears lexical stress. He is instructed to type a single inverted comma (') in front of the lexically stressed syllable of each word that should, in his opinion, receive a pitch accent. In the near future, it will be sufficient to locate the single inverted comma at the beginning of the whole word.

As was stated before, this synthesis system used diphones as elementary building blocks. These are stored in a memory in formant-coded form, in frames of 10 ms duration, together with markings with respect to segment boundaries. Thus, the standardized position of each of the pitch movements, e.g. for a rise '1' from 70 ms before to 50 ms after the vowel onset, can be accounted for automatically. Since the duration of each of the diphones is known, the entire duration of the clause or sentence that is to be synthesized can be calculated as soon as the typing in of the string of characters has been finished. On that basis, the slope of the declination line can be calculated, as is explained in chapter 5.

Clearly, the system has a number of limitations. Since the contours obtained are all based on one variant of the hat pattern, the melodic variation is not very impressive. But if we keep in mind that the relative frequency of occurrence of the hat pattern, even in spontaneous speech, is nearly 70 per cent, this limitation is less severe than might have been the case if the various different basic patterns had been evenly distributed. Another drawback is that, although quite a few things are controlled automatically, the locations of pitch accents and clause boundaries have to be fed in manually. This drawback is compensated to a certain extent, however, since the user can evoke special effects by using a pitch-accent distribution different from a standard solution as generated by a rule system.

7.1.4 Application in linguistic and phonetic research

Our contribution to the study of pitch in speech constitutes a necessary, but only modest, first step towards tackling more central issues of intonation. Our analysis has only brought to light which variations of F_0 can occur in speech; it has only to a limited extent answered the question under which conditions which pitch movements can take place, or the question under which conditions which basic patterns are used. And although we know now how accentuation and the marking of prosodic boundaries are connected to particular melodic phenomena, we do not know which words should or may be accented in a given context, or whether or not a given syntactic boundary should or may be marked intonationally. Yet, it is our conviction that the more central issues can hardly be approached fruitfully without the tools lower-level analysis has provided: it is useless to try to examine why or under what conditions potentially communicatively relevant events occur in intonation as long as the means to describe these events adequately are lacking. Quite a few authors have shown that they share this opinion by using our results in their own investigations. For instance, Boves and Jansen (1973) used our notational system and our grammar of intonation in an attempt to interpret the planning of intonation in a fragment of spontaneous speech, in which F_0 was measured by means of a cepstrum technique. Van Katwijk (1974), Kruyt (1985), Terken (1985), Baart (1987), Nooteboom and Kruyt (1987) and Terken and Nooteboom (1987) did their experiments on the accentuation of Dutch with the aid of artificial contours built according to our rules. Likewise did De Rooij (1979), in his study on marking of prosodic boundaries; and Geluykens (1985, 1987) in his on the relation between [± Question] and intonation, in British English (see also ch. 4). Maeda (1976), in his study of the intonation of American English, was strongly inspired by the stylization method which is the core of the IPO approach, and was the first to show that this method can also be fruitful in the analysis of the intonation of languages other than Dutch. The implementation of his rules in Klatt's (1980) synthesis system has given a substantial improvement to its intonation, as compared with the earlier performance. Maassen (1985) evaluated the gain in intelligibility of speech of deaf children by, among other things, providing their speech with intonation according to our rules (see also Maassen and Povel, 1985). Keijsper (1984a, 1984b) has tried to give an account of some relations between forms of Dutch pitch contours (described by means of our transcription system), on the one hand, and syntactic structure, and hence various aspects of interpretation, on the other. Earlier (1983), she tried to translate Bryzgunova's (1977) description of Russian intonation into IPO terminology. Two other authors who wanted to develop a further linguistic analysis of the phonetic data from IPO have already been mentioned in chapter 6: Ladd (1983a) and Gussenhoven (1988). Finally, Van Wijk and Kempen (Van Wijk and Kempen, 1985; Van Wijk, 1987) have incorporated our results in a psycholinguistic model for the generation of sentences.

We believe that the substantial improvement of the possibilities of giving an adequate auditory transcription of speech pitch is largely due to the fact that a set of suitable descriptive units have become available. In principle, it has now become possible for investigators who do not have computer facilities at their disposal, to participate in intonation research on a much firmer basis than in the past. Of course, the transcriber should first make himself familiar with the inventory of the movements, and with the combination restrictions as recorded in the grammar. The familiarity should be so intense that the transcriber has learnt to recognize the various movements. In this, help can be offered in specific training, which has now become possible, thanks to the explicitness of the description, as can be found in our 'Cursus Nederlandse Intonatie'.

7.2 Potential applications

7.2.1 Second-language acquisition by Dutch students

For quite a number of languages, intonation research has resulted in intonation courses on behalf of those who want to study any of these languages as a second language. British English has a long and rich tradition in intonation research, witness the two rather recent intonation courses by Halliday (1970) and O'Connor and Arnold (1973). Well known also are, for example, the courses by Von Essen (1956) and by Stock and Zacharias (1982) for German, and the one by Bryzgunova (1977) for Russian intonation.

These courses have in common that, due to the lack of technical facilities at the time they were written, they are based largely on auditory observations by the authors, and not on an experimental analysis as has become possible nowadays. We believe that on the basis of the IPO approach, with its emphasis on the perceptually relevant pitch movements, it should be possible to design intonation courses for foreign languages in which very explicit instructions are given about where to produce which kinds of pitch movement. Moreover, since the intonation of the target language has been (British English) or is being (presently German and Russian) analysed by means of the same experimental techniques as applied in the study of Dutch intonation, the intonation systems of Dutch, on the one hand, and of each of the target languages, on the other, can be compared in a feasible and reliable way. This may make it easier to take into account mother-tongue interferences that can be expected to occur.

7.2.2 Automatic stylization for use in feedback systems

At the end of section 7.1.1, we made the supposition that the use of stylized contours in the visual presentation of a teacher's model intonation and in the visual feedback of the student's imitations would give better results than can be obtained with only slightly smoothed F_0 curves. This introduces the challenge of trying to develop algorithms with which close-copy stylizations, or even standardized stylizations, can be derived automatically from the output of a pitch meter (Hermes and 't Hart, 1987). We believe that it is worthwhile trying to take up that challenge, especially in view of tackling the problem of teaching intonation to congenitally deaf children. For them, feedback seems indispensible if one wants to correct the very abnormal F_0 variations they usually produce. The wish to apply such correction has recently found support in an investigation by Maassen (1985; also Maassen and Povel, 1985) in which it is shown that, although correction of the intonation alone does not notably improve the intelligibility of the speech of the deaf, there is a tremendous positive interaction between segmental and suprasegmental correction, if applied together.

7.2.3 Synthesis by rule

In our laboratory, a number of computer programs are available for making artificial pitch contours. These can be divided into two categories: viz. programs for expert users and programs for those people who, for some reason or other, want spoken output with intonation of their choice, but who are not phoneticians themselves, let alone have specialized knowledge of intonation. The former programs offer facilities ranging from full freedom in every respect, as is necessary for making close-copy stylizations, to freedom only with respect to the combinatory possibilities of the movements, which themselves have standard specifications. In the latter programs, the intonation grammar (for either Dutch or British English) is built in, to the effect that all variants of all basic patterns can be made in fully standardized form, with the automatic exclusion of ungrammaticalities. As can be seen in the literature of the past, investigators wanting to do psycholinguistic experiments on sentence comprehension, and fearing that (improper) intonation might constitute a disturbing factor, often avoided using stimuli with very large variations of F_0. That is, in principle at least, no longer necessary when use is made of these programs.

However, necessary input requirements for the latter programs are the choice of a basic pattern, the locations of vowel onsets of syllables that will be accented, of boundaries one wishes to mark, and of the end of voicing of syllables that are to receive a continuation rise or a final rise. Additionally, there are a great number of options for the generation of any of the variants of the basic patterns, as far as these are grammatically correct in the chosen melodic context. Although the grammatical constraints are monitored by the program itself, non-expert researchers who want intoned spoken output still have to take care of quite a few detailed input requirements beyond their primary interest. This brings us to the point that, ultimately, one wants to have at one's disposal a system in which intonation can be generated entirely by rule. As will be clear, such a system has a far wider field of application than is covered by expert and non-expert researchers: in the foreseeable future, computer systems and other apparatus will communicate with their users partly in spoken language, rather than exclusively in written form on a screen.

Within phonetic research, synthesis by rule is not only an aim in itself, viz. a demonstration that the acoustic analysis of the speech signal in terms of the properties that are relevant and indispensable for perception is mastered. It also has a heuristic value, since it shows the limits of one's knowledge, in the sense that incomplete knowledge will betray itself sooner or later in the generation of unacceptable output. We will elaborate on this by means of a few examples about boundary marking.

The sentence in (1) is taken from 'The fable of the north wind and the sun' (IPA, 1962):

(1) [Ze kwamen over<u>een</u> [dat degene [die het <u>eerst</u> erin zou
S_0 – – – – – – S_1 – – – – S_2 – – – – – –
     They   agreed   that the one   who   the   first   in it   would

slagen [de reiziger zijn mantel te doen <u>uit</u> trekken,]]   de
   – – S_3 – – – – 0   0   0 0   0   1   ∅   ∅ S_3 S_2 ∅
succeed the traveller his cloak to make take off,   the

sterkste zou worden geacht.]]
  A   0   0   0 0   0 0 S_1 S_0
strongest would be considered.

The general tendency to connect the last two accents by means of a 'flat hat' (rise '1', high declination line, fall 'A') is so strong, that the syntactic boundary between the two accents, here between *uittrekken* and *de sterkste*, is not intonationally marked. We have observed this phenomenon in many more cases.

Of course, the speaker keeps the option to mark the boundary by means of a temporal cue (pause, or preboundary lengthening, or both). In the example given, it is, for that matter, quite possible to make an additional intonational marking, e.g. in one of the ways in (2):

(2) . . . te doen uittrekken, de sterkste . . .

0	0	1	Ø Ø	B	1&A	0	
0	0	1&A	0 2B	0	1&A	0	
0	0	1&A	0 2	Ø	A	0	

Surprisingly, despite this strong general tendency, the use of a flat hat may in some cases lead to an unintended interpretation, or simply to unacceptability. An example of the first is (3):

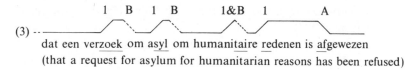

(3) -- dat een verzoek om asyl om humanitaire redenen is afgewezen
(that a request for asylum for humanitarian reasons has been refused)

in which it seems as if the grounds for the refusal were humanitarian reasons. It is not yet clear under which general conditions the use of a flat hat for the last two accents should be avoided.

In the sentence from the fable, we have seen that intonational marking of the boundary between *uittrekken* and *de sterkste* is optional. That is not the case with another boundary in this sentence, viz. the one between *die het eerst erin zou slagen* and *de reiziger zijn mantel te doen uittrekken*. If one wishes to mark that boundary, the simplest way to do it is to use a fall 'B' between *slagen* and *de reiziger* (in our usual terminology, it would read: early in *de*). The alternative to such a location of 'B', that is to say if one does not wish to mark the boundary, consists in having 'B' follow immediately after the preceding rise (of type '1'), which occurs on the word *eerst* in this sentence. After resynthesis with a standardized contour, it appeared that marking the boundary by means of a fall 'B' on *de* sounds unacceptable, and that not marking it (making '1&B' on 'eerst') is the only acceptable solution.

This is an example of a clear syntactic boundary, which may very well be marked temporally, but nevertheless must not be marked by intonational means. This restriction seems to be related to the fact that this boundary is situated within the subordinate clause *die het eerst . . . te doen uittrekken*:

intonational marking would unjustly evoke the suggestion in the listener that a return to the main clause takes place.

Apart from the problem of determining which boundaries should be marked, may be marked or should not be marked, much the same problem exists for accentuation. But, of late, this problem has been studied intensively, also in the Netherlands (Kruyt, 1985; Terken, 1985; Baart, 1987; Nooteboom and Kruyt, 1987; Terken and Nooteboom, 1987), and the results justify the expectation that in future text-to-speech systems the number of errors (incorrect accentuation and also incorrect de-accentuation) can be kept limited, and that such errors will not always be very disturbing to the listener.

Synthesis by rule is now being implemented in a project (SPICOS) in which Siemens Munich, Philips Research in Brussels and Hamburg and IPO are cooperating in order to develop office computer-systems with spoken input and output, using the German language. The assignment of pitch accents is partly based on a syntactic analysis of the message the system is going to produce as output. In order to enable the system to formulate a correct answer to the question spoken by the user, this input message is submitted to a semantic analysis. This offers the possibility of basing the pitch-accent assignment also on the content of the input message (Van Hemert, Adriaens-Porzig and Adriaens, 1987).

As has been mentioned already, speech synthesis by rule can be used as a heuristic device. Suppose, for instance, that we want to test a specific hypothesis about the location of a pitch accent, or of a boundary marker and/or a declination reset, or about variable sizes in a sequence of pitch movements. These are all examples of phenomena not accounted for by the rules of the grammar of intonation. An immediate test is then possible by means of artificially generated pitch contours, partly built according to the rules of the grammar, partly according to the hypotheses to be tested. If the resulting contours sound well-formed, the hypothesis is confirmed, if not, it must be rejected. The direct verdict is possible by virtue of the grammatical correctness of the generated contours: the aspect of them that is constructed according to the hypothesis is, so to say, the only experimental variable. The judgment about whether or not the resulting contours sound well-formed can be achieved rather easily by virtue of the extreme stylization, which will lay bare any error in a contour in a most merciless way. Thus, what once constituted a research objective has now found an application as a research tool to develop rules for higher structural properties of the prosodic system.

7.2.4 Application in automatic speech recognition

It is widely appreciated that in automatic speech recognition a useful contribution should be expected from prosodic analysis. As it is explained in a very thoughtful review by Lea (1980), prosodic analysis can be helpful in, roughly, three different respects:

1. The detection of stressed syllables may serve to provide 'islands of phonetic reliability' (p. 170) or 'anchors for reliable phonetic analysis' (p. 201): their segmental phonetic analysis can be trusted more than that of other syllables.
2. As far as the speech-recognition system makes an appeal to syntactic information, 'prosodic analysis offers an independent way of acoustically detecting some aspects of syntactic structure' (p. 167), i.e. one is not confined to basing the segmental analysis on potentially incorrectly recognized words. Therefore, it should be considered profitable to try to divide discourse into sentences, and sentences into clauses and phrases.
3. Prosodic features constitute cues to voicing, to locations of syllable nuclei (vowels), to occurrences of glottal stops, etc.

However plausible this may be, three important requirements should be met in order to make a prosodic analysis applicable. First of all, as a matter of course, the technical facilities should be sufficiently refined to detect the sometimes very subtle effects of prosody on the speech signal. The second requirement is that the analysis system must be instructed what to look for; in order to be able to recognize a specific contribution of any of the prosodic parameters, the underlying prosodic system of the language at issue should be sufficiently known. The third requirement is that it should be possible to evaluate the extent to which the prosodic analyser is successful as such, and the extent to which it contributes to the automatic speech-recognition process.

We will try to illustrate these points. To find out where pitch accents have been realized, it is not enough to look for rather abrupt changes of F_0, since, as we know, the position with respect to the syllable is a critical parameter. Therefore, apart from changes of F_0, syllable boundaries and vowel onsets and offsets have to be detected with sufficient accuracy. Rietveld (1983) reports that in a first evaluation test of a pitch-accent detector, with short sentences spoken by two male speakers, a hitting percentage of 93.5 was achieved, with 5.9 per cent false alarm. Upon the inclusion of longer sentences and two more (male) speakers, these percentages became 85.8 and 10 respectively. Such figures can only be obtained in a comparison to human accent assignment, but even the use of a panel of trained listeners does not warrant unequivocal results. This explains some of the discrepancies between automatic and human accent detection. Anyway, we must fear that finding the 'islands of phonetic reliability' may constitute a problem in itself.

In prosodic analysis aiming at the detection of aspects of syntactic structure, recognition of boundary markers plays an important part. One of the boundary markers of Dutch, viz. the continuation rise followed by a fall, will, especially in rapid speech, readily be confused with the complex '1&A' (or 'pointed hat'). Thus, for this problem it is also necessary to apply a syllabification algorithm, in order to decide whether the rise (and the subsequent fall) is situated early or late in the syllable, and in order to establish syllable lengthening. For the latter, it is, furthermore, necessary to know how long syllables are when not lengthened before a boundary.

Probably, it will be very difficult to detect a boundary marker that takes the form of a declination reset. In as far as listeners are able to detect this phenomenon at all, they might be considered to do this on the basis of an analysis of a rather long stretch of speech, large enough to make an estimation of the course of the lower declination line. If the identification of a declination reset in the acoustic signal cannot take place until a close-copy stylization has first been made, and that is the present situation, one can imagine that its automatic detection will only become a possibility once the technique of automatic stylization has been sufficiently mastered.

For Dutch, there is as yet no experience with automatic recognition of prosodic boundary markers. It should be expected that it will be difficult to evaluate the performance of such a detection algorithm, since there is no certainty about which boundary may or should be marked, and which may or should not.

Although it is beyond doubt that prosodic features constitute cues to voicing, to locations of vowels, to occurrences of glottal stops, etc., it remains to be seen whether even the best pitch meters, which operate with a time window of several tens of milliseconds, are able to measure these subtle phenomena in a reliable way. And apart from that, although quite a bit is known about the perceptual processing of these cues, their acoustic characterization is established to a far lesser extent.

We have discussed above mainly the technical problems of prosodic analysis, the lack of background knowledge in some cases, and the potential difficulties in evaluating the prosodic analyser. No wonder, then, that as yet nobody has got round to the second part of the third requirement listed earlier in this subsection, viz. the evaluation of the contribution of prosodic analysis to automatic speech recognition.

But, in any case, from these considerations it appears that accepting this single challenge, viz. the application of prosodic analysis for the use of automatic speech recognition, confronts us with quite a few more fundamental problems that also need to be brought to a solution for the use of other applications.

7.3 Conclusions

At the end of this chapter, especially of its second part, we feel we cannot escape the conclusion that there is a tremendous amount of work still to be done. For instance, the writing of a course for Dutch students of British English has not yet been started, although that was one of the main objectives from the very outset of our study of British English intonation. Much the same holds for Russian. At some time, an experiment will have to be done to provide support for our conviction that an explicit, cognitive course of intonation will appear to be more helpful than the traditional listen-and-repeat method.

Our efforts to achieve automatic stylization have seen good progress, but in order to be applicable in speech training for deaf children, it should be implemented in hardware, to make real-time operation possible. Next, a training programme will have to be designed that will cope with many uncertainties, among others those resulting from the fact that congenitally deaf people do not know what pitch is. Only then can a beginning be made on the evaluation of both the apparatus and the training programme.

The stylization method was developed originally as a tool to analyse the intonation system in terms of feasible descriptive units. Thanks to the continuous application of a perceptual criterion, even the standardized stylizations sound acceptable, to the effect that, although the primary aim of the analysis was not to collect precepts for the control of F_0 in synthetic speech, yet our findings can successfully be used in the generation of artificial speech. However, when it comes to the synthesis of entire texts, the repetition of standard contours, derived from only one basic pattern, may give rise to a lower acceptability than is measured in an experiment with isolated sentences, with a systematic alternation of basic patterns. Therefore, efforts are still being invested in attempts to develop rules for variation of excursion, and for a feasible alternation of boundary markers (Collier and Terken, 1987). Moreover, experiments are being carried out to examine the conditions in which microintonation phenomena (including vowel-intrinsic pitch) may contribute to liveliness and naturalness in artificial intonation.

As for the application of prosodic analysis in automatic speech recognition, we have pointed out in 7.2.4 that even before an investigation of the question whether or not such an analysis may give a favourable contribution, a lot of problems inherent to the analysis itself will have to be solved first.

Nevertheless, the finding of a solution to each of the many problems still extant would have been far more remote without the results of the work done in the past.

8

Conclusion

In this final chapter we would like to assess the main points that we have tried to make in establishing the feasibility of approaching pitch in speech from a mainly perceptual point of view.

This focussing on perception was initially inspired by the dissatisfaction we felt with the state of the art at the start of our programme. At this juncture, in the concluding chapter of this book, we wish to sketch briefly, by way of summary, the main considerations that have led to the choice of our approach. These are to be found in the inadequacy of the methods used within a linguistic framework, based on the primacy of semantic functioning, the principle of distinctivity (8.1).

In close connection with this we were faced also with the lack of an adequate apparatus to account for the melodic properties of the surface phenomenon of intonation, which were generally dealt with in an impressionistic way (8.2). By means of the technique of experimental phonetics, in studying the listeners' intonational skill, we believe we are in a better position to account ultimately for the way language users cope with speech melody (8.3; 8.4).

In the following sections we will deal successively with the two major lines of approach, prevalent in the field, which can be indicated as top down versus bottom up, leading to our endeavour to reconcile them in our own attempt at modelling the listeners' way of processing intonational cues in speech.

8.1 Top down

If it is the legitimate object of the linguistic approach to account for the language users' competence, this should include the prosodic domain. However, contrary to the situation in phonology and morphosyntax, heuristic devices are not so easy to come by within the field of prosody. Indeed, at the start of our endeavour some twenty years ago, the linguistic literature had not provided the kind of consensus in this field as compared to that established in studying segmental phenomena based on the criterion of distinctivity. The age-old device of distinguishing between statements, questions and commands, constituting the handiwork in linguistic studies of earlier generations has clearly been shown to be too poor a means to account for the rich details in cueing points of interest by prosodic means.

The broad field of prosodic cues allows a large amount of freedom to language users to alter or modify their intended vocal expressions in any number of dimensions, including mood, awareness of purpose to elicit reactions from a partner in a dialogue, to reach and convince an audience, to emphasize and contrast any chosen part of a message, none of which clearly can be accounted for within a purely linguistic framework. Such a narrow linguistic approach would seem to run the risk of seriously underdifferentiating important intonational cues.

Moreover, the principle of distinctivity, which proved to be such a helpful tool in clearly discriminating discrete differences in meaning on the phonological level, cannot easily be upheld: here the existence of a lexicon provides a reliable criterion to decide whether or not observed segmental differences give rise to differences in meaning of words; such a yardstick is not available in intonational matters. Indeed, the principle of distinctivity is incapable of differentiating the subtle shades of meaning involved on a prosodic level. Moreover, in order to account for attitudinal meaning, one needs a gradual scale instead of all-or-none decisions.

We therefore decided, for the time being, to lay aside this top-down approach, and to start from the other end, working bottom up. This option in reality involved shelving the principle of distinctivity until later and concentrating on trying to discover structural properties of the phenomenal attributes of intonation in terms of melodic characteristics, to be established in perceptual experiments.

The reason for staying clear of the allegedly straight and narrow path of linguistic distinctivity is not so much the intricacy inherent in meaning as such, formidable as it is, in particular with respect to intonation, but rather the absence of a reliable tool with which to reveal the actual pitch phenomena that are supposed to represent the various shades of meaning. Therefore, the major reason for adopting our own way of dealing with intonation was that, at the start of our efforts, the basic groundwork, on which a reliable description of the characteristics of intonation would have to depend, was lacking.

8.2 Bottom up

In attempting to set up the necessary framework for acquiring reliable tools in describing intonational features we were aware of the opposite danger to underdifferentiation: viz. that of overdifferentiating pitch cues that may be shown to obtain in the speech signal under laboratory conditions in a psychoacoustic setting. What we find in looking at pitch from the experimental-phonetic point of view is an embarrassing wealth of details as can be found in an accurate acoustic rendering of the fluctuations of the vocal cords. To be able to see the wood for the trees, we felt the need to try to reduce the available acoustic data within a manageable framework. In the words of Bolinger (1986), as compared with the segmental field, where there is a consensus about the descriptive entities, nothing so ready to hand is found in intonation and therefore, 'More than anywhere else structure has to be imposed', (Preface, viii).

Now the question arises: how can this structure be brought about? We believe we have solved this in trying to establish, by experimental means, a model of how listeners deal with pitch cues in speech. For this purpose we rather heavily leaned on what we termed our basic assumption. This implied that only those F_0 changes would be regarded as possible candidates for a descriptive model of pitch for which a link could be established with commands to the vocal-cord mechanism, which as such are under the speaker's control. The notion of this link was subsequently backed by studying, of necessity, the production aspect of intonation, including that of declination.

Within this setting the task of mapping a model of the listener's behaviour with regard to pitch in speech could be envisaged. The decision as to what is relevant for the listener has resulted from the outcome of listening experiments with the help of manipulated pitch contours. In this way, we were able to sustain our conviction that whatever information is ultimately carried by pitch is not confined to linguistic distinctivity.

Through this bottom-up approach, we arrived at the perceptually relevant pitch movements on which to base the descriptive device we were looking for.

In this respect an analogy with the practice found in segmental phonetics may be helpful. In this field it has long been common practice to distinguish in phonetic transcription between 'broad' and 'narrow'. In prosodic matters, a broad framework would allow one to distinguish such categories as exclamation, question, surprise, etc. A narrow approach, in its attempt to account for more detailed information, runs the risk of bringing to light small variations whose communicative significance remains unclear.

Returning to the segmental level, the issue of narrow vs broad can be easily decided. For phonological purposes there is every reason to confine oneself to a broad framework of transcription, based on the principle of distinctivity. Within such an approach, there would be no need to distinguish the various free variants of the /r/ phoneme, e.g. as flapped, rolled or fricative. In our experimental approach towards intonational phenomena, we found that there is a fairly large amount of freedom to opt for variants belonging to one and the same basic intonation pattern. Since many of these variants have been shown

186

to be perceptually distinct, they cannot be left out of the account. The notation of such variants is provided for in a narrow transcription. In this connection the expressive means used in writing through bold type, italics and the conventions of punctuation can be seen to illustrate a broad approach. As such, they are insufficient to indicate specific renderings for which a narrow transcription would have to be made available.

There are two limiting conditions that have to be regarded. On the one hand, there are the psychoacoustic thresholds and tolerances that have to be accounted for in any perceptually based study of pitch. On the other hand, there are the clear cases of linguistic relevance that *ipso facto* deserve to be included. As such, these two limiting conditions are the first candidates to be seriously considered in any attempt to map the universal characteristics making up a theory of intonation.

8.3 Reconciling top down and bottom up

It is in the intermediate field between psychoacoustics and linguistics that we believe the mapping of intonational features can best be undertaken. To a large extent this field was almost *terra incognita* when we started our efforts. The main problem to be solved was to make available a reliable descriptive tool that was so far missing. Earlier attempts had been based on impressionistic data which may be unreliable, as was shown by the well-known study of Lieberman (1965). The other issue to be squarely faced was that of the relationship between phonetic and functional aspects. As illustrated by Crystal (1969), starting from function proved to be very tricky indeed. Our solution to the dilemma was to make perceptual tolerances the decisive factor in setting up criteria for how to cut up the pitch continuum into discrete pitch movements. This could only be achieved by means of the basic assumption, the link with commands to the vocal apparatus. It enabled us to come up eventually with a tool kit of pitch movements, being the discrete descriptive units, and a firm link with listeners' judgments about the acceptability of synthesized contours. This method of analysis by synthesis afforded us a powerful means of carrying out data reduction from the wealth of details found in any acoustic recording. So, sticking to our tools of the experimental phonetician, but with a clear eye for the need to regard functional aspects, we have come up with a grammar of intonation, a model of possible and perceptually tested intonation patterns that are the core of the native speakers' intonational competence. It allows them to make contact with the verbal content by means of well-formed intonational features afforded by the intonation grammar and impinging, as far as pitch accents are involved, on segments selected by both pragmatic and syntactic requirements.

187

There are a number of issues that have been decided on the way, and which may be mentioned once more in an effort to characterize the way in which our approach is intended to be taken as a proper means of tackling the overall problem of accounting for pitch in speech. It is the pitch movements, rather than levels, which provide the cues to listeners for whatever segment in an utterance is supposed to be made salient by carrying a pitch accent. We believe that the proper way of dealing with the acoustic correlate of pitch, F_0, should be rendered in terms of semitones rather than Hertz, due to the mechanism of the auditory apparatus. The phenomenological datum that pitch is heard as a continuum in spite of the presence of voiceless and therefore pitchless interludes is taken care of by means of the notion of pitch contours. The sequential regularities involved in such contours are generated by the intonation grammar. The concentration on pitch as one of the prosodic features at the exclusion of others has been a working hypothesis that has stood the test very well. This is by no means intended to imply that a proper study of the contribution of temporal features, including pauses, can be overlooked. On the contrary, our efforts in working towards a fully automated text-to-speech conversion have taught us that a lot can and should be gained by just such a study. However, the absence of a reliable frame for rendering pitch has forced us to take this restricted approach.

So far, we have only mentioned the way in which we believe we have succeeded in bridging a gap that was apparent through the absence of a reliable, thoroughly tested tool to account for the possible and acceptable pitch patterns characteristic of any particular language. We feel that we have supplied an overall framework for dealing with the intonational features of not only Dutch, but also of British English, German and Russian, as subsequent studies have shown.

Studies in the field of what has come to be known as language and speech technology have already constituted a touchstone for what we believe we know and, even more stringently, for what we do not yet know about the interface between linguistic parameters and phonetic output. For instance, these studies have created the necessity of establishing rules for, among other things, accentuation in an ultimate text-to-speech conversion. But what is still lacking is a model of how to make sure where the accents should fall in a verbal message. It is in this context that linguistic analyses can be experimentally verified for their validity in attributing markers for prosodic implementation: since the output is speech, rather than the end product of a set of rules written on paper, a text-to-speech conversion system provides a very strict and instructive criterion for the adequacy of the linguistic analysis.

Extracting the information about accentuation and boundary marking automatically, as is required in a complete text-to-speech conversion system, is a research aim in which we are at present engaged in a nationally coordinated programme, set up for this specific aim. In this endeavour we have come to realize, more strongly than we felt it beforehand, that the relations between linguistic and phonetic aspects, or in broader terms between language and speech, constitute an exciting and perennial problem. In the course of working to its solution we feel sure that only co-operation between linguists and phoneticians working in concert can hope to bear fruit.

8.4 Integrating the linguistic code and the speech signal

In this final section we will once more face the problem of how to match considerations from the formal and functional points of view. Instead of allowing the primacy of a structural-linguistic approach, we have arrived at the conclusion that the communicative function is of paramount importance in tackling the task of putting structure on the recalcitrant phenomena of pitch cues in speech.

Our general position is the following.

We firmly believe that speech as such is the most natural way in which linguistically encoded messages can be framed. As in every coding system, the resulting messages are prone to errors coming from three possible sources: the encoder, the decoder, and what can be indicated as noise. This noise can be either external, due to unfavourable communication conditions, for example noisy surroundings, or internal, as for example caused by inherent ambiguity of the linguistically encoded message. The way to overcome these disturbing influences is constituted by the introduction of redundant information, so that parts of the message that are obscured can still be decoded successfully by making use of the redundancies supplied in it. Natural speech is an extremely efficient code in this respect, since it is usually abundant in just this matter of supplying extra cues to secure communication. Prosodic features as such are eminently capable of taking care of this aspect. After all, most language communication can also be brought about in written form in which prosodic cues are not involved. Intonation, as one of the constituents of speech prosody, can be removed from a speech message without seriously damaging the linguistic content of the message. Such is, for example, the case in speech which is artificially supplied with a monotone. Nevertheless, since natural speech is accompanied by pitch modifications, it stands to reason to study this phenomenon in an effort to impose a structure on the seemingly capricious pitch excursions of the vocal mechanism. What the student of intonation is faced with, therefore, is the task of grasping the impact of how this extra information contained in the surface output of natural speech is brought about. It is our conviction that while intonation is always embedded in a linguistically couched frame, clauses, sentences and the like, it follows its own rules, which differ from one language to another. Nevertheless, these rules will

189

always be determined to a certain extent by the same abstract properties inherent in all intonation systems. Hence it falls legitimately within the scope of linguistics. On the other hand, since intonation is an observable property of speech, it stands to reason that its study falls within the field of phonetics.

As we see it, intonation highlights the background information that is provided by the linguistically encoded message. Through the wear and tear of speech communication over the ages, intonation is eminently suited to fulfil this additional role of providing extra cues to safeguard efficient transmission of linguistic information contained in the verbal message. On the one hand, it enables listeners in noisy surroundings, where more speakers are involved, to focus on the message carried by one speaking source. On the other hand, it will help in assessing the frame of mind in which speakers address them.

What we have tried in our endeavours is to acknowledge the various layers that can be observed in the multitude of possible intonational functions that are concomitant with the linguistic message. We have tried as much as possible to focus on the most rewarding aspect in order to provide an opening to disentangle this complex phenomenon. We believe we have found this in concentrating on the perceptual point of view, since speech is, after all, meant to be heard. We have come up with a descriptive model in which the regularities that can be observed in studying what listeners make of intonational cues can be accounted for. The resulting intonation grammar occupies the borderline between speech and language, since the linguistic background and the intonational capacity of foregrounding should be seen to match as closely as possible. However, since there is a great amount of freedom for language users to choose patterns of their own for pragmatic reasons, no obvious one-to-one relationships can be expected between linguistic background and phonetic foreground. The study of this pragmatic aspect and the way it impinges on the actual choice of patterns and configurations being made is an interesting research objective for the near future. Such research will therefore have to concentrate on high-quality synthesis in fully automated text-to-speech systems. As indicated above, such systems will make greater demands than can be supplied by the availability of a melodical model. Nevertheless, we expect that the strategy of assigning a central role to the perceptual criterion will continue to prove fruitful.

We have experienced that, in spite of generally large tolerances, the selective acuity of the perceptual mechanism forces us to supply information over and above that of assigning proper placement of pitch accents. In particular, additional information is required regarding direction, slope, and temporal alignment of pitch movements in quantitative terms. With this object in mind, we are once again back on phonetic ground, from which we started our research effort in the first place.

References

Abramson, A.S. 1978. Static and dynamic acoustic cues in distinctive tones. *Language and Speech* 21: 319–25.

Adriaens L.M.H. 1984. A preliminary description of German intonation. *IPO Annual Progress Report* 19: 36–41.

Appels, R. 1985. Een productiemodel voor declinatie en onderzoek naar declinatie-resets binnen spraakuitingen. Internal report no. 498, Institute for Perception Research (IPO).

Armstrong, L.E. and I.C. Ward 1926. *A handbook of English intonation.* Leipzig/Berlin: Teubner; Cambridge: Heffer, 1931.

Atal, B.S. and S.L. Hanauer 1971. Speech analysis and synthesis by linear prediction of the speech wave. *Journal of the Acoustical Society of America* 50: 637–55.

Atkinson, J. 1978. Correlation analysis of the physiological features controlling fundamental voice frequency. *Journal of the Acoustical Society of America* 63: 211–22.

Baart, J.L.G. 1987. Focus, syntax, and accent placement. Unpublished doctoral dissertation, University of Leyden.

Bachem, A. 1937. Various types of absolute pitch. *Journal of the Acoustical Society of America* 9: 146–51.

Baer, T. 1979. Reflex activation of laryngeal muscles by sudden induced subglottal pressure changes. *Journal of the Acoustical Society of America* 65: 1271–5.

Basmajian, J. and G. Stecko 1962. A new bipolar indwelling electrode for electromyography. *Applied Physiology* 17: 849ff.

Berg, J. van den 1968. Mechanism of the larynx and the laryngeal vibrations. In B. Malmberg (ed.) *Manual of phonetics*, 278–308. Amsterdam: North Holland.

Bezooijen, R.A.M.G. van 1984. *Characteristics and recognizability of vocal expressions of emotion.* Dordrecht: Foris.

Bolinger, D.L. 1957/8. Intonation and grammar. *Language Learning* 8: 31–7.

1958. A theory of pitch accent in English. *Word* 14: 109–49.

1986. *Intonation and its parts*, vol. 1. Stanford: Stanford University Press.

Borden, G. and K.S. Harris 1983. *Speech science primer: physiology, acoustics and perception of speech.* Baltimore/London: Wilkins and Wilkins.

Borst, J.M. and F.S. Cooper 1957. Speech research devices based on a channel vocoder. *Journal of the Acoustical Society of America* 29: 777 (abstract).

Bot, C. de 1982. Visuele feedback van intonatie. Unpublished doctoral dissertation, Catholic University of Nijmegen.

References

Bouma, H. 1979. Perceptual functions. In J.A. Michon, E.G.J. Eijkman and L.F.W. de Klerk (eds.) *Handbook of psychonomics*, vol. 1, 427–531. Amsterdam, New York, Oxford: North Holland.

Boves, L. and P. Jansen 1973. Onderzoek van de intonatie in spontane spraak. In S.G. Nooteboom (ed.) *Proceedings of the Spring meeting of the Dutch Society of Phonetic Sciences, May 25, 1973*, 9–20.

Breckenridge, J. 1977. The declination effect. *Journal of the Acoustical Society of America* 61, supplement 1: S90 (abstract).

and M.Y. Liberman 1977. The declination effect in perception. Unpublished paper, available from Bell Laboratories, Murray Hill, N.J.

Bryzgunova, E.A. 1977. *Zvuki i intonacija russkoj reci, 3-e izdanie, pererabotannoe.* Moskva: Russkij Jazyk.

Burns, E.M. 1974. In search of the *shruti*. *Journal of the Acoustical Society of America* 56, supplement 1: S26 (abstract).

Cardozo, B.L. 1972. Topics in audition. *IPO Annual Progress Report* 7: 1–4.

and R.J. Ritsma 1965. Short-time characteristics of periodicity pitch. In D.E. Commins (ed.) *Proceedings of the fifth International Congress on Acoustics, Liège, 1964*, paper B37.

Chomsky, N. 1957. *Syntactic structures.* Janua Linguarum 4. 's-Gravenhage: Mouton.

Cohen, A., R. Collier and J. 't Hart 1982. Declination: construct or intrinsic feature of speech pitch? *Phonetica* 39: 254–73.

and J. 't Hart 1965. Perceptual analysis of intonation patterns. In D.E. Commins (ed.) *Proceedings of the fifth International Congress on Acoustics, Liège, 1964*, paper A16.

1967. On the anatomy of intonation. *Lingua* 19: 177–92.

Collier, R. 1970. The optimum position of prominence-lending pitch rises, *IPO Annual Progress Report* 5: 82–5.

1972. From pitch to intonation. Unpublished doctoral dissertation, Catholic University of Leuven.

1974. Laryngeal muscle activity, subglottal air pressure, and the control of pitch in speech. *Status report on speech research, Haskins Laboratories* 39/40: 137–70.

1975a. Physiological correlates of intonation patterns. *Journal of the Acoustical Society of America* 58: 249–55.

1975b. Perceptual and linguistic tolerance in intonation. *IRAL* 13: 293–308.

1977a. La Perception de l'intonation anglaise par des anglophones et néerlando-phones. *Actes des 8èmes journées d'étude sur la parole, Aix-en-Provence*, 139–46.

1977b. The perception of English intonation by Dutch and English listeners. *IPO Annual Progress Report* 12: 69–73.

1983. Some physiological and perceptual constraints on tonal systems. In B. Butterworth, B. Comrie and O. Dahl (eds.) *Explanation for language universals.* Amsterdam: Mouton.

1984. Fysiologische verklaringen voor F_0-declinatie. In A.C.M. Rietveld (ed.) *Proceedings of the Autumn meeting of the Dutch Society of Phonetic Sciences*, 14–20.

1985. The setting and resetting of the baseline. *Annual Bulletin of the Research Institute of Logopedics and Phoniatrics, Tokyo* 19: 111–32.

1987. F_0 declination: the control of its setting, resetting and slope. In T. Baer, C.

Sasaki and K.S. Harris (eds.) *Laryngeal function in phonation and respiration*, 403–21. Boston: Little and Brown.

1989. On the phonology of Dutch intonation. In F.J. Heyvaert and F. Steurs (eds.) *Worlds behind words, Essays in honour of Prof. Dr F.G. Droste*, 245–59. Louvain: Leuven University Press.

and C.E. Gelfer 1984. Physiological explanations of F_0 declination. In M.P.R. van den Broecke and A. Cohen (eds.), *Proceedings of the tenth International Congress of Phonetic Sciences*, 354–60, Dordrecht/Cinnaminson: Foris.

and J. 't Hart 1971. A grammar of pitch movements in Dutch intonation. *IPO Annual Progress Report* 6: 17–21.

and J. 't Hart 1972. Perceptual experiments on Dutch intonation. In A. Rigault and R. Charbonneau (eds.) *Proceedings of the seventh International Congress of Phonetic Sciences, Montreal 1971*, 880–4. The Hague/Paris: Mouton.

and J. 't Hart 1975. The role of intonation in speech perception. In A. Cohen and S.G. Nooteboom (eds.) *Structure and process in speech perception*, 107–23. Berlin/Heidelberg/New York: Springer.

and J. 't Hart 1981. *Cursus Nederlandse Intonatie*. Leuven/Amersfoort: Acco/De Horstink.

and J.M.B. Terken 1987. Intonation by rule in text-to-speech applications. In J. Laver and M.A. Jack (eds.), *Proceedings of the European Conference on Speech Technology, Edinburgh, 1987*, vol. 2, 165–8.

Cooper, F.S. 1962. Speech synthesizers. In A. Sovijärvi and P. Aalto (eds.), *Proceedings of the fourth International Congress of Phonetic Sciences, Helsinki, 1961*, 3–13. The Hague: Mouton.

Cooper, W.E. and J.M. Sorensen 1977. Fundamental frequency contours at syntactic boundaries. *Journal of the Acoustical Society of America* 62: 682–92.

1981. *Fundamental frequency in sentence production*. New York/Heidelberg/Berlin: Springer.

Cranen, B. and L. Boves 1985. Pressure measurements during speech production using semiconductor miniature pressure transducers: impact on models for speech production. *Journal of the Acoustical Society of America* 77: 1543–51.

Cruttenden, A. 1986. *Intonation*, Cambridge: Cambridge University Press.

Crystal, D. 1969. *Prosodic systems and intonation in English*. Cambridge: Cambridge University Press.

1975. *The English tone of voice*. London: Edward Arnold.

and R. Quirk 1964. *Systems of prosodic and paralinguistic features in English*. The Hague: Mouton.

Deliege, R.J.H. 1989. An experimental keyboard-to-speech system for the speech impaired. *Speech Communication* 8: 81–90.

and R.P. Waterham 1986. Application of speech synthesis and resynthesis in two speech communication aids. *IPO Annual Progress Report* 21: 110–15.

I.M.A.F. Speth-Lemmens and R.P. Waterham 1988. Ontwikkeling en evaluatie van twee communicatiehulpmiddelen met spraakuitvoer. *Logopedie en Foniatrie* 60: 220–4.

Di Cristo, A. and M. Chafcouloff 1977. Les faits microprosodiques du français: voyelles, consonnes, coarticulation. *Actes des 8èmes journées d'étude sur la parole, Aix-en-Provence*, 147–58.

References

and D. Hirst 1986. Modelling French micromelody. *Phonetica* 43: 11–30.

Dorman, M.F., L.J. Raphael and A.M. Liberman 1979. Some experiments on the sound of silence in phonetic perception. *Journal of the Acoustical Society of America* 65: 1518–32.

Dudley, H.W. 1935. Signal transmission. USA patent 2,151,091.

Duifhuis, H., L.F. Willems and R.J. Sluyter 1978. Measuring pitch in speech. *IPO Annual Progress Report* 13: 24–30.

  1982. Measurement of pitch in speech: an implementation of Goldstein's theory of pitch perception. *Journal of the Acoustical Society of America* 71: 1568–80.

Essen, O. von 1956. *Grundzüge der hochdeutschen Satzintonation*. Ratingen: A. Henn.

Flanagan, J.L. and M.G. Saslow 1958. Pitch discrimination for synthetic vowels. *Journal of the Acoustical Society of America* 30: 435–42.

Fujisaki, H. 1960. Automatic extraction of fundamental period of speech by auto-correlation analysis and peak detection. *Journal of the Acoustical Society of America* 32: 1518 (abstract).

  and H. Sudo 1971. Synthesis by rule of prosodic features of connected Japanese. In *Proceedings of the seventh International Congress on Acoustics*, vol. 3, 133–6. Budapest: Akadémiai Kiadó.

Gandour, J. and B. Weinberg 1982. Perception of contrastive stress in alaryngeal speech. *Journal of Phonetics* 10: 347–59.

Geel, R.C. van 1983. Pitch inflection in electrolaryngeal speech. Unpublished doctoral dissertation, University of Utrecht.

Gelfer, C.E., K.S. Harris and T. Baer 1987. Controlled variables in sentence intonation. In T. Baer, C. Sasaki and K.S. Harris (eds.), *Laryngeal function in phonation and respiration*, 422–35. Boston: Little and Brown.

Gelfer, C.E., K.S. Harris, R. Collier and T. Baer 1985. Is declination actively controlled? In I. Titze and R. Scherer (eds.), *Vocal fold physiology: biomechanics, acoustics and phonatory control*, 113–26. Denver: Denver Center for the Performing Arts.

Geluykens, R. 1985. Questioning intonation. MA thesis, University of Reading.

  1987. Intonation and speech act type. An experimental approach to rising intonation in queclaratives. *Journal of Pragmatics* 11: 483–94.

Gill, J.S. 1959. Automatic extraction of the excitation function of speech with particular reference to the use of correlation methods. In L. Cremer (ed.), *Proceedings of the third International Congress of Acoustics, Stuttgart, 1959*, 217–20. Amsterdam (1962): Elsevier.

Gold, B. 1962. Computer program for pitch extraction. *Journal of the Acoustical Society of America* 34: 916–21.

Goldstein, J.L. 1973. An optimum processor theory for the central formation of the pitch of complex tones. *Journal of the Acoustical Society of America* 54: 1496–516.

Greiffenberg, M. and N. Reinholt Petersen 1982. The effect of high and low vowels on the fundamental frequency: some preliminary observations. *Annual Report of the Institute of Phonetics of the University of Copenhagen* 16: 101–11.

Grützmacher, M. and W. Lottermoser 1937. Über ein Verfahren zur trägheitsfreien Aufzeichnung von Melodiekurven. *Akustische Zeitschrift* 2: 242–8.

Gussenhoven, C. 1984. *On the grammar and semantics of sentence accents*. Dordrecht: Foris.

194

1988. Adequacy in intonation analysis: the case of Dutch. In N. Smith and H. van der Hulst (eds.) *Autosegmental studies on pitch accent*, 95–121. Dordrecht: Foris.

Hadding-Koch, K. and M. Studdert-Kennedy 1964. An experimental study of some intonation contours. *Phonetica* 11: 175–85.

Halliday, M.A.K. 1970. *A course in spoken English: intonation*. London: Oxford University Press.

Harris, K.S. 1981. Electromyography as a technique for laryngeal investigation. In C.L. Ludlow and M.O. Hart (eds.) *ASHA reports: proceedings of the Conference on the Assessment of Vocal Pathology*, vol. 11, 70–86.

't Hart, J. 1976a. Psychoacoustic backgrounds of pitch contour stylization. *IPO Annual Progress Report* 11: 11–19.

1976b. How distinctive is intonation? In Rudolf Kern (ed.) *Löwen und Sprachtiger*, 367–83. Louvain: Edition Peeters.

1981. Differential sensitivity to pitch distance, particularly in speech. *Journal of the Acoustical Society of America* 6: 811–21.

and A. Cohen 1973. Intonation by rule: a perceptual quest. *Journal of Phonetics* 1: 309–27.

and R. Collier 1975. Integrating different levels of intonation analysis. *Journal of Phonetics* 3: 235–55.

and R. Collier 1979. On the interaction of accentuation and intonation in Dutch. In E. Fischer-Jørgensen, J. Rischel and N. Thorsen (eds.) *Proceedings of the ninth International Congress of Phonetic Sciences, Copenhagen*, vol. 2, 395–402.

S.G. Nooteboom, L.L.M. Vogten and L.F. Willems 1982. Manipulations with speech sounds. *Philips Technical Review* 40: 134-45.

Hemert, J.P. van, U. Adriaens-Porzig and L.M.H. Adriaens 1987. Speech synthesis in the SPICOS project. In H.G. Tillmann and G. Willée (eds.) *Analyse und Synthese gesprochener Sprache: Vorträge im Rahmen der Jahrestagung 1987 der Gesellschaft für linguistische Datenverarbeitung e.V., Bonn*, 34–9. Hildesheim: Olms.

Henning, G.B. 1966. Frequency discrimination of random-amplitude tones. *Journal of the Acoustical Society of America* 39: 336–9.

Hermes, D.J. 1988. Measurement of pitch by subharmonic summation. *Journal of the Acoustical Society of America* 83: 257–64.

and J. 't Hart 1987. Visual feedback of intonation for the deaf by means of automatically stylized contours. *Research News – International Journal of Rehabilitation Research* 10: 457–8.

Hess, W. 1983. *Pitch determination of speech signals*. Berlin/Heidelberg/New York/Tokyo: Springer.

Hill, D.R. and N.A. Reid 1977. An experiment on the perception of intonational features. *International Journal of Man–Machine Studies* 9: 337–47.

Hirst, D.J., Y. Nishinuma, and A. Di Cristo 1979 (abstract). The estimation of intrinsic F_0: a comparative study. In E. Fischer-Jørgensen, J. Rischel and N. Thorsen (eds.) *Proceedings of the ninth International Congress of Phonetic Sciences, Copenhagen*, vol. I, 381.

Hombert, J.-M. 1976. Development of tones from vowel height. *UCLA Working Papers* 33: 55–66.

House, A.S. and G. Fairbanks 1953. The influence of consonant environment upon the secondary acoustical characteristics of vowels. *Journal of the Acoustical Society of America* 25: 105–13.

References

Houtsma, A.J.M. 1980. Pitch of harmonic two-tone complexes of unequal amplitudes. *Journal of the Acoustical Society of America* 68, supplement 1: S110 (abstract).
Hunt, F.V. 1935. A direct-reading frequency meter for high speed recording. *The Review of Scientific Instruments* 6: 43–6.
IPA 1962. The principles of the International Phonetic Association. Dept of Phonetics, University College, London.
Issachenko, A.V. and H.-J. Schädlich 1970. *A model of standard German intonation.* The Hague/Paris: Mouton.
Johnson, S.C. 1967. Hierarchical clustering schemes. *Psychometrica* 32, no. 3: 241–54.
Jones, D. 1909. *Intonation curves.* Leipzig: Teubner.
  1957. *An outline of English phonetics*, 8th edn. Cambridge: Heffer.
Kaiser, L. 1940. Biological and statistical research concerning the speech of 216 Dutch students. *Archives Néerlandaises de Phonétique Experimentale*, vol. 16: 1–211.
Katwijk, A.F.V. van 1974. *Accentuation in Dutch.* Assen: Van Gorcum.
  and G.A. Govaert 1967. Prominence as a function of the location of pitch movement. *IPO Annual Progress Report* 2: 115–17.
Keijsper, C.E. 1983. Comparing Dutch and Russian pitch contours. *Russian Linguistics* 7: 101–54.
  1984a. Vorm en betekenis in Nederlandse toonhoogtecontouren I. *Forum der Letteren* 25: 20–37.
  1984b. Vorm en betekenis in Nederlandse toonhoogtecontouren II. *Forum der Letteren* 25: 113–26.
Klatt, D.H. 1973. Discrimination of fundamental frequency contours in synthetic speech: implications for models of pitch perception. *Journal of the Acoustical Society of America* 53: 8–16.
  1980. Real-time synthesis by rule. *Journal of the Acoustical Society of America* 68, supplement: S18 (abstract).
Kruyt, J.G. 1985. Accents from speakers to listeners. Unpublished doctoral dissertation, University of Leyden.
Ladd, D.R. 1980. *The structure of intonational meaning: evidence from English.* Bloomington: Indiana University Press.
  1983a. Phonological features and intonational peaks. *Language* 59: 721–59.
  1983b. Levels vs configurations, revisited. In F.B. Agard, G. Kelly, A. Makkai and V. Becker Makkai (eds.) *Essays in honour of Charles F. Hockett*, 49–59. Leiden: Brill.
  1984. Declination: a review and some hypotheses. *Phonology Yearbook* 1: 53–74.
  and K.E.A. Silverman 1984. Vowel intrinsic pitch in connected speech. *Phonetica* 41: 31–40.
Ladefoged, P. 1967. *Three areas of experimental phonetics.* London: Oxford University Press.
Lea, W.A. 1980. Prosodic aids to speech recognition. In W.A. Lea (ed.) *Trends in speech recognition*, 166–205. Englewood Cliffs, NJ: Prentice Hall.
Ledeboer van Westerhoven, L.F. 1939. Melodie und Tonbewegung im Niederländischen. In E. Blanquaert and W. Pée (eds.) *Proceedings of the third International Congress of Phonetic Sciences, Ghent, 1938*, 489–96. Ghent: Laboratory of Phonetics.
Lehiste, I. 1970. *Suprasegmentals.* Cambridge, MA: MIT Press.

1975. The phonetic structure of paragraphs. In A. Cohen and S.G. Nooteboom (eds.) *Structure and process in speech perception*, 195–206. Berlin/Heidelberg/New York: Springer.

and G.E. Peterson 1961. Some basic considerations in the analysis of intonation. *Journal of the Acoustical Society of America* 33: 419–25.

Léon, P. and Ph. Martin 1969. *Prolégomènes à l'étude des structures intonatives*. Studia Phonetica 2. Montréal/Paris/Bruxelles: Marcel Didier.

Leroy, L. 1984. The psychological reality of fundamental frequency declination. *Antwerp Papers in Linguistics* no. 40, University of Antwerp, Belgium.

Liberman, A. and I. Mattingly 1985. The motor theory of speech perception revised. *Cognition* 21: 1–36.

Lieberman, Ph. 1965. On the acoustic basis of the perception of intonation by linguists. *Word* 21: 40–54.

1967. *Intonation, perception and language*. Cambridge, MA: MIT Press.

Maassen, B.A.M. 1985. Artificial corrections to deaf speech. Unpublished doctoral dissertation, Catholic University of Nijmegen.

and D.-J. Povel 1985. The effect of segmental and suprasegmental correction on the intelligibility of deaf speech. *Journal of the Acoustical Society of America* 78: 877–86.

Maeda, S. 1976. A characterization of American English intonation. Unpublished PhD thesis, MIT, Cambridge, MA.

Mead, J., A. Bouhuys and D.F. Proctor 1968. Mechanisms generating subglottic pressure. In M. Krauss, M. Hammar and A. Bouhuys (eds.) *Sound production in man. Annals of the New York Academy of Sciences*, vol. 155, art. 1: 177–81.

Meyer, E.A. 1911. Ein neues Verfahren zur graphischen Bestimmung des musikalischen Akzents. *Medizinisch-pädagogische Monatsschrift für die gesamte Sprachheilkunde*.

Nabelek, I, and I.J. Hirsh 1969. On the discrimination of frequency transitions. *Journal of the Acoustical Society of America* 45: 1510–19.

Noll, A.M. 1964. Short time spectrum and 'cepstrum' techniques for vocal pitch detection. *Journal of the Acoustical Society of America* 36: 296–302.

Nooteboom, S.G. 1972. Production and perception of vowel duration; a study of durational properties of vowels in Dutch. Unpublished doctoral dissertation, University of Utrecht.

and J.G. Kruyt 1987. Accents, focus distribution and the perceived distribution of given and new information. *Journal of the Acoustical Society of America* 82: 1512–24.

Nordmark, J.O. 1968. Mechanisms of frequency discrimination. *Journal of the Acoustical Society of America* 44: 1533–40.

Obata, J. and R. Kobayashi 1937. A direct-reading pitch recorder and its applications to music and speech. *Journal of the Acoustical Society of America* 9: 156–61.

1938. An apparatus for direct-recording the pitch and intensity of sound. *Journal of the Acoustical Society of America* 10: 147–9.

1940. Further applications of our direct-reading pitch and intensity recorder. *Journal of the Acoustical Society of America* 12: 188–92.

O'Connor, J.D. and G.F. Arnold 1973. *Intonation of colloquial English*, 2nd edn. London: Longman.

197

References

Odé, C. 1986. Towards a perceptual analysis of Russian intonation. *Dutch Studies in Russian Linguistics* (= *Studies in Slavic and General Linguistics*, vol. 8), 395–443. Amsterdam: Rodopi.

1987. A perceptual analysis of Russian intonation. In Ü. Viks (ed.), *Proceedings of the eleventh International Congress of Phonetic Sciences*, vol. 3, 194–7. Tallinn: Academy of Sciences of the Estonian SSR.

1988. Rising pitch accents in Russian intonation: an experiment. *Dutch Contributions to the tenth International Congress of Slavists, Sofia, Linguistics* (= *Studies in Slavic and General Linguistics*, vol. 11), 421–35. Amsterdam: Rodopi.

1989. *Russian intonation: a perceptual description.* Amsterdam/Atlanta GA: Rodopi.

Ohala, J.J. 1970. Aspects of the control and production of speech. *UCLA Working Papers in Phonetics* 15: 1–192.

1978. Production of tone. In V. Fromkin (ed.) *Tone, a linguistic survey.* New York: Academic Press.

and W.G. Ewan, 1973. Speed of pitch change. *Journal of the Acoustical Society of America* 53: 345 (abstract).

O'Shaughnessy D. 1976. Modelling fundamental frequency, and its relationship to syntax, semantics and phonetics. Unpublished PhD thesis, MIT.

1979; Linguistic features in fundamental frequency patterns. *Journal of Phonetics* 7: 119–45.

Palmer, H.E. 1933. *A new classification of English tones.* Institute for Research in English Teaching, Tokyo.

Parmenter, C.E. and S.N. Treviño 1932. A technique for the analysis of pitch in connected discourse. *Archives néerlandaisses de phonétique expérimentale* 7: 1–29.

Pée, E. and W. Pée 1932. Beitrag zum Studium der niederländischen Intonation, I. *Archives Néerlandaises de Phonétique Expérimentale* 7: 71–103.

1933. Beitrag zum studium der niederländischen Intonation, II. *Archives néerlandaises de phonétique expérimentale* 8/9: 11–67.

Peterson, G.E. and H.L. Barney 1952. Control methods used in a study of the vowels. *Journal of the Acoustical Society of America* 24: 175–84.

Pickett, J.M. 1980. *The sounds of speech communication: a primer of acoustic phonetics and speech perception.* Baltimore: University Park Press.

Pierrehumbert, J. 1979. The perception of fundamental frequency declination. *Journal of the Acoustical Society of America* 66: 363–9.

1980. The phonology and phonetics of English intonation. Unpublished PhD thesis, MIT.

Pijper, J.R. de 1983. *Modelling British English intonation.* Dordrecht/Cinnaminson: Foris.

Pike, K.L. 1945. *The intonation of American English.* Ann Arbor, MI: University of Michigan Press.

Plomp, R., W.A. Wagenaar and A.M. Mimpen 1973. Musical interval recognition with simultaneous tones. *Acustica* 29: 101–9.

Pollack, I. 1968. Detection of rate of change of auditory frequency. *Journal of Experimental Psychology* 77: 535–41.

Rabiner, L.R. 1977. On the use of autocorrelation analysis for pitch detection. *IEEE Transactions ASSP* 25: 24–33.

M.J. Cheng, A.E. Rosenberg and C.A. McGonegal 1976. A comparative performance study of several pitch detection algorithms. *IEEE Transactions ASSP* 24: 399–418.

Rakowsky, A. 1971. Pitch discrimination at the threshold of hearing. *Proceedings of the seventh International Congress on Acoustics, Budapest*, vol. 3, 20H6: 373–6.

Reinholt Petersen, N. 1986. Perceptual compensation for segmentally conditioned fundamental frequency perturbation. *Phonetica* 43: 31–42.

Riesz, R.R. 1936. Wave translation. USA patent 2,183,248.

Rietveld, A.C.M. 1983 Syllaben, kemtonen en de automatische detectie van beklemtoonde syllaben in het Nederlands. Unpublished doctoral dissertation, Catholic University of Nijmegen.

 and C. Gussenhoven 1985. On the relation between pitch excursion size and prominence. *Journal of Phonetics* 13: 299–308.

Ritsma, R.J. 1965. Pitch discrimination and frequency discrimination. In D.E. Commins (ed.) *Proceedings of the fifth International Congress on Acoustics, Liège*, paper B22.

 1967. Frequencies dominant in the perception of the pitch of complex sounds. *Journal of the Acoustical Society of America* 42: 191–9.

 B.L. Cardozo, G. Domburg and J.J.M. Neelen 1966. The build-up of the pitch percept. *IPO Annual Progress Report* 1: 12–15.

Rooij, J.J. de 1979. Speech punctuation. Unpublished doctoral dissertation, University of Utrecht.

Rossi, M. 1971. Le seuil de glissando ou seuil de perception des variations tonales pour les sons de la parole. *Phonetica* 23: 1–33.

 1978. La perception des glissandos descendants dans les contours prosodiques (The perception of falling glissandos in prosodic contours). *Phonetica* 35: 11–40.

 and M. Chafcouloff 1972. Recherche sur le seuil différentiel de fréquence fondamentale dans la parole. *Travaux de l'Institut de Phonétique d'Aix* 1: 179–85.

Rousselot, P. 1908. *Principes de phonétique expérimentale*. Paris: Didier.

Schouten, H.E.M. 1985. Identification and discrimination of sweep tones. *Perception and Psychophysics* 37: 369–76.

Schouten, J.F. 1940. The residue and the mechanism of hearing. *Proceedings Koninklijke Nederlandse Akademie van Wetenschappen* 43: 991–9.

Schroeder, M.R. 1968. Period histogram and product spectrum: new methods for fundamental-frequency measurement. *Journal of the Acoustical Society of America* 43: 829–34.

Schutte, H.K. 1980. The efficiency of voice production. Unpublished doctoral dissertation, University of Groningen.

Scott, N.N. 1861. *Inscription automatique des sons de l'air au moyen d'une oreille artificielle*. Paris: Annales du Conservatoire des Arts et Métiers.

Scripture, E.W. 1902. Studies of melody in English speech. *Philosophische Studien* 19: 599–615.

Sergeant, R.L. and J.D. Harris 1962. Sensitivity to unidirectional frequency modulation. *Journal of the Acoustical Society of America* 34: 1625–8.

Silverman, K.E.A. 1986. F_0 segmental cues depend on intonation: the case of the rise after voiced stops. *Phonetica* 43: 76–91.

Shower, E.G. and R. Biddulph 1931. Differential pitch sensitivity of the ear. *Journal of the Acoustical Society of America* 3: 275–87.

References

Sondhi, M.M. 1968. New methods of pitch extraction. *IEEE Transactions AU* 16: 262–6.

Sorensen, J.M. and W.E. Cooper 1980. Syntactic coding of fundamental frequency in speech. In R.A. Cole (ed.) *The perception and production of fluent speech*, 399–440. Hillsdale, NJ: Lawrence Erlbaum Associates.

Sreenivas, T.V. and P.V.S. Rao 1979. Pitch extraction from corrupted harmonics of the power spectrum. *Journal of the Acoustical Society of America* 65: 223–8.

Steele, J. 1775. *An essay towards establishing the melody and measure of speech, to be expressed and perpetuated by peculiar symbols.* London: Bowyer and Nichols.
   1779. *Prosodia rationalis, or: an essay towards establishing the melody and measure of speech, to be expressed and perpetuated by peculiar symbols. The Second Edition, Emended and Enlarged.* London: Nichols.

Steele, S.A. 1986. Interaction of vowel F_0 and prosody. *Phonetica* 43: 92–105.

Stevens, S.S. and J. Volkman 1940. The relation of pitch to frequency: a revised scale. *American Journal of Psychology* 53: 329–53.

Stock, E. and Chr. Zacharias 1982. *Deutsche Satzintonation*, 3rd edn. Leipzig: Enzyklopädie.

Stone, R.B. and G.M. White 1963. Digital correlation detects voice fundamental. *Electronics* 36: 26–30.

Stumpf, C. 1890. *Tonpsychologie.* Leipzig: Hirzel.

Sundberg, J. 1979. Maximum speed of pitch changes in singers and untrained subjects. *Journal of Phonetics* 7: 71–9.

Terhardt, E. 1979. Calculating virtual pitch. *Hearing Research* 1: 155–82.

Terken, J.M.B. 1985. Use and function of accentuation. Unpublished doctoral dissertation, University of Leyden.
   and S.G. Nooteboom 1987. Opposite effects of accentuation and deaccentuation on verification latencies for given and new information. *Language and Cognitive Processes* 2: 145–63.

Thorsen, N. 1980. A study of the perception of sentence intonation – evidence from Danish. *Journal of the Acoustical Society of America* 67: 1014–30.

Thorsen, N. Grønnum 1985. Intonation and text in standard Danish. *Journal of the Acoustical Society of America* 77: 1205–16.
   1986. Sentence intonation in textual context – supplementary data. *Journal of the Acoustical Society of America* 80: 1041–7.

Titze, I.R. 1983. Symposium 3: models of the larynx. In M.P.R. van den Broecke and A. Cohen (eds.) *Proceedings of the tenth International Congress of Phonetic Sciences*, 162ff. Dordrecht/Cinnaminson: Foris.

Trager, G.L. and H.L. Smith 1951. *An outline of English structure*, Studies in Linguistics, Occasional Papers 3, Norman, OK: Battenburg Press.

Vaissière, J. 1983. Language-independent prosodic features. In A. Cutler and D.R. Ladd (eds.) Prosody: *models and measurements*, 53–66. Heidelberg: Springer.

Vanderslice, R. and P. Ladefoged 1971. Binary suprasegmental features. *UCLA Working Papers in Phonetics* 17: 6–24.

Wanner E. and M. Maratsos 1978. An ATN approach to comprehension. In M. Halle, J. Bresnan and G.A. Miller (eds.) *Linguistic theory and psychological reality*, 119–61. Cambridge, MA: MIT Press.

Wijk, C.H. van 1987. Speaking, writing and sentence form. Unpublished doctoral dissertation, Catholic University of Nijmegen.

    and G. Kempen 1985. From sentence structure to intonation contour – an algorithm for computing pitch contours on the basis of sentence accents and syntactic structure. In B. Müller (ed.) *Sprachsynthese*, 157–82. Hildesheim: Olms.

Willems, N.J. 1982. *English intonation from a Dutch point of view*. Dordrecht/Cinnaminson: Foris.

    1983. Towards an objective course in English intonation: standardized precepts. In M. van den Broecke, V. van Heuven and W. Zonneveld (eds.) *Sound structures, studies for Antonie Cohen*, 281–96. Dordrecht/Cinnaminson: Foris.

    R. Collier and J. 't Hart 1988. A synthesis scheme for British English intonation. *Journal of the Acoustical Society of America* 84: 1250–61.

Zelle, H.W., J.R. de Pijper and J. 't Hart 1984. Semi-automatic synthesis of intonation for Dutch and British English. In M.P.R. van den Broecke and A. Cohen (eds.) *Proceedings of the tenth International Congress of Phonetic Sciences, Utrecht*, 247–51. Dordrecht/Cinnaminson: Foris.

Author index

Subject index

Absolute threshold of pitch change, 29, 31
Abstract intonation patterns, 66, 120
Abstract pitch targets, 168
Abstract properties of intonation, 120
Accent-lending pitch movements, 96f.
Accentual (dis-)similarity, 100
Accentuation, 95, 98, 109, 160f., 164, 172,
    175, 180, 188, *see also* Pitch
    accentuation; Sentence accentuation
  and intonation, 96ff., 115
  and syntax, 114, 118, 161
  degree of, 76
Acceptability, 52ff., 64, 187
  test(s), 552
Acoustic features, perceptually relevant, 5
Acquisition of intonation of second
    language, 170, 176f.
Air expenditure, 133, 135
Ambiguity, 107, 109, 131f., 146
  awareness of, 110
  interpretation of syntactically ambiguous
    utterances, 109
American English intonation, 125, 175
Analysis by synthesis, 187
Anticipatory dip, 124
Applications, 169ff.
  existing, 170ff.
  potential, 176ff.
Artificial intonation, liveliness of, 183
Arytenoid (cartilage), 11
Association of Text and Tune, 160ff.
Atomistic features, 66
Atomistic features of pitch movements, 151
Atomistic levels of analysis, 72
Auditory impression(s), 4, 5
  descriptions of, 4, 187
Auto-signcorrelation, 22
Autocorrelation technique, 22
Automatic speech recognition, 180, 182
Automatic stylization, 177, 182f.

Baseline, 8, 41, 71, 76, 125f., 128, 141f., *see*
    also Declination
  concave course of, 129
  convex course of, 129

Basic assumption, 39, 70, 95, 123, 150, 186f.
Bernoulli effect, 12, 14
Block, Continuation, 79
  End, 79
  Prefix, 79
Bottom-up (approach), 66, 119, 167, 185ff.
Boundaries, clause, 102, 130, 149, 158, 162,
    173
  melodic marking of, 115, 173
  resets at, 130f.
  variation in marking, 173
  clause internal, 103, 162
  melodic marking of, 103
  markers, 181f.
  temporal and intonational, 108
  marking, 120, 172, 178, 188
  phrase, 173
  prosodic, 107f., 109, 166
  marking of, 103, 175
  segment, 174
  syllable, 181
  syntactic, 100f., 105, 140, 163f., 175, 179
  melodic highlighting of, 163
  tone, low, 165f.
Boyle's law, 135
British English intonation, 44, 53, 76, 80,
    125f., 134, 146, 163, 173, 175f., 188
  grammar, 59

Cadence, 96
Canonical form of contour, 168
Cap pattern, 84
Categorical differences, 48
Categorically different groups, 50
Cepstrum, 22
Clause, 72, 79, 100, 154, 158, 163, *see also*
    Boundaries
  main, 180
  subordinate, 179
Cognitive approach to teaching, 170
  course of intonation, 183
Communicative aspects, 145
  function, 1, 5, 148, 189
  relevance, 25

206